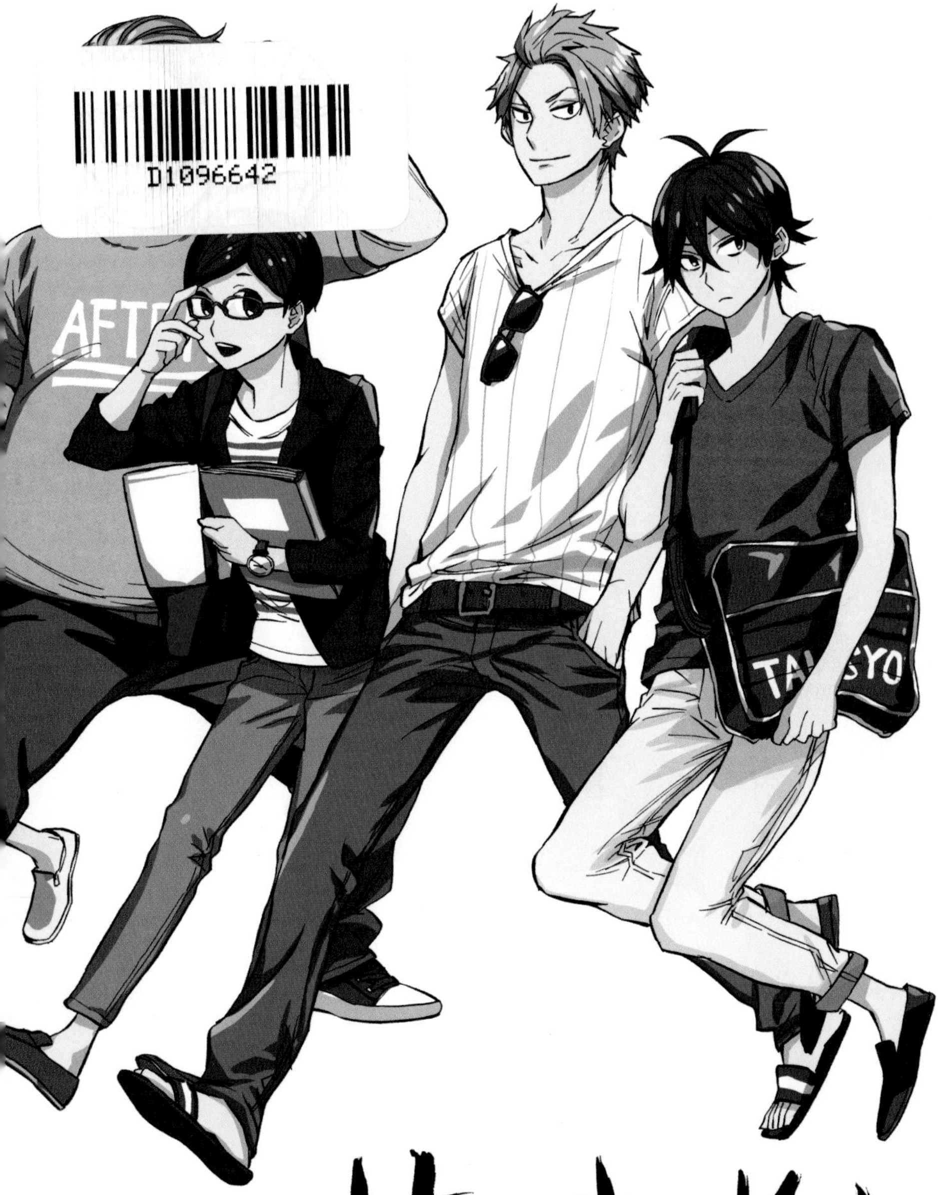

Handa-Kun

Volume Seven

SATSUKI YOSHINO

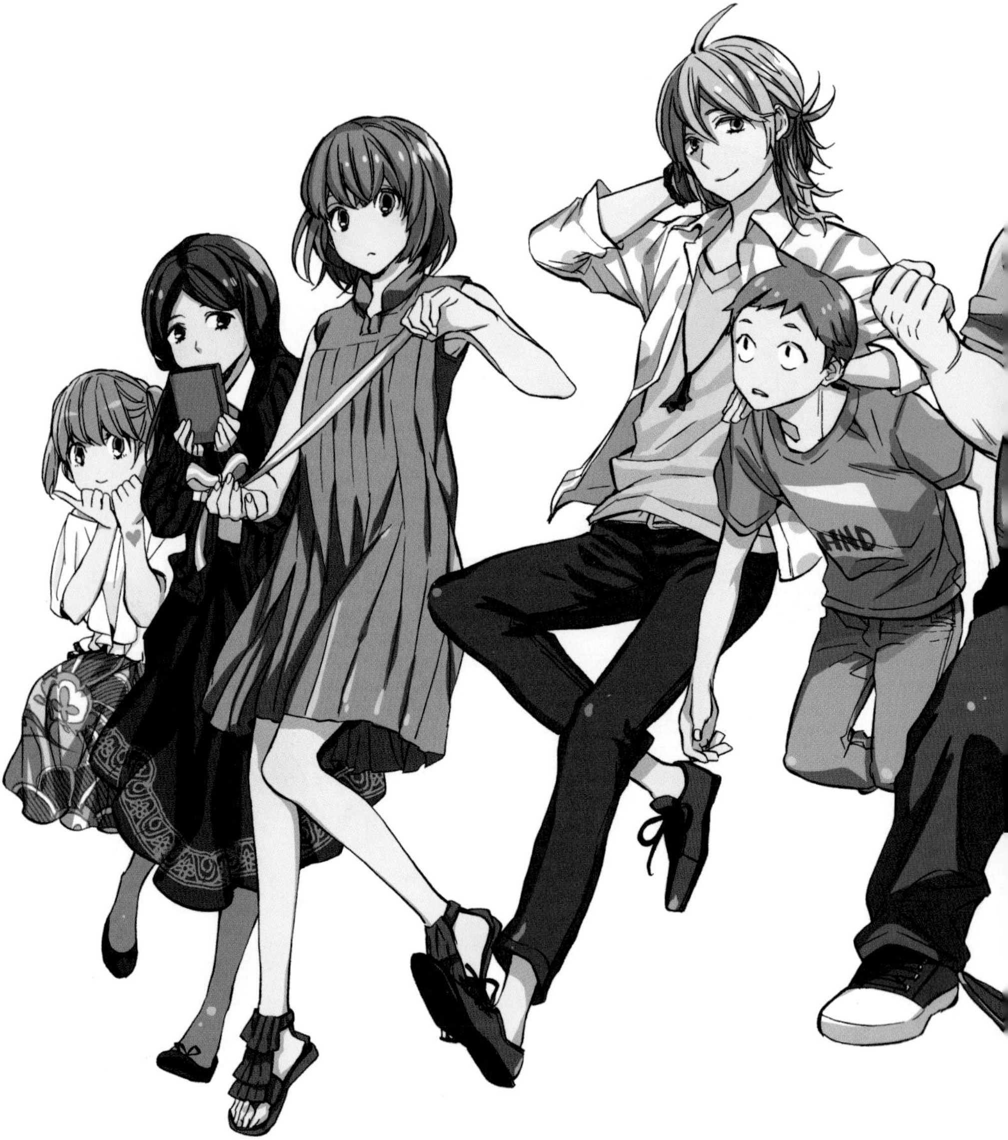

SPECIAL COMIC GALLERY

These are all the color manga that had previously been published only in *Monthly Shonen Gangan*, presented here in one fell swoop!

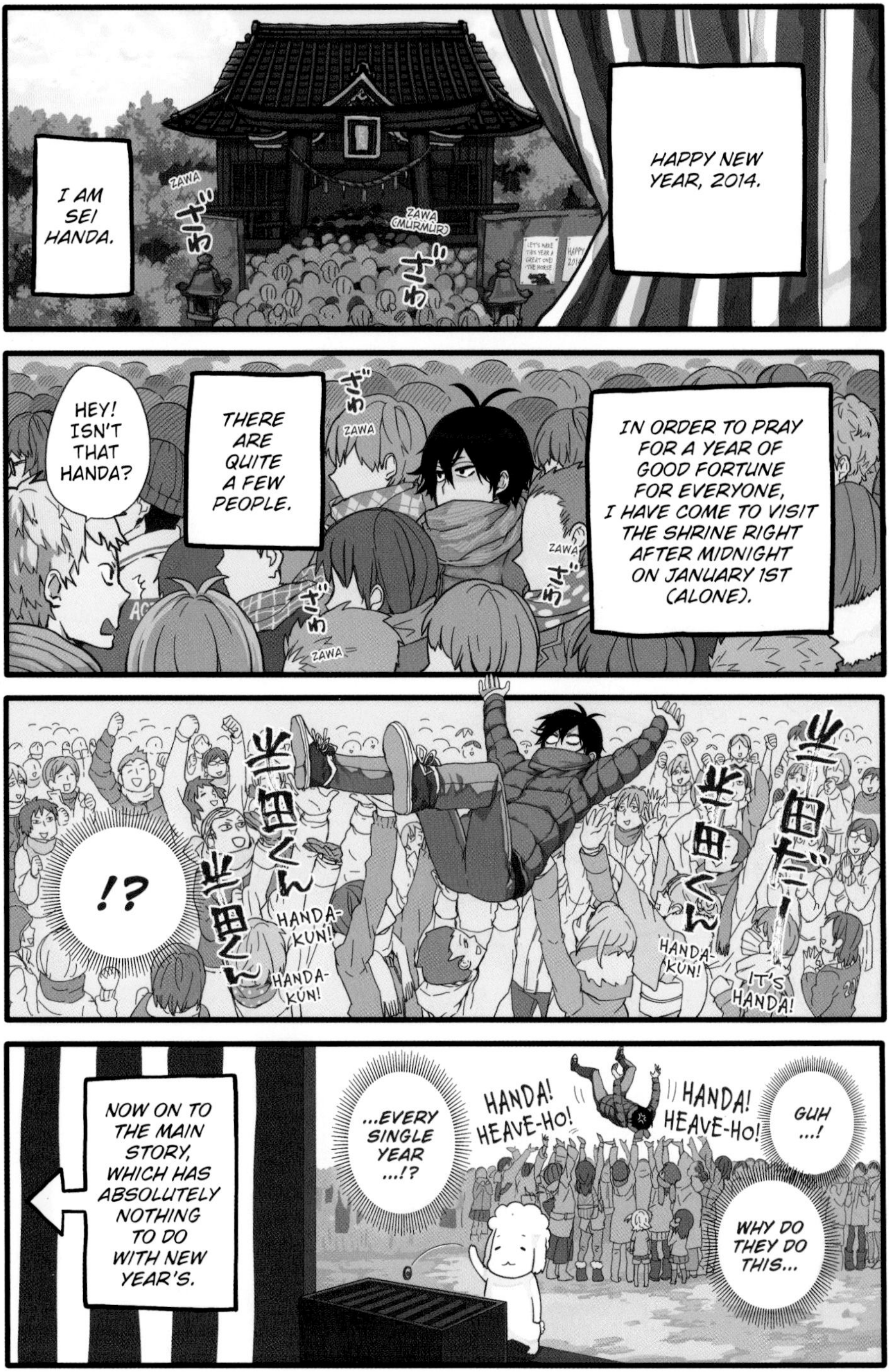
HAPPY NEW YEAR, 2014.
ZAWA (MURMUR)
ざわ
ZAWA
ざわ
I AM SEI HANDA.
IN ORDER TO PRAY FOR A YEAR OF GOOD FORTUNE FOR EVERYONE, I HAVE COME TO VISIT THE SHRINE RIGHT AFTER MIDNIGHT ON JANUARY 1ST (ALONE).
ZAWA
ざわ
ざわ
ZAWA
ざわ
ZAWA
THERE ARE QUITE A FEW PEOPLE.
HEY! ISN'T THAT HANDA?
半田だー!
IT'S HANDA!
半田くん
HANDA-KUN!
半田くん
HANDA-KUN!
半田くん
HANDA-KUN!
!?
GUH ...!
WHY DO THEY DO THIS...
HANDA! HEAVE-HO!
HANDA! HEAVE-HO!
...EVERY SINGLE YEAR ...!?
NOW ON TO THE MAIN STORY, WHICH HAS ABSOLUTELY NOTHING TO DO WITH NEW YEAR'S.

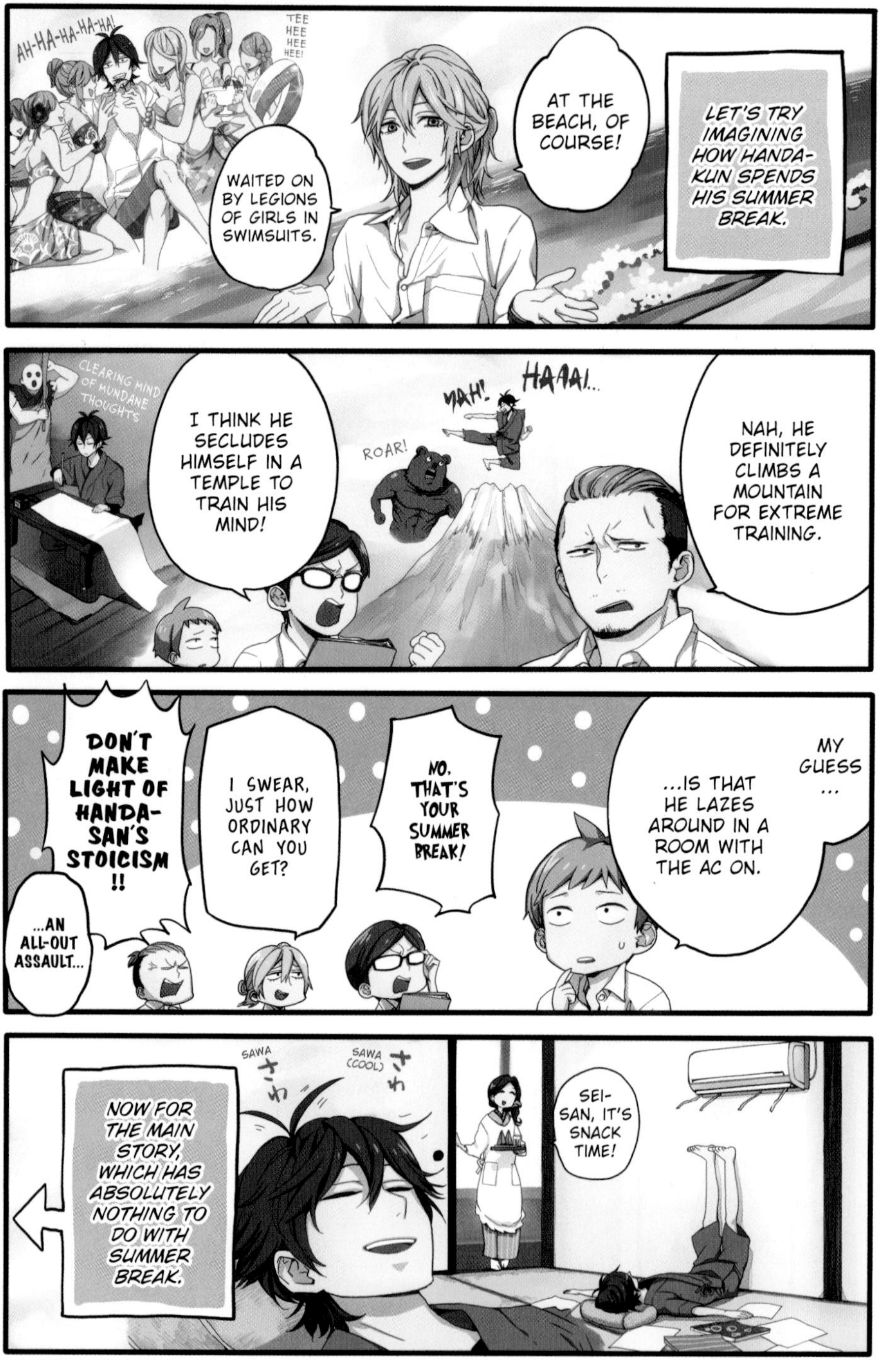
LET'S TRY IMAGINING HOW HANDA-KUN SPENDS HIS SUMMER BREAK.
AT THE BEACH, OF COURSE!
WAITED ON BY LEGIONS OF GIRLS IN SWIMSUITS.
TEE HEE HEE HEE!
AH-HA-HA-HA-HA!
NAH, HE DEFINITELY CLIMBS A MOUNTAIN FOR EXTREME TRAINING.
HAAAI...
NAH!
ROAR!
I THINK HE SECLUDES HIMSELF IN A TEMPLE TO TRAIN HIS MIND!
CLEARING MIND OF MUNDANE THOUGHTS
MY GUESS ...
...IS THAT HE LAZES AROUND IN A ROOM WITH THE AC ON.
NO. THAT'S YOUR SUMMER BREAK!
I SWEAR, JUST HOW ORDINARY CAN YOU GET?
DON'T MAKE LIGHT OF HANDA-SAN'S STOICISM!!
...AN ALL-OUT ASSAULT...
SEI-SAN, IT'S SNACK TIME!
SAWA (COOL)
さわ
SAWA
さわ
NOW FOR THE MAIN STORY, WHICH HAS ABSOLUTELY NOTHING TO DO WITH SUMMER BREAK.

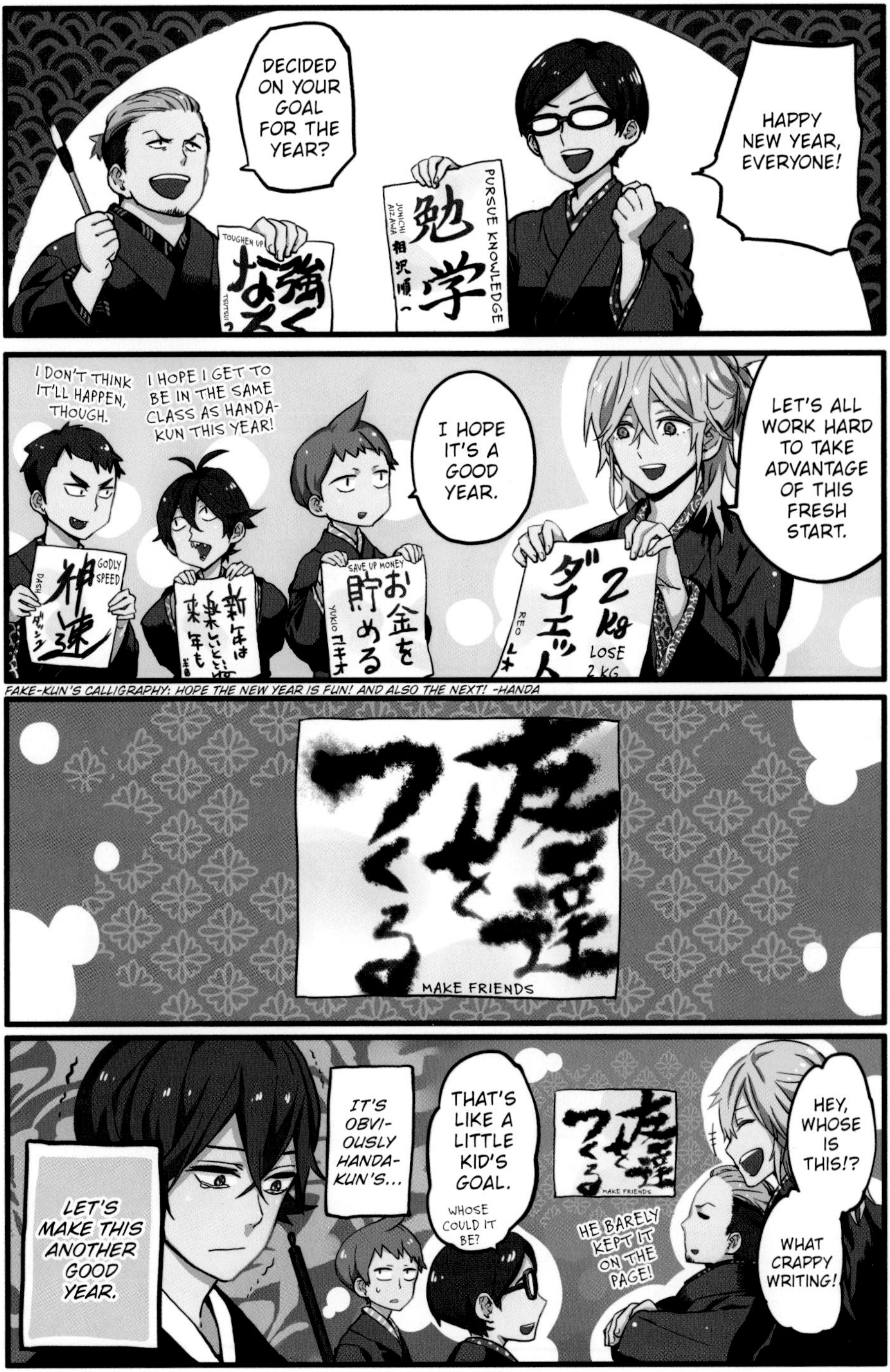
HAPPY NEW YEAR, EVERYONE!
PURSUE KNOWLEDGE
JUNICHI AIZAWA
DECIDED ON YOUR GOAL FOR THE YEAR?
TOUGHEN UP
TSUTSUI
LET'S ALL WORK HARD TO TAKE ADVANTAGE OF THIS FRESH START.
2 kg
LOSE 2 KG
REO
I HOPE IT'S A GOOD YEAR.
SAVE UP MONEY
YUKIO
I HOPE I GET TO BE IN THE SAME CLASS AS HANDA-KUN THIS YEAR!
I DON'T THINK IT'LL HAPPEN, THOUGH.
GODLY SPEED
DASH
FAKE-KUN'S CALLIGRAPHY: HOPE THE NEW YEAR IS FUN! AND ALSO THE NEXT! -HANDA
MAKE FRIENDS
HEY, WHOSE IS THIS!?
WHAT CRAPPY WRITING!
HE BARELY KEPT IT ON THE PAGE!
MAKE FRIENDS
THAT'S LIKE A LITTLE KID'S GOAL.
WHOSE COULD IT BE?
IT'S OBVI-OUSLY HANDA-KUN'S...
LET'S MAKE THIS ANOTHER GOOD YEAR.

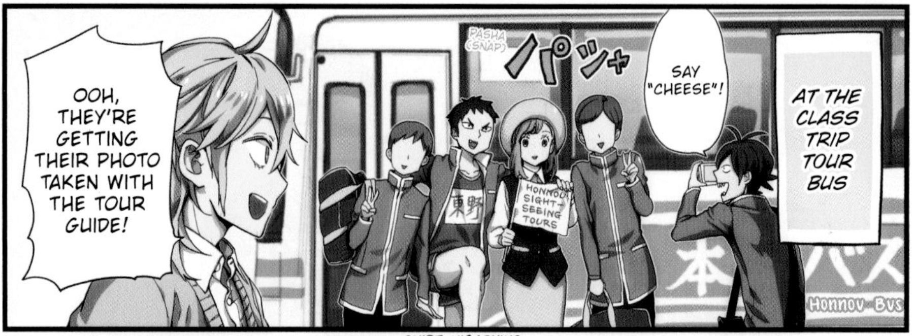
AT THE CLASS TRIP TOUR BUS
SAY "CHEESE"!
PASHA (SNAP)
パシャ
OOH, THEY'RE GETTING THEIR PHOTO TAKEN WITH THE TOUR GUIDE!
HONNOU SIGHT-SEEING TOURS
東野
本 バス
Honnou Bus

SHIRT: HIGASHINO

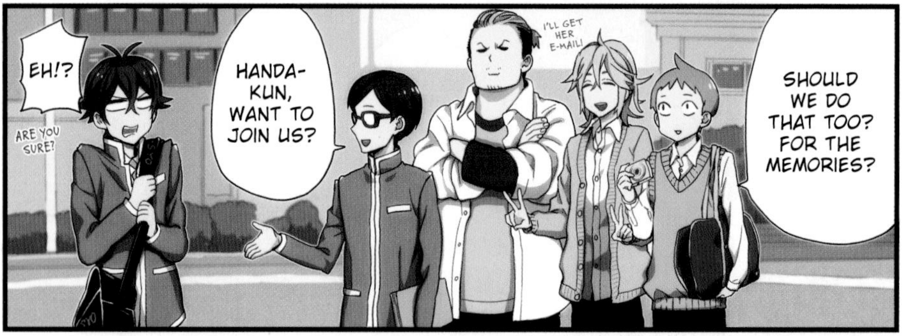
SHOULD WE DO THAT TOO? FOR THE MEMORIES?
I'LL GET HER E-MAIL!
HANDA-KUN, WANT TO JOIN US?
EH!?
ARE YOU SURE?

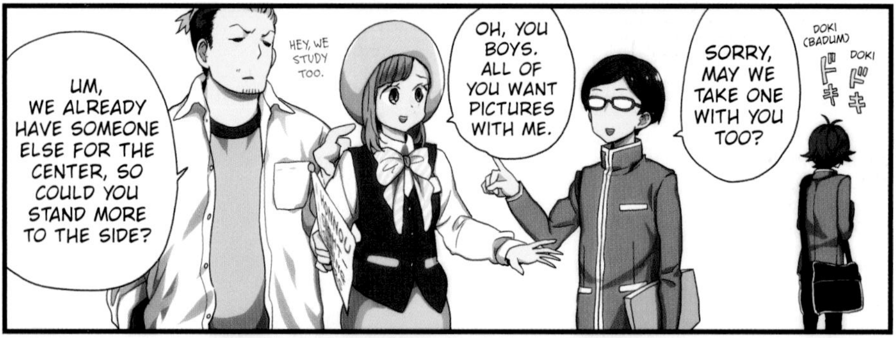
DOKI (BADUM) DOKI
ドキ ドキ
SORRY, MAY WE TAKE ONE WITH YOU TOO?
OH, YOU BOYS. ALL OF YOU WANT PICTURES WITH ME.
HEY, WE STUDY TOO.
UM, WE ALREADY HAVE SOMEONE ELSE FOR THE CENTER, SO COULD YOU STAND MORE TO THE SIDE?

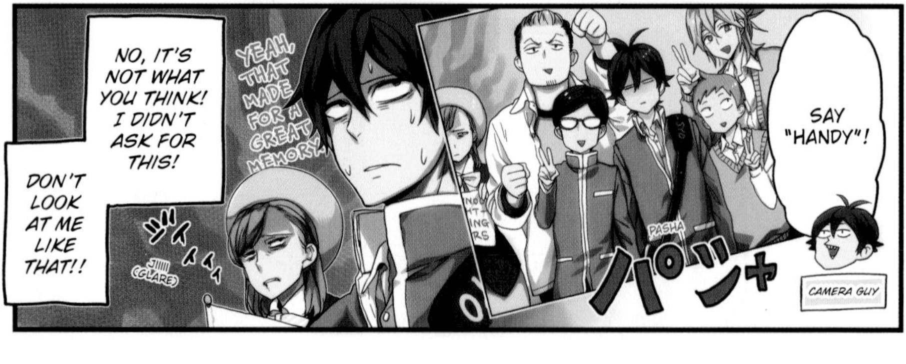
SAY "HANDY"!
CAMERA GUY
PASHA
パシャ
YEAH, THAT MADE FOR A GREAT MEMORY.
NO, IT'S NOT WHAT YOU THINK! I DIDN'T ASK FOR THIS!
DON'T LOOK AT ME LIKE THAT!!
ジィィィ
JIIIII (GLARE)

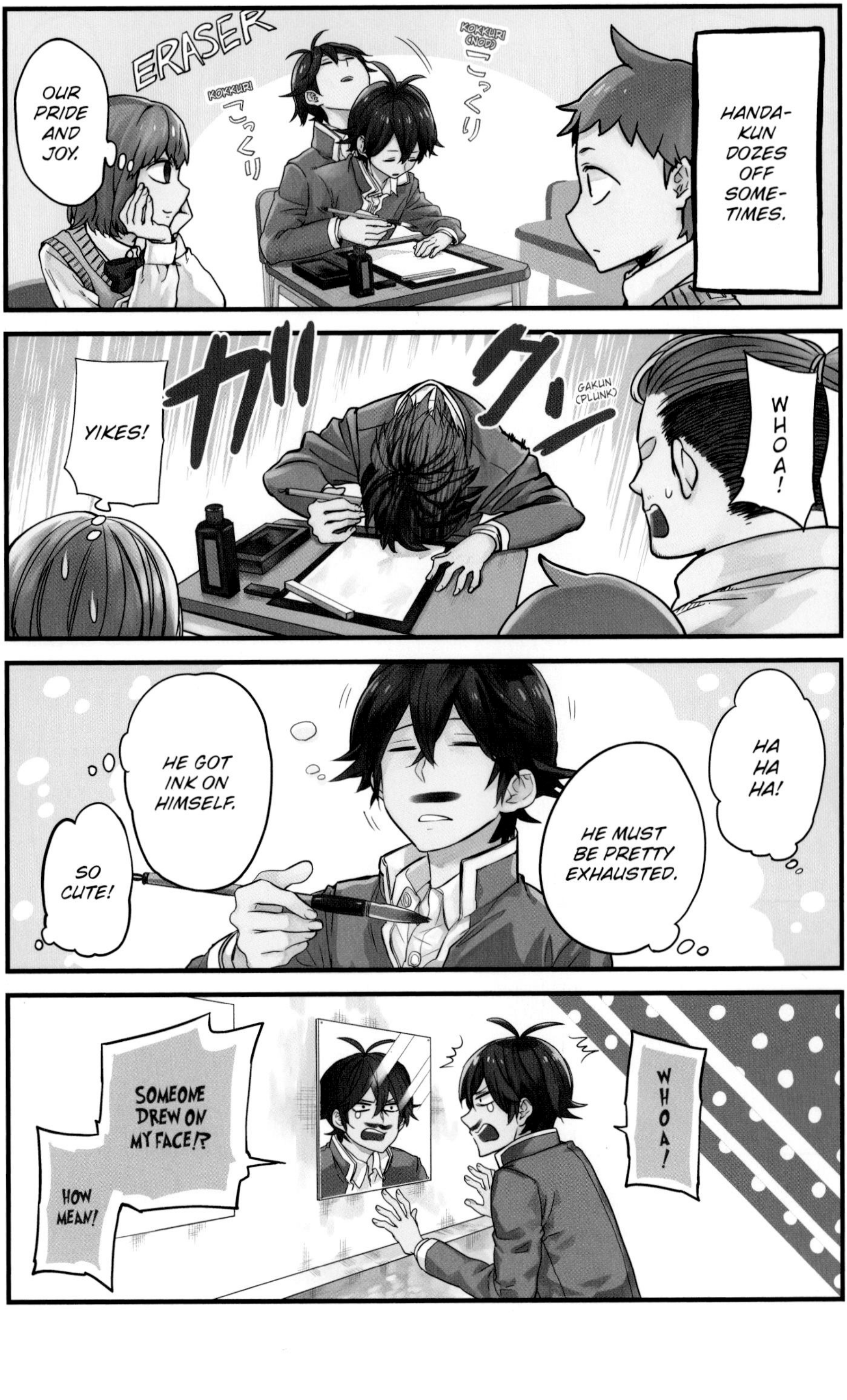
HANDA-KUN DOZES OFF SOMETIMES.
KOKKURI (NOD)
こっくり
KOKKURI
こっくり
ERASER
OUR PRIDE AND JOY.
WHOA!
GAKUN (PLUNK)
YIKES!
HA HA HA!
HE MUST BE PRETTY EXHAUSTED.
HE GOT INK ON HIMSELF.
SO CUTE!
WHOA!
SOMEONE DREW ON MY FACE!?
HOW MEAN!

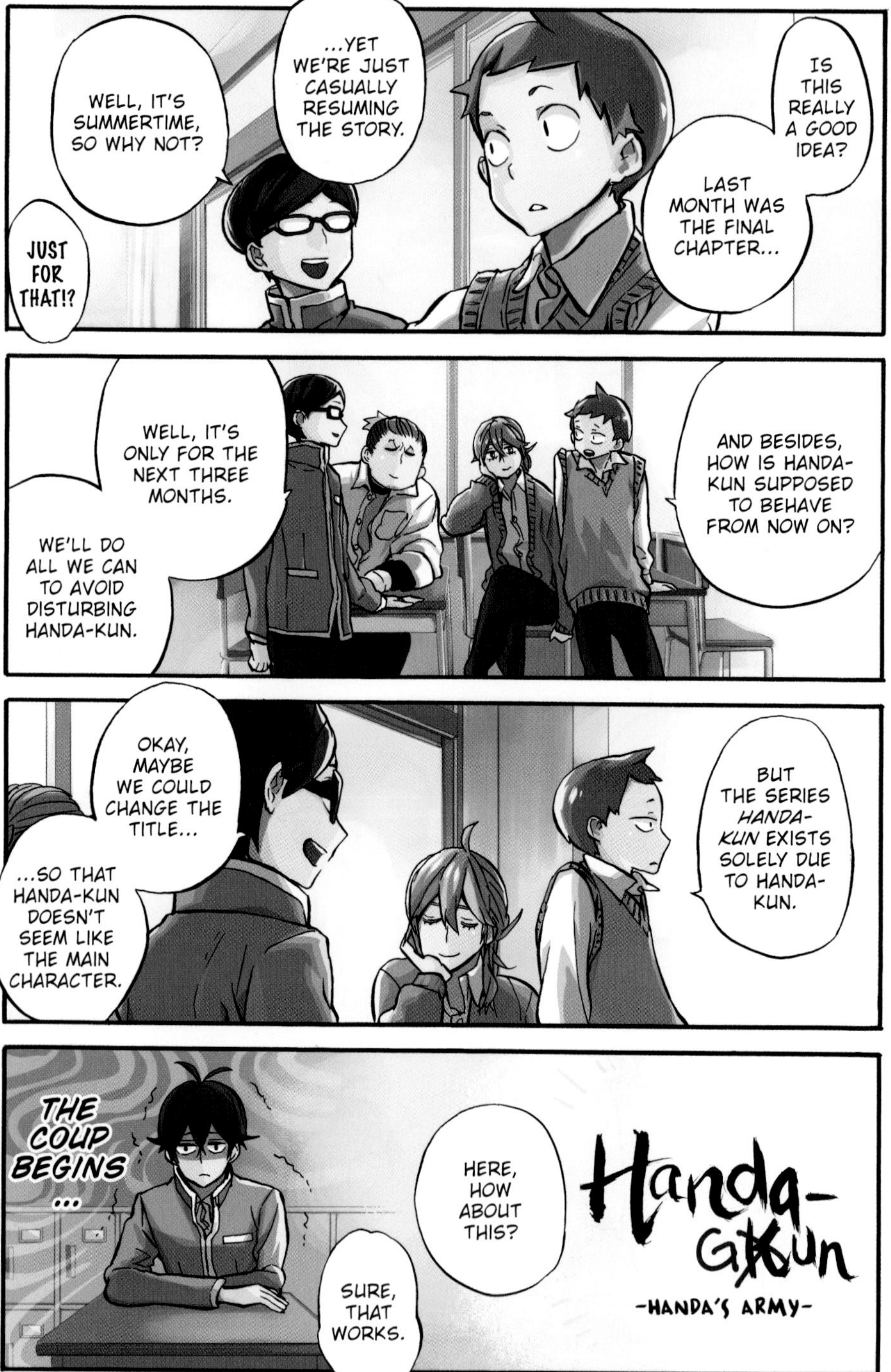
IS THIS REALLY A GOOD IDEA?
LAST MONTH WAS THE FINAL CHAPTER...
...YET WE'RE JUST CASUALLY RESUMING THE STORY.
WELL, IT'S SUMMERTIME, SO WHY NOT?
JUST FOR THAT!?
AND BESIDES, HOW IS HANDA-KUN SUPPOSED TO BEHAVE FROM NOW ON?
WELL, IT'S ONLY FOR THE NEXT THREE MONTHS.
WE'LL DO ALL WE CAN TO AVOID DISTURBING HANDA-KUN.
BUT THE SERIES *HANDA-KUN* EXISTS SOLELY DUE TO HANDA-KUN.
OKAY, MAYBE WE COULD CHANGE THE TITLE...
...SO THAT HANDA-KUN DOESN'T SEEM LIKE THE MAIN CHARACTER.
Handa-G~~K~~un
-HANDA'S ARMY-
HERE, HOW ABOUT THIS?
SURE, THAT WORKS.
THE COUP BEGINS...

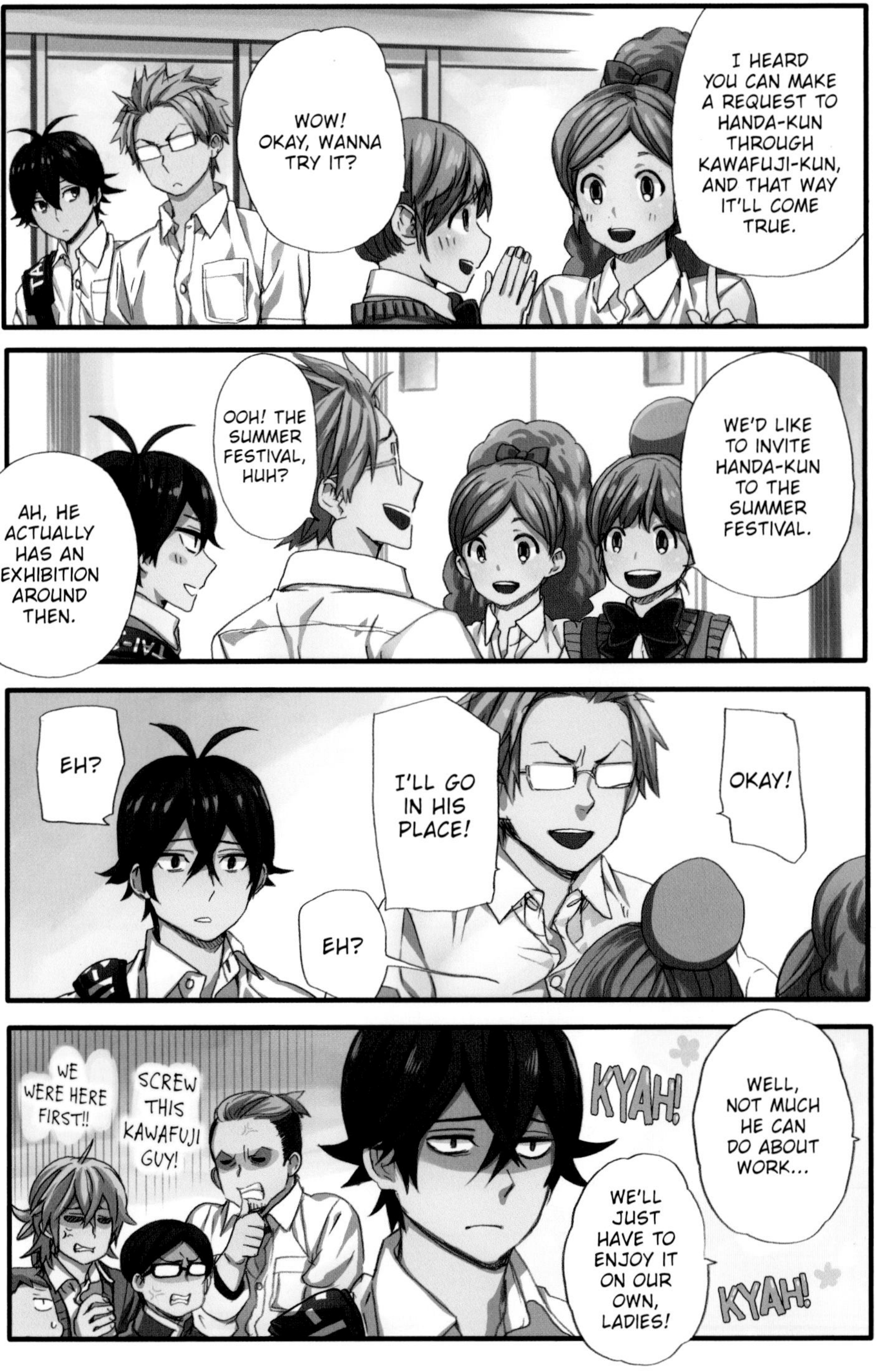
I HEARD YOU CAN MAKE A REQUEST TO HANDA-KUN THROUGH KAWAFUJI-KUN, AND THAT WAY IT'LL COME TRUE.
WOW! OKAY, WANNA TRY IT?
WE'D LIKE TO INVITE HANDA-KUN TO THE SUMMER FESTIVAL.
OOH! THE SUMMER FESTIVAL, HUH?
AH, HE ACTUALLY HAS AN EXHIBITION AROUND THEN.
OKAY!
I'LL GO IN HIS PLACE!
EH?
EH?
WELL, NOT MUCH HE CAN DO ABOUT WORK...
KYAH!
WE'LL JUST HAVE TO ENJOY IT ON OUR OWN, LADIES!
KYAH!
SCREW THIS KAWAFUJI GUY!
WE WERE HERE FIRST!!

Contents

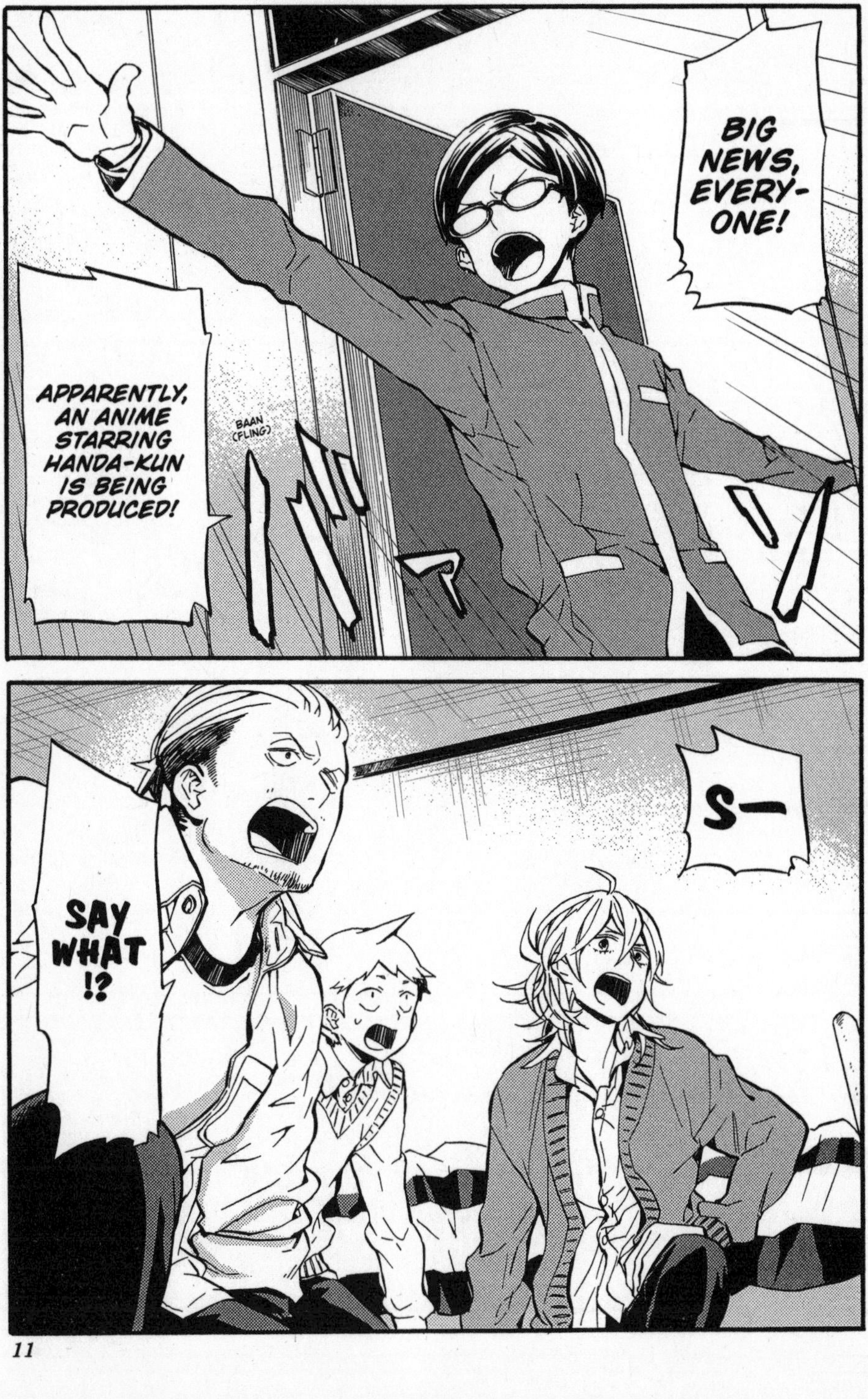
BIG NEWS, EVERYONE!
BAAN (FLING)
APPARENTLY, AN ANIME STARRING HANDA-KUN IS BEING PRODUCED!
S—
SAY WHAT!?

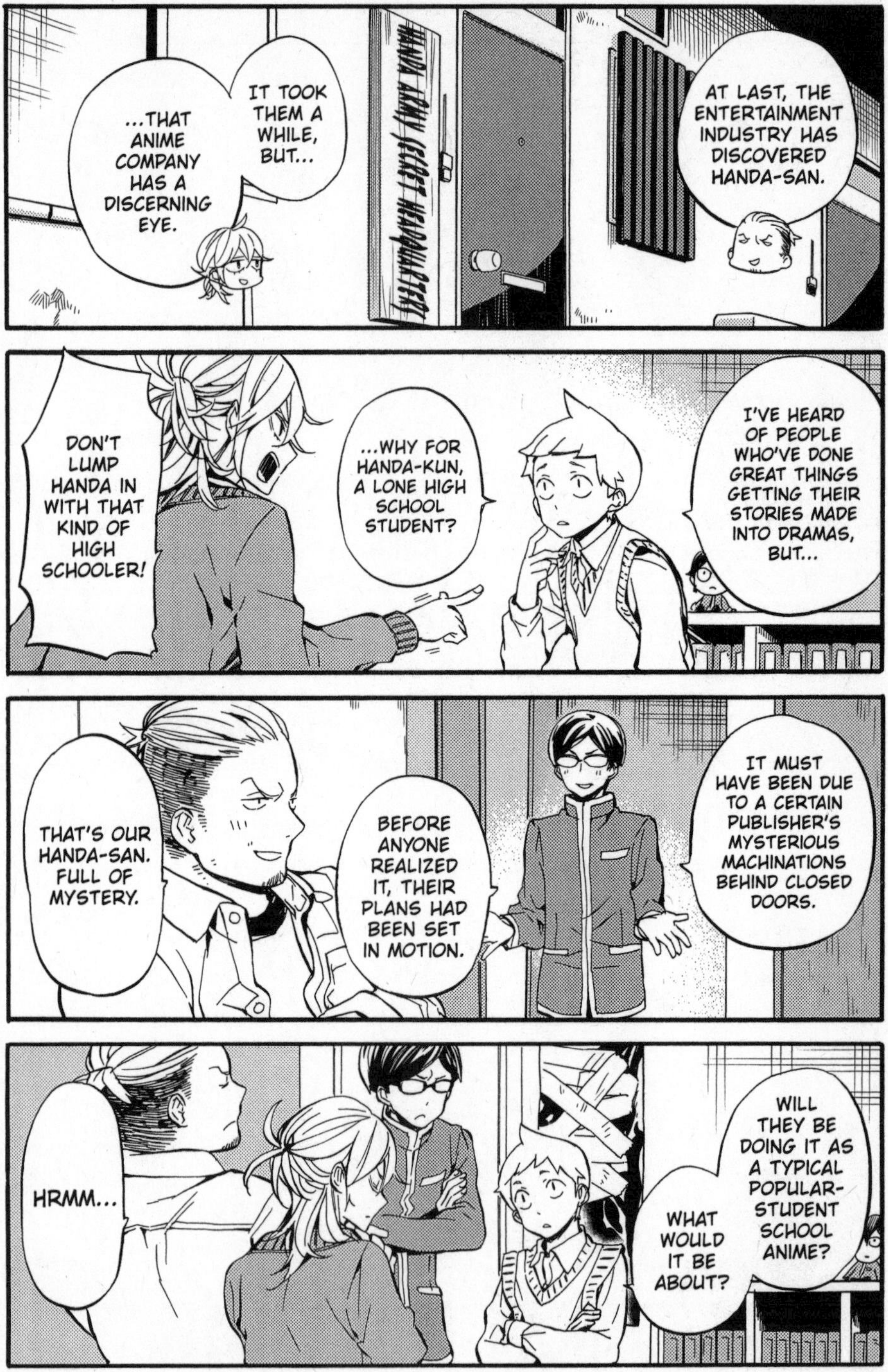
AT LAST, THE ENTERTAINMENT INDUSTRY HAS DISCOVERED HANDA-SAN.
HANDA ARMY SECRET HEADQUARTERS
IT TOOK THEM A WHILE, BUT...
...THAT ANIME COMPANY HAS A DISCERNING EYE.
I'VE HEARD OF PEOPLE WHO'VE DONE GREAT THINGS GETTING THEIR STORIES MADE INTO DRAMAS, BUT...
...WHY FOR HANDA-KUN, A LONE HIGH SCHOOL STUDENT?
DON'T LUMP HANDA IN WITH THAT KIND OF HIGH SCHOOLER!
IT MUST HAVE BEEN DUE TO A CERTAIN PUBLISHER'S MYSTERIOUS MACHINATIONS BEHIND CLOSED DOORS.
BEFORE ANYONE REALIZED IT, THEIR PLANS HAD BEEN SET IN MOTION.
THAT'S OUR HANDA-SAN. FULL OF MYSTERY.
WILL THEY BE DOING IT AS A TYPICAL POPULAR-STUDENT SCHOOL ANIME?
WHAT WOULD IT BE ABOUT?
HRMM...

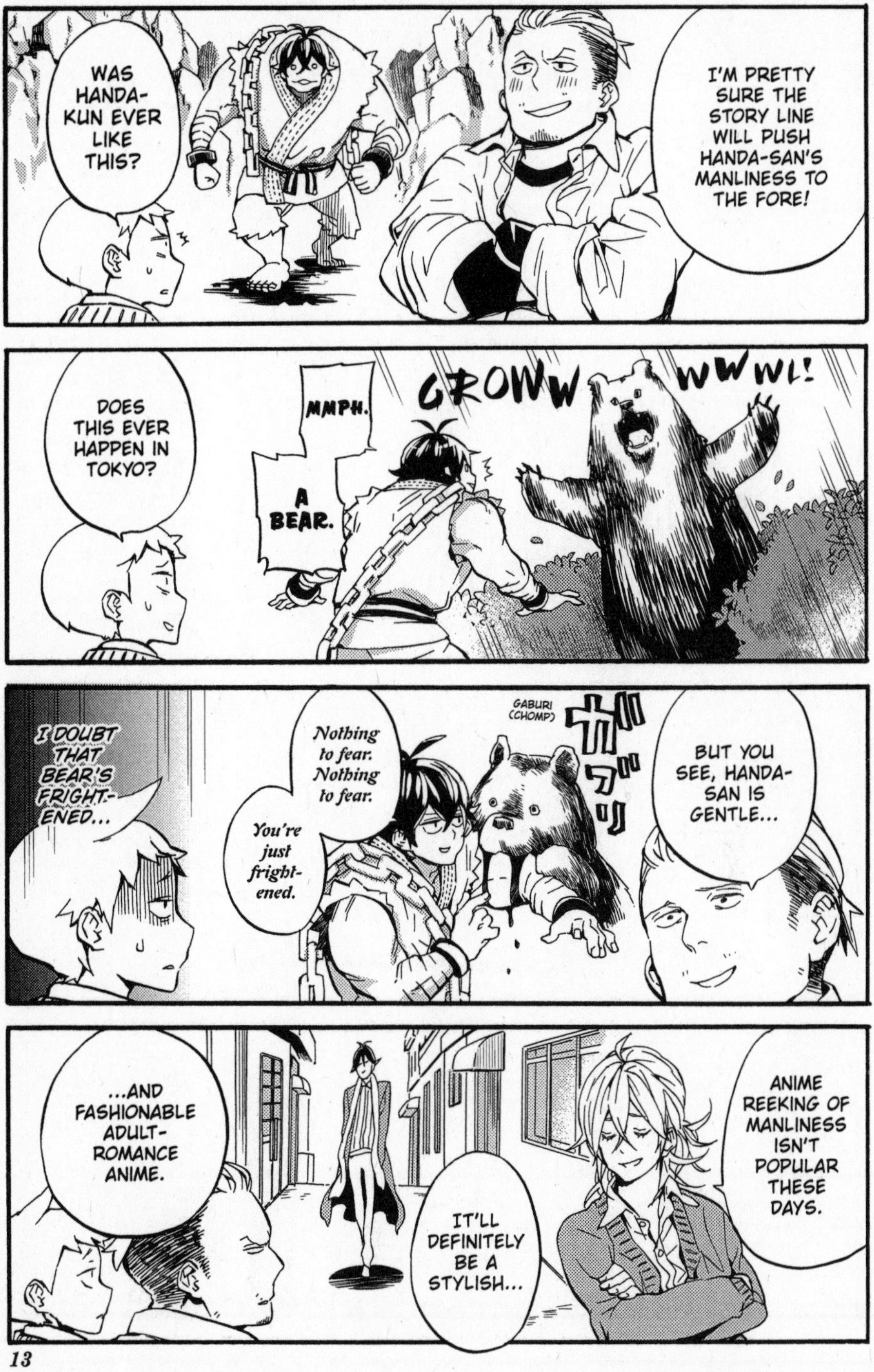
I'M PRETTY SURE THE STORY LINE WILL PUSH HANDA-SAN'S MANLINESS TO THE FORE!
WAS HANDA-KUN EVER LIKE THIS?
GROWW WWWL!
MMPH.
A BEAR.
DOES THIS EVER HAPPEN IN TOKYO?
BUT YOU SEE, HANDA-SAN IS GENTLE...
ガブリ
GABURI (CHOMP)
Nothing to fear. Nothing to fear.
You're just fright-ened.
I DOUBT THAT BEAR'S FRIGHT-ENED...
ANIME REEKING OF MANLINESS ISN'T POPULAR THESE DAYS.
IT'LL DEFINITELY BE A STYLISH...
...AND FASHIONABLE ADULT-ROMANCE ANIME.

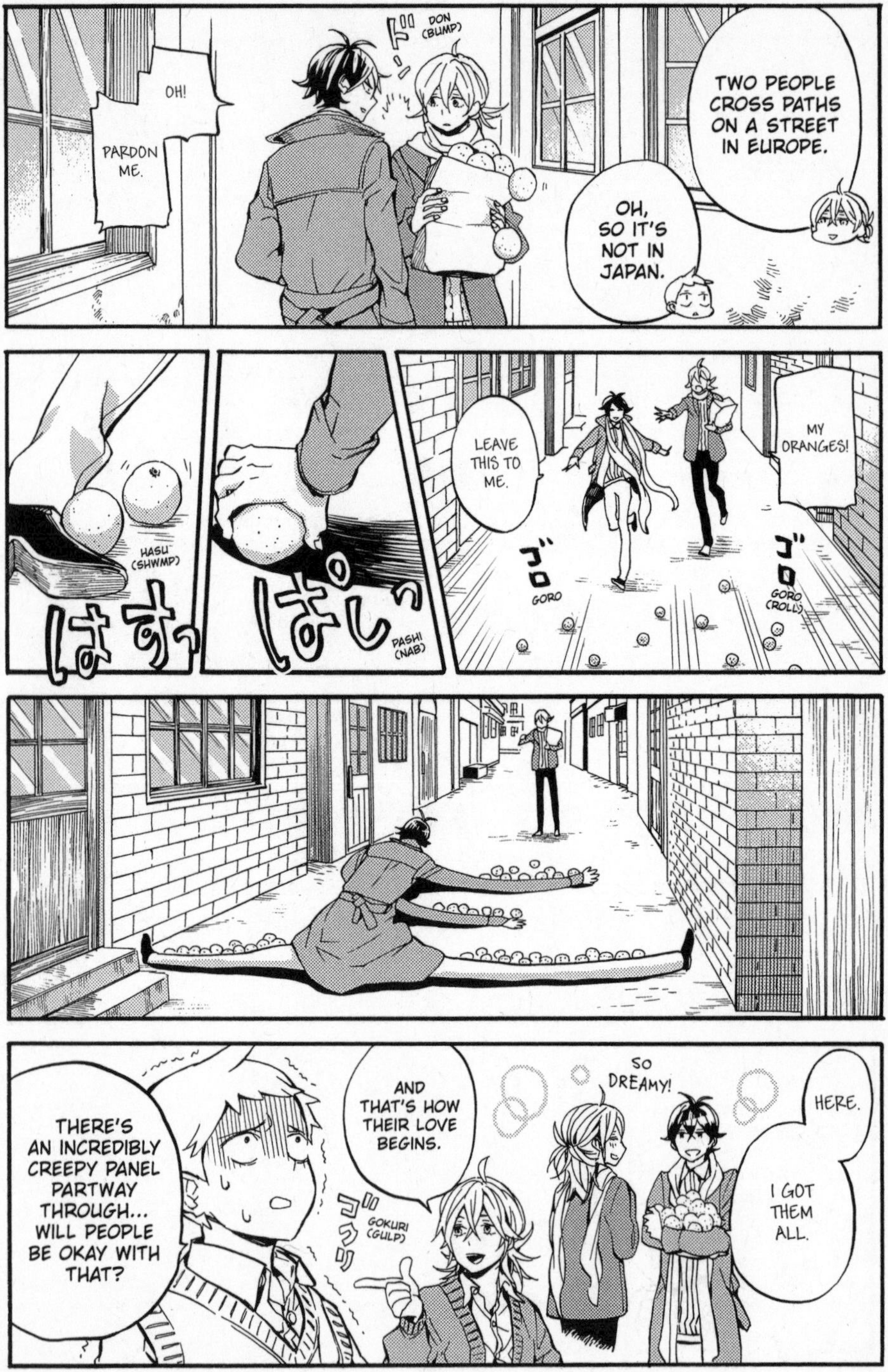

TWO PEOPLE CROSS PATHS ON A STREET IN EUROPE.
OH, SO IT'S NOT IN JAPAN.
ド
DON (BUMP)
OH!
PARDON ME.
MY ORANGES!
LEAVE THIS TO ME.
ゴロ
GORO (ROLL)
ゴロ
GORO
ぱしっ
PASHI (NAB)
はすっ
HASU (SHWMP)
HERE.
I GOT THEM ALL.
SO DREAMY!
AND THAT'S HOW THEIR LOVE BEGINS.
ゴクリ
GOKURI (GULP)
THERE'S AN INCREDIBLY CREEPY PANEL PARTWAY THROUGH... WILL PEOPLE BE OKAY WITH THAT?

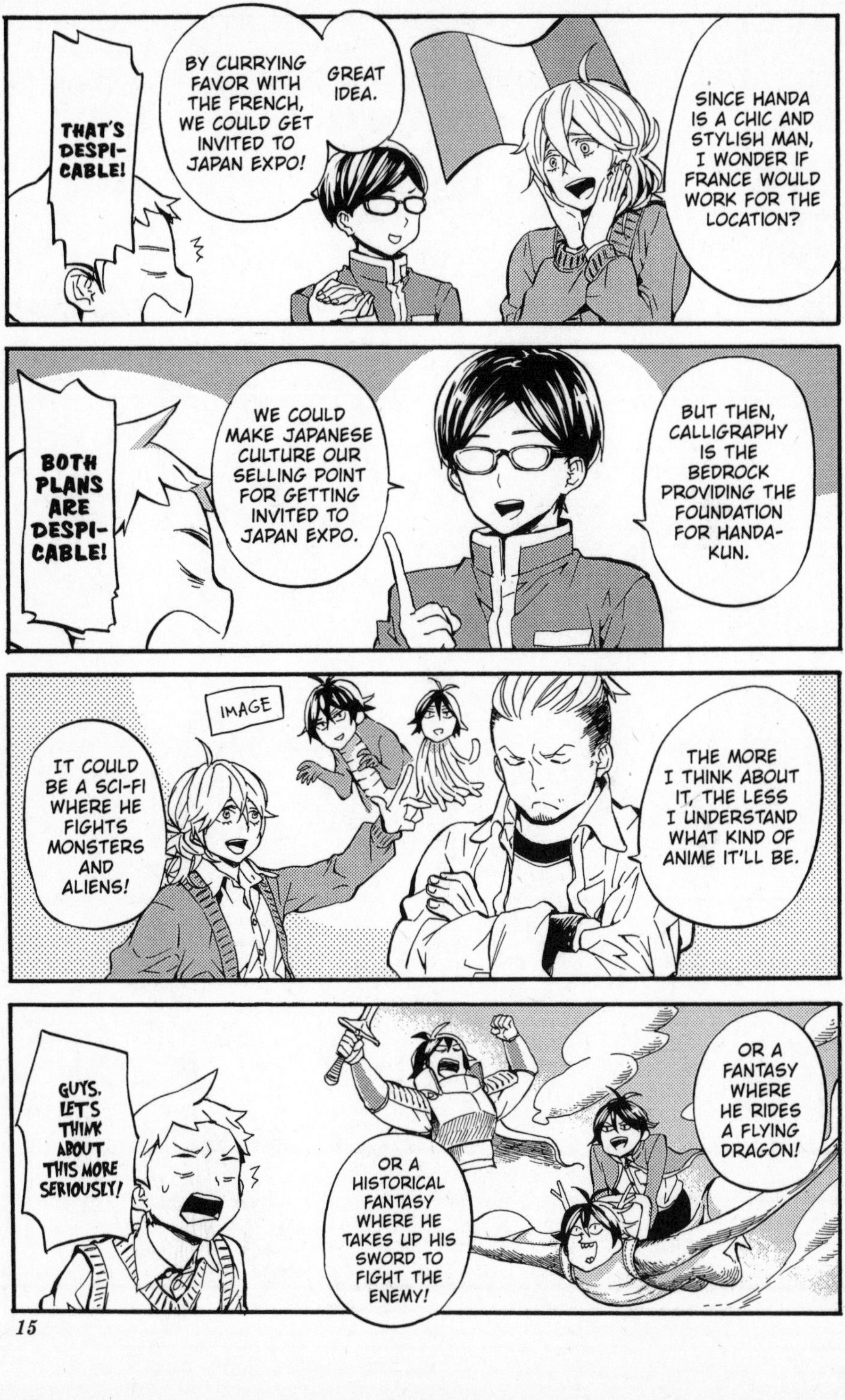
SINCE HANDA IS A CHIC AND STYLISH MAN, I WONDER IF FRANCE WOULD WORK FOR THE LOCATION?
GREAT IDEA.
BY CURRYING FAVOR WITH THE FRENCH, WE COULD GET INVITED TO JAPAN EXPO!
THAT'S DESPI-CABLE!
BUT THEN, CALLIGRAPHY IS THE BEDROCK PROVIDING THE FOUNDATION FOR HANDA-KUN.
WE COULD MAKE JAPANESE CULTURE OUR SELLING POINT FOR GETTING INVITED TO JAPAN EXPO.
BOTH PLANS ARE DESPI-CABLE!
THE MORE I THINK ABOUT IT, THE LESS I UNDERSTAND WHAT KIND OF ANIME IT'LL BE.
IMAGE
IT COULD BE A SCI-FI WHERE HE FIGHTS MONSTERS AND ALIENS!
OR A FANTASY WHERE HE RIDES A FLYING DRAGON!
OR A HISTORICAL FANTASY WHERE HE TAKES UP HIS SWORD TO FIGHT THE ENEMY!
GUYS. LET'S THINK ABOUT THIS MORE SERIOUSLY!

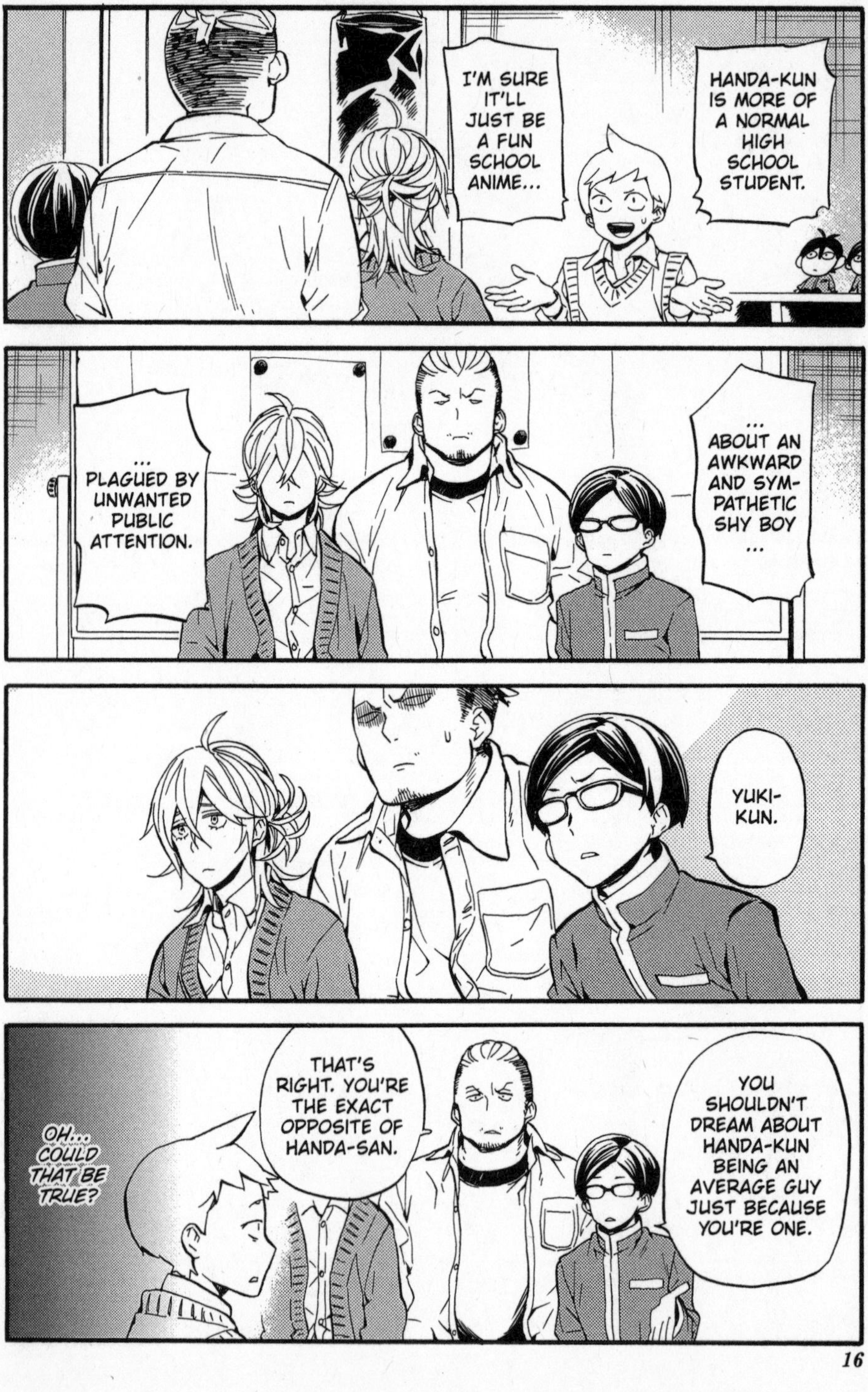
HANDA-KUN IS MORE OF A NORMAL HIGH SCHOOL STUDENT.
I'M SURE IT'LL JUST BE A FUN SCHOOL ANIME...
...ABOUT AN AWKWARD AND SYM-PATHETIC SHY BOY...
...PLAGUED BY UNWANTED PUBLIC ATTENTION.
YUKI-KUN.
YOU SHOULDN'T DREAM ABOUT HANDA-KUN BEING AN AVERAGE GUY JUST BECAUSE YOU'RE ONE.
THAT'S RIGHT. YOU'RE THE EXACT OPPOSITE OF HANDA-SAN.
OH... COULD THAT BE TRUE?

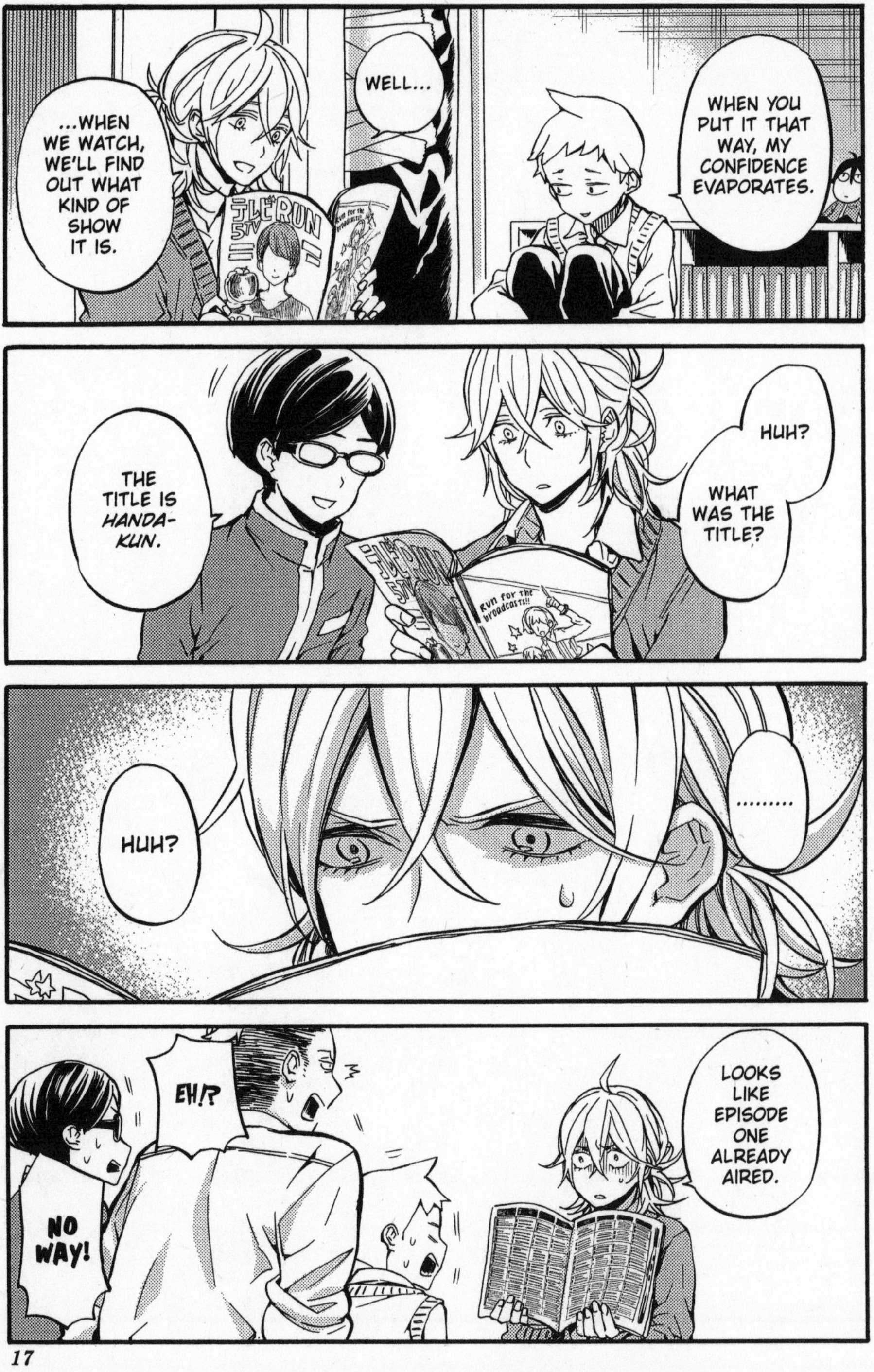

WHEN YOU PUT IT THAT WAY, MY CONFIDENCE EVAPORATES.
WELL...
...WHEN WE WATCH, WE'LL FIND OUT WHAT KIND OF SHOW IT IS.
HUH?
WHAT WAS THE TITLE?
THE TITLE IS *HANDA-KUN*.
Run for the broadcasts!!
....
HUH?
LOOKS LIKE EPISODE ONE ALREADY AIRED.
EH!?
NO WAY!

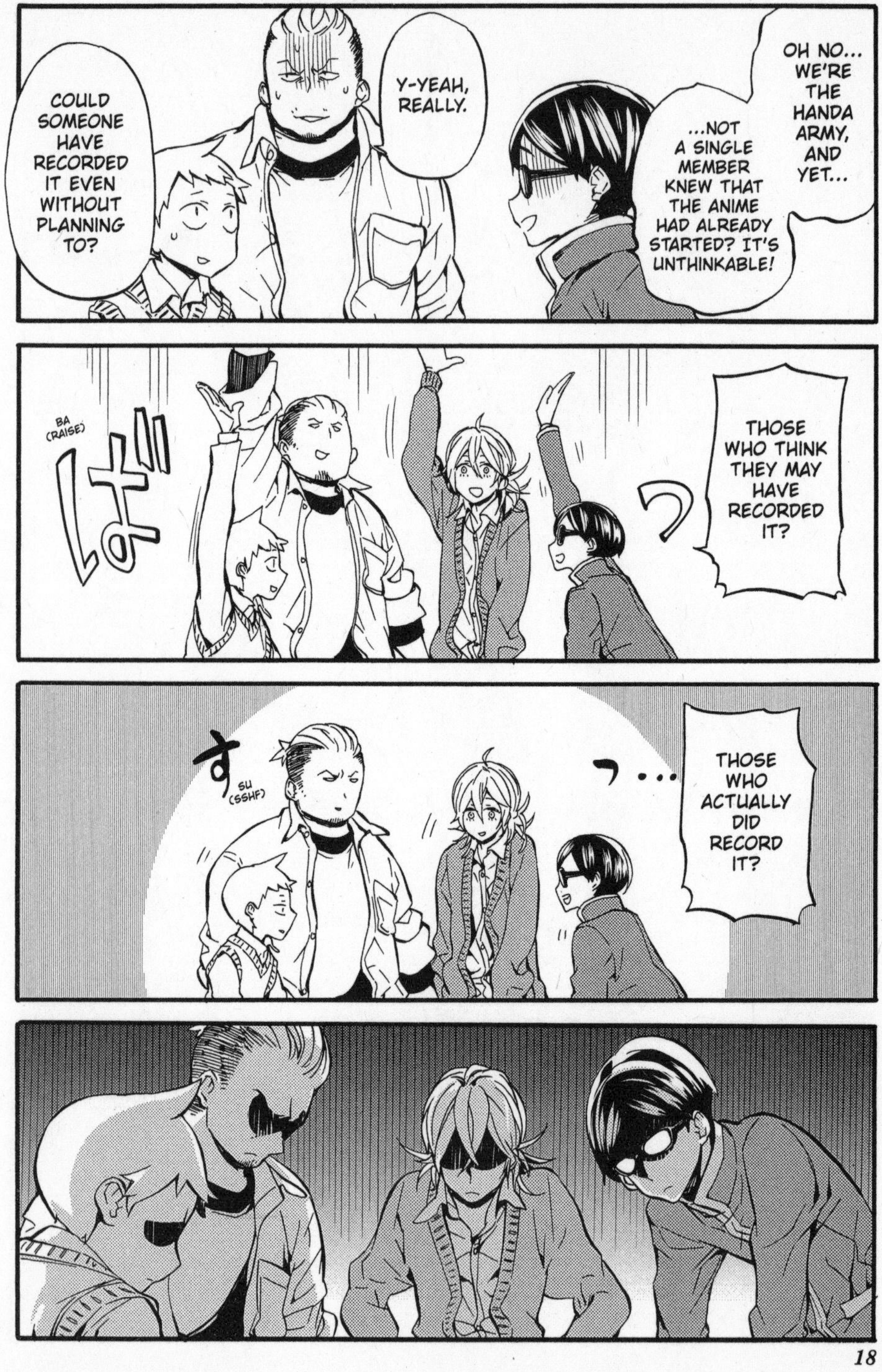
OH NO... WE'RE THE HANDA ARMY, AND YET...
...NOT A SINGLE MEMBER KNEW THAT THE ANIME HAD ALREADY STARTED? IT'S UNTHINKABLE!
Y-YEAH, REALLY.
COULD SOMEONE HAVE RECORDED IT EVEN WITHOUT PLANNING TO?
THOSE WHO THINK THEY MAY HAVE RECORDED IT?
っ
ば
BA (RAISE)
THOSE WHO ACTUALLY DID RECORD IT?
っ...
す
SU (SSHF)

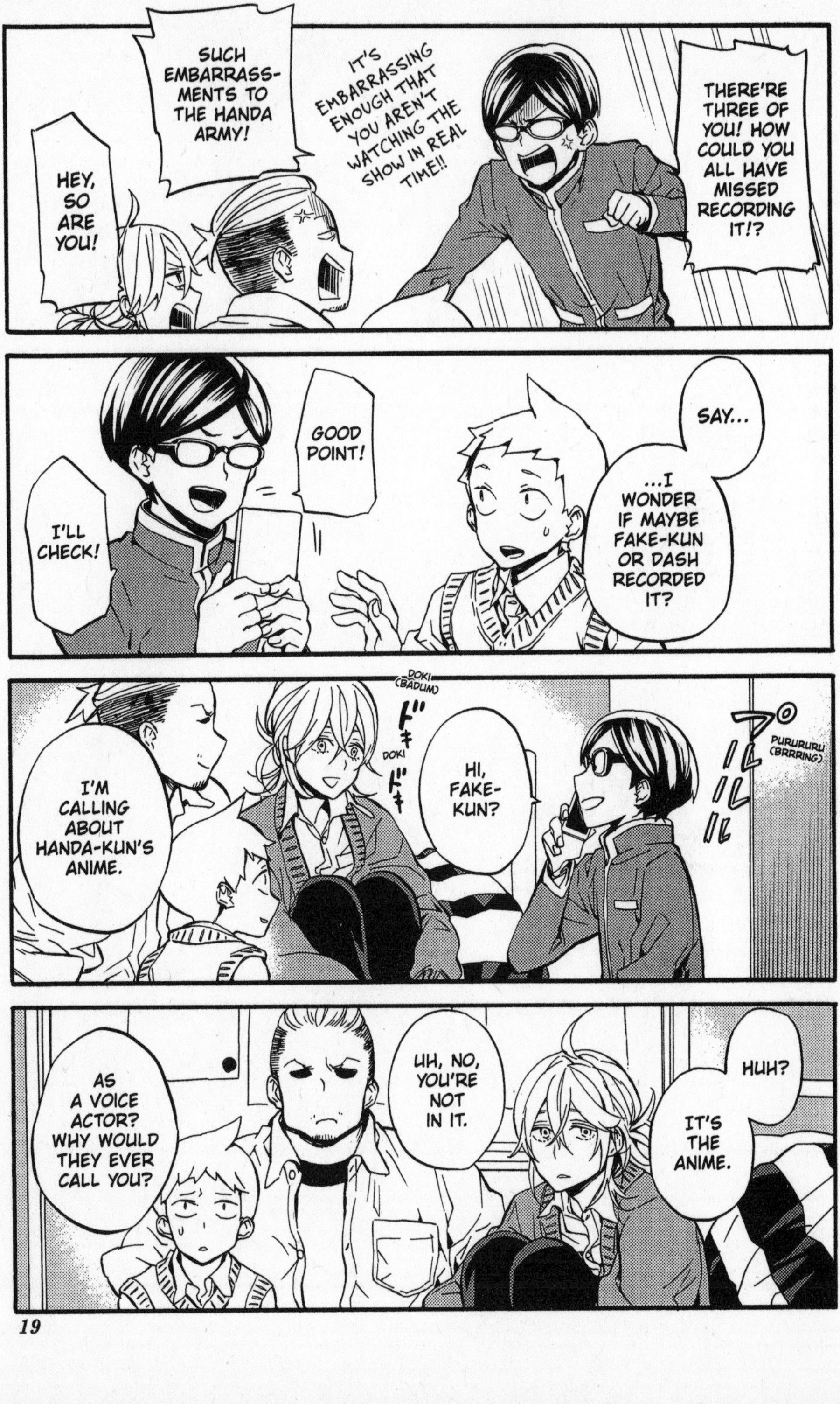
THERE'RE THREE OF YOU! HOW COULD YOU ALL HAVE MISSED RECORDING IT!?
IT'S EMBARRASSING ENOUGH THAT YOU AREN'T WATCHING THE SHOW IN REAL TIME!!
SUCH EMBARRASS-MENTS TO THE HANDA ARMY!
HEY, SO ARE YOU!
SAY...
...I WONDER IF MAYBE FAKE-KUN OR DASH RECORDED IT?
GOOD POINT!
I'LL CHECK!
PURURURU (BRRRING)
HI, FAKE-KUN?
DOKI (BADUM)
DOKI
I'M CALLING ABOUT HANDA-KUN'S ANIME.
HUH?
IT'S THE ANIME.
UH, NO, YOU'RE NOT IN IT.
AS A VOICE ACTOR? WHY WOULD THEY EVER CALL YOU?

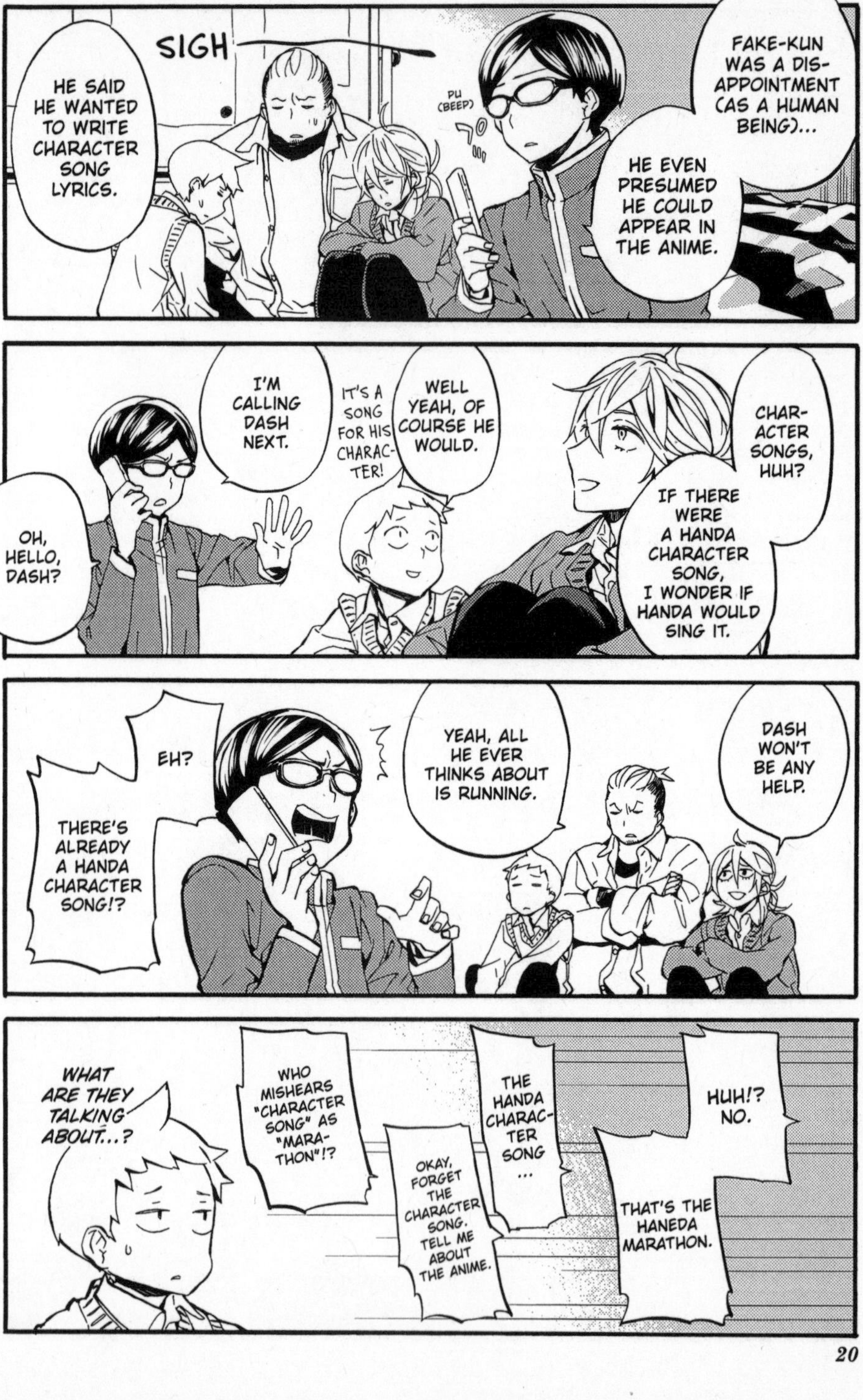
FAKE-KUN WAS A DIS-APPOINTMENT (AS A HUMAN BEING)...
HE EVEN PRESUMED HE COULD APPEAR IN THE ANIME.
PU (BEEP)
SIGH
HE SAID HE WANTED TO WRITE CHARACTER SONG LYRICS.
CHAR-ACTER SONGS, HUH?
IF THERE WERE A HANDA CHARACTER SONG, I WONDER IF HANDA WOULD SING IT.
WELL YEAH, OF COURSE HE WOULD.
IT'S A SONG FOR HIS CHARAC-TER!
I'M CALLING DASH NEXT.
OH, HELLO, DASH?
DASH WON'T BE ANY HELP.
YEAH, ALL HE EVER THINKS ABOUT IS RUNNING.
EH?
THERE'S ALREADY A HANDA CHARACTER SONG!?
HUH!? NO.
THAT'S THE HANEDA MARATHON.
THE HANDA CHARACTER SONG ...
OKAY, FORGET THE CHARACTER SONG. TELL ME ABOUT THE ANIME.
WHO MISHEARS "CHARACTER SONG" AS "MARA-THON"!?
WHAT ARE THEY TALKING ABOUT...?

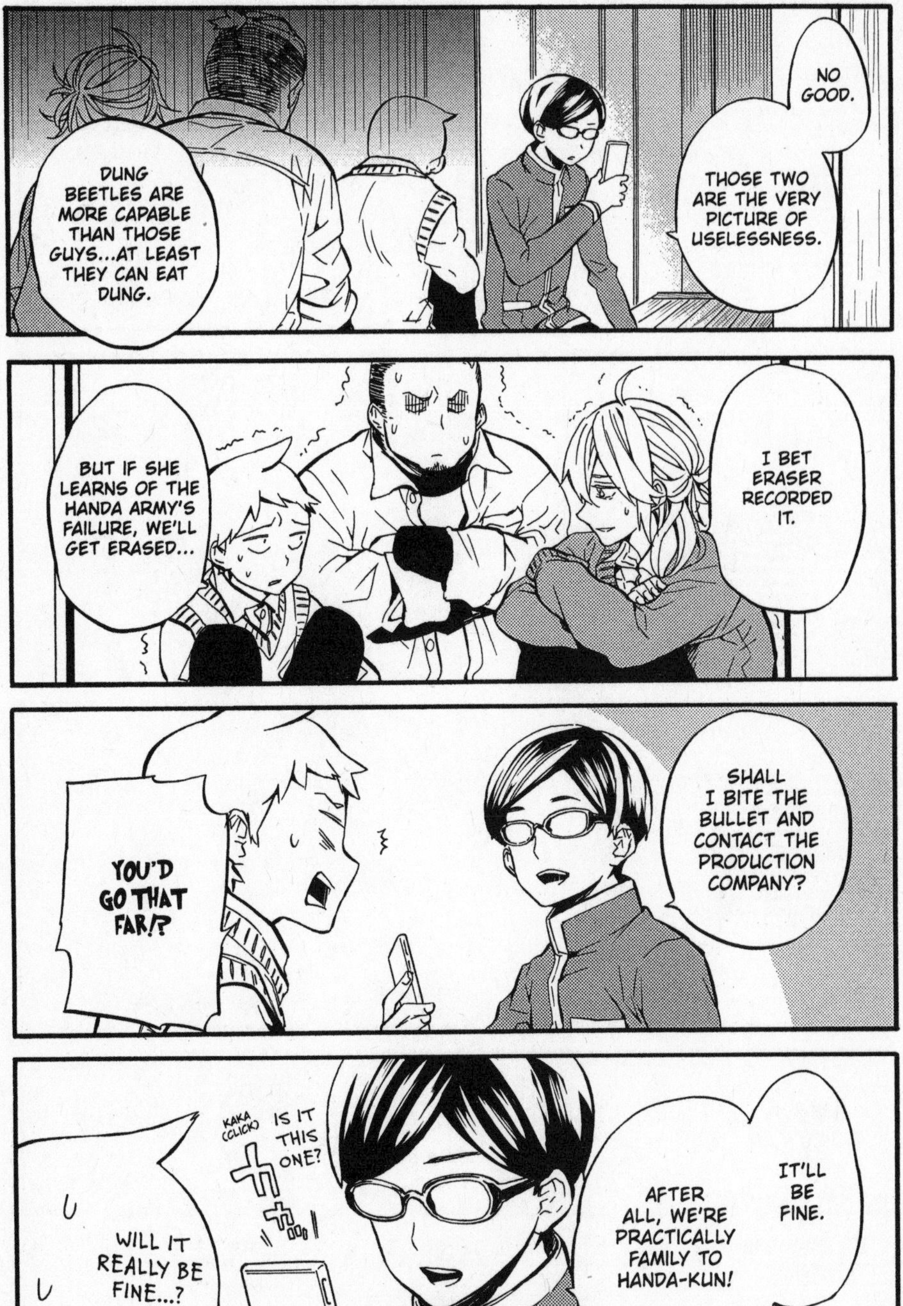
NO GOOD.
THOSE TWO ARE THE VERY PICTURE OF USELESSNESS.
DUNG BEETLES ARE MORE CAPABLE THAN THOSE GUYS...AT LEAST THEY CAN EAT DUNG.
I BET ERASER RECORDED IT.
BUT IF SHE LEARNS OF THE HANDA ARMY'S FAILURE, WE'LL GET ERASED...
SHALL I BITE THE BULLET AND CONTACT THE PRODUCTION COMPANY?
YOU'D GO THAT FAR!?
IT'LL BE FINE.
AFTER ALL, WE'RE PRACTICALLY FAMILY TO HANDA-KUN!
KAKA (CLICK)
IS IT THIS ONE?
WILL IT REALLY BE FINE...?

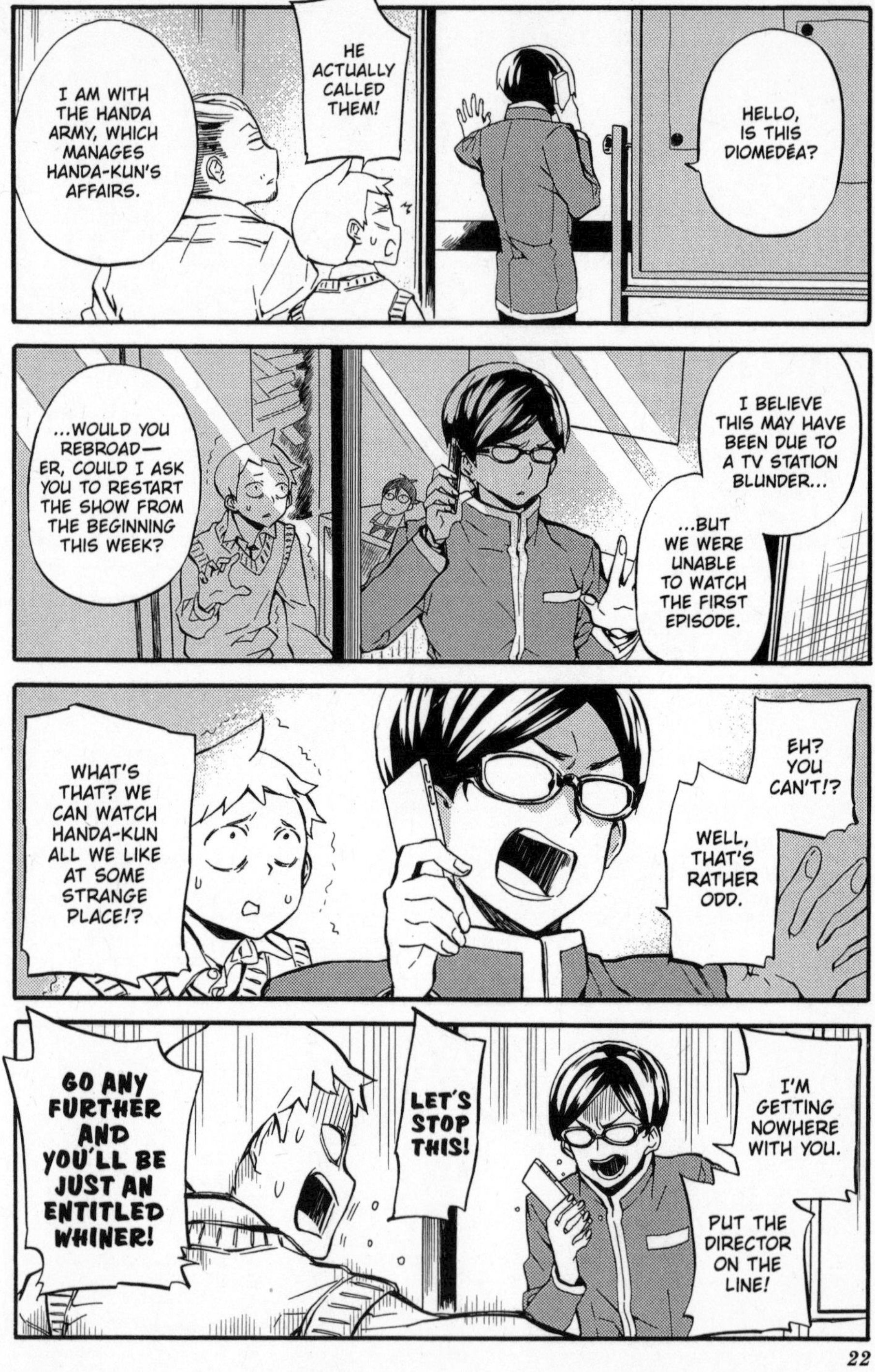
HELLO, IS THIS DIOMEDÉA?
HE ACTUALLY CALLED THEM!
I AM WITH THE HANDA ARMY, WHICH MANAGES HANDA-KUN'S AFFAIRS.
I BELIEVE THIS MAY HAVE BEEN DUE TO A TV STATION BLUNDER...
...BUT WE WERE UNABLE TO WATCH THE FIRST EPISODE.
...WOULD YOU REBROAD— ER, COULD I ASK YOU TO RESTART THE SHOW FROM THE BEGINNING THIS WEEK?
EH? YOU CAN'T!?
WELL, THAT'S RATHER ODD.
WHAT'S THAT? WE CAN WATCH HANDA-KUN ALL WE LIKE AT SOME STRANGE PLACE!?
I'M GETTING NOWHERE WITH YOU.
PUT THE DIRECTOR ON THE LINE!
LET'S STOP THIS!
GO ANY FURTHER AND YOU'LL BE JUST AN ENTITLED WHINER!

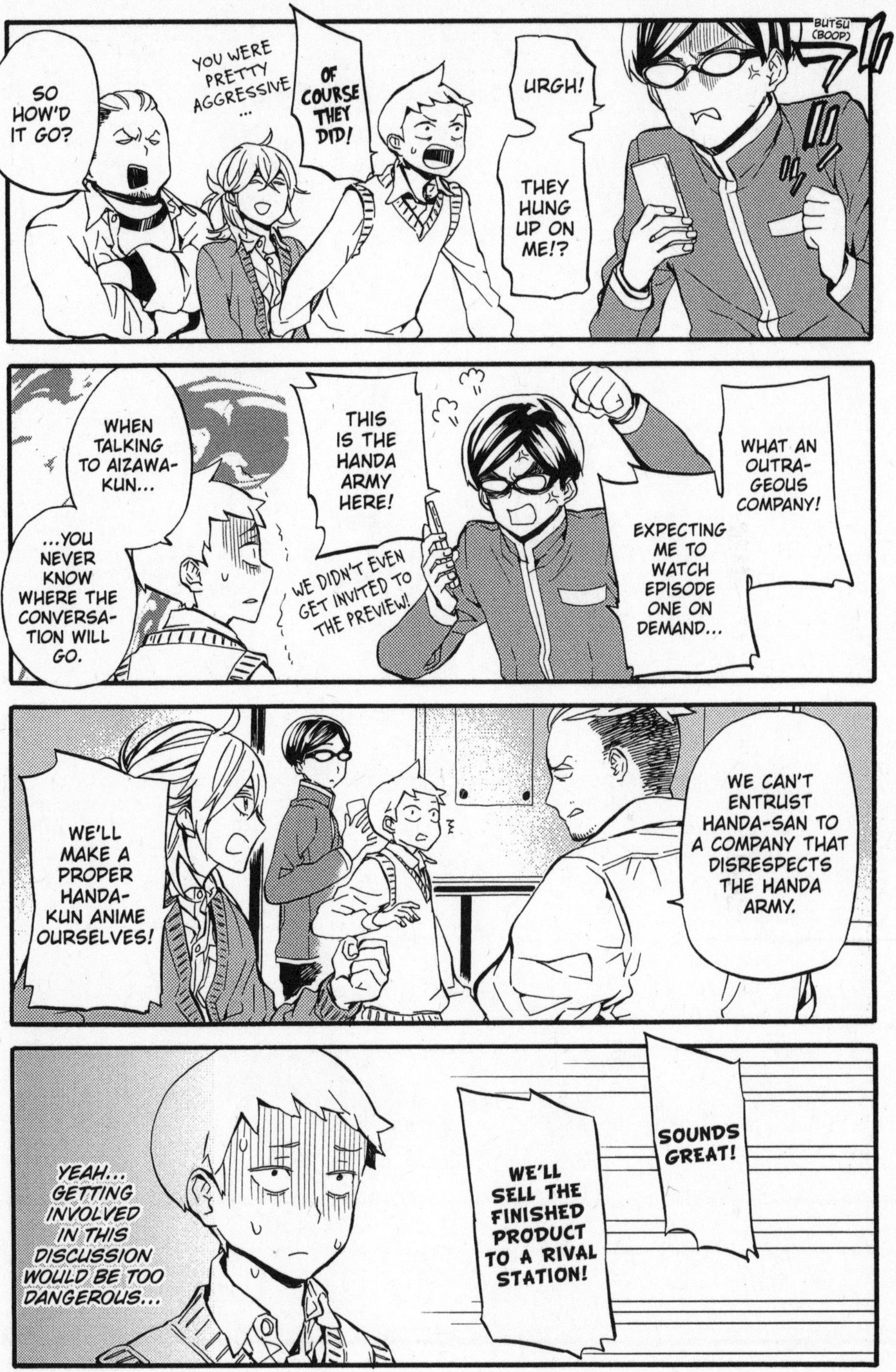
BUTSU (BOOP)
URGH!
THEY HUNG UP ON ME!?
OF COURSE THEY DID!
YOU WERE PRETTY AGGRESSIVE...
SO HOW'D IT GO?
WHAT AN OUTRAGEOUS COMPANY!
EXPECTING ME TO WATCH EPISODE ONE ON DEMAND...
THIS IS THE HANDA ARMY HERE!
WE DIDN'T EVEN GET INVITED TO THE PREVIEW!
WHEN TALKING TO AIZAWA-KUN...
...YOU NEVER KNOW WHERE THE CONVERSATION WILL GO.
WE CAN'T ENTRUST HANDA-SAN TO A COMPANY THAT DISRESPECTS THE HANDA ARMY.
WE'LL MAKE A PROPER HANDA-KUN ANIME OURSELVES!
SOUNDS GREAT!
WE'LL SELL THE FINISHED PRODUCT TO A RIVAL STATION!
YEAH... GETTING INVOLVED IN THIS DISCUSSION WOULD BE TOO DANGEROUS...

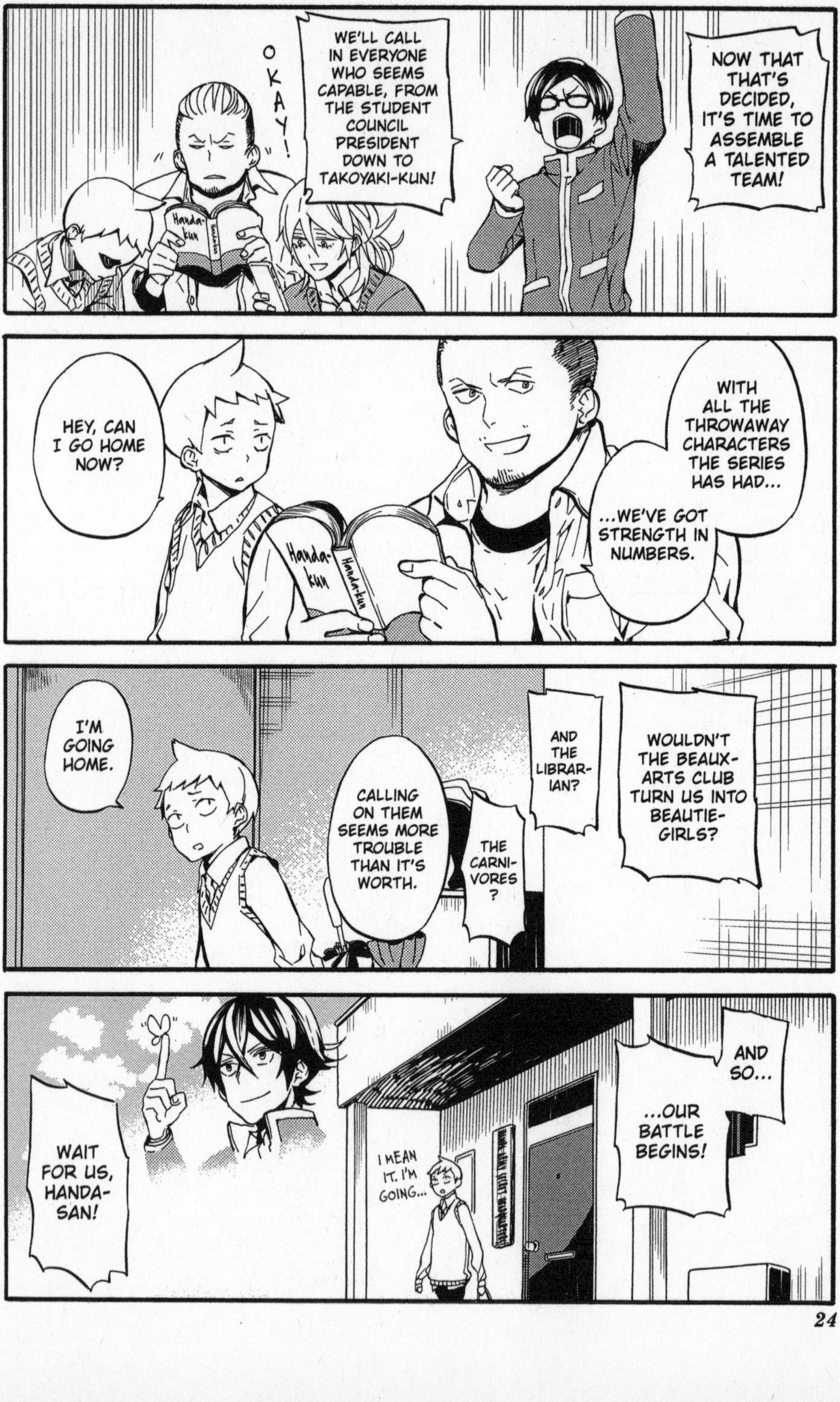
NOW THAT THAT'S DECIDED, IT'S TIME TO ASSEMBLE A TALENTED TEAM!
WE'LL CALL IN EVERYONE WHO SEEMS CAPABLE, FROM THE STUDENT COUNCIL PRESIDENT DOWN TO TAKOYAKI-KUN!
OKAY!
Handa-kun
WITH ALL THE THROWAWAY CHARACTERS THE SERIES HAS HAD...
...WE'VE GOT STRENGTH IN NUMBERS.
Handa-kun
Handa-kun
HEY, CAN I GO HOME NOW?
WOULDN'T THE BEAUX-ARTS CLUB TURN US INTO BEAUTIE-GIRLS?
AND THE LIBRARIAN?
THE CARNIVORES?
CALLING ON THEM SEEMS MORE TROUBLE THAN IT'S WORTH.
I'M GOING HOME.
AND SO...
...OUR BATTLE BEGINS!
I MEAN IT. I'M GOING...
WAIT FOR US, HANDA-SAN!

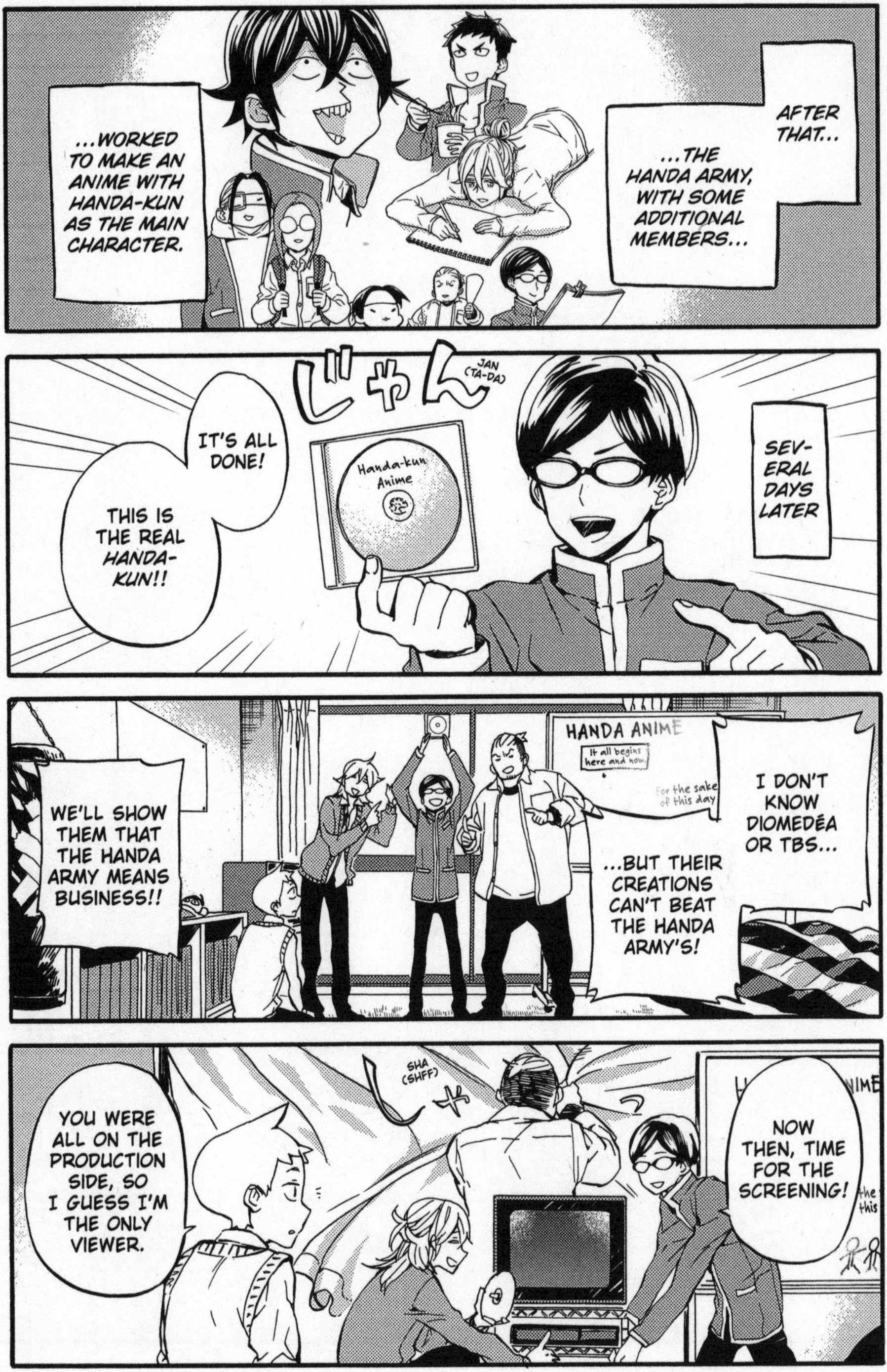
AFTER THAT...
...THE HANDA ARMY, WITH SOME ADDITIONAL MEMBERS...
...WORKED TO MAKE AN ANIME WITH HANDA-KUN AS THE MAIN CHARACTER.
SEVERAL DAYS LATER
じゃん
JAN (TA-DA)
Handa-kun Anime
IT'S ALL DONE!
THIS IS THE REAL HANDA-KUN!!
I DON'T KNOW DIOMEDÉA OR TBS...
...BUT THEIR CREATIONS CAN'T BEAT THE HANDA ARMY'S!
HANDA ANIME
It all begins here and now.
For the sake of this day
WE'LL SHOW THEM THAT THE HANDA ARMY MEANS BUSINESS!!
NOW THEN, TIME FOR THE SCREENING!
しャ
SHA (SHFF)
YOU WERE ALL ON THE PRODUCTION SIDE, SO I GUESS I'M THE ONLY VIEWER.

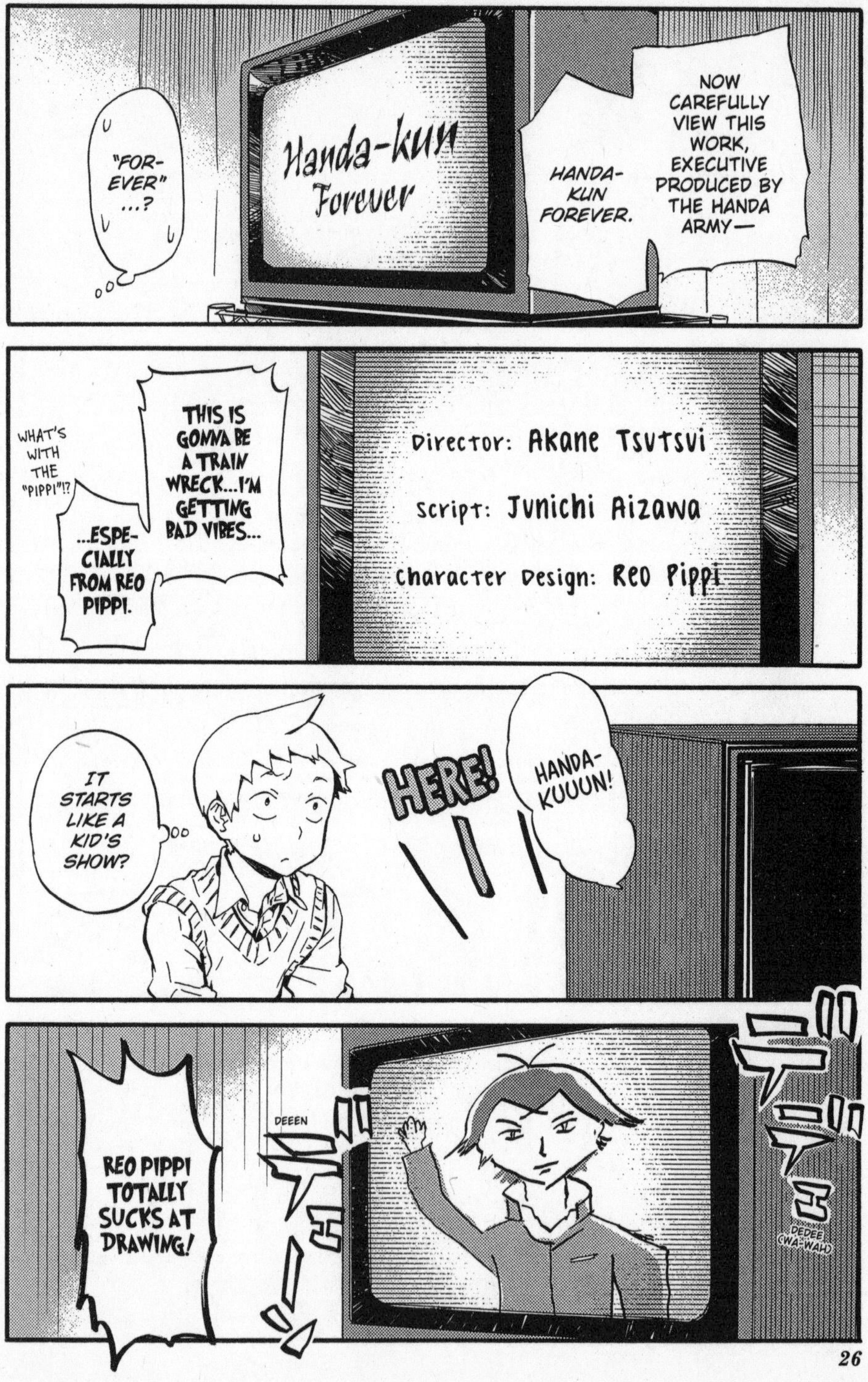
NOW CAREFULLY VIEW THIS WORK, EXECUTIVE PRODUCED BY THE HANDA ARMY—
HANDA-KUN FOREVER.
Handa-kun Forever
"FOR-EVER" ...?
Director: Akane Tsutsui
Script: Junichi Aizawa
Character Design: Reo Pippi
THIS IS GONNA BE A TRAIN WRECK...I'M GETTING BAD VIBES...
...ESPE-CIALLY FROM REO PIPPI.
WHAT'S WITH THE "PIPPI"!?
HANDA-KUUUN!
HERE!
IT STARTS LIKE A KID'S SHOW?
DEDEE (WA-WAH)
DEEEN
REO PIPPI TOTALLY SUCKS AT DRAWING!

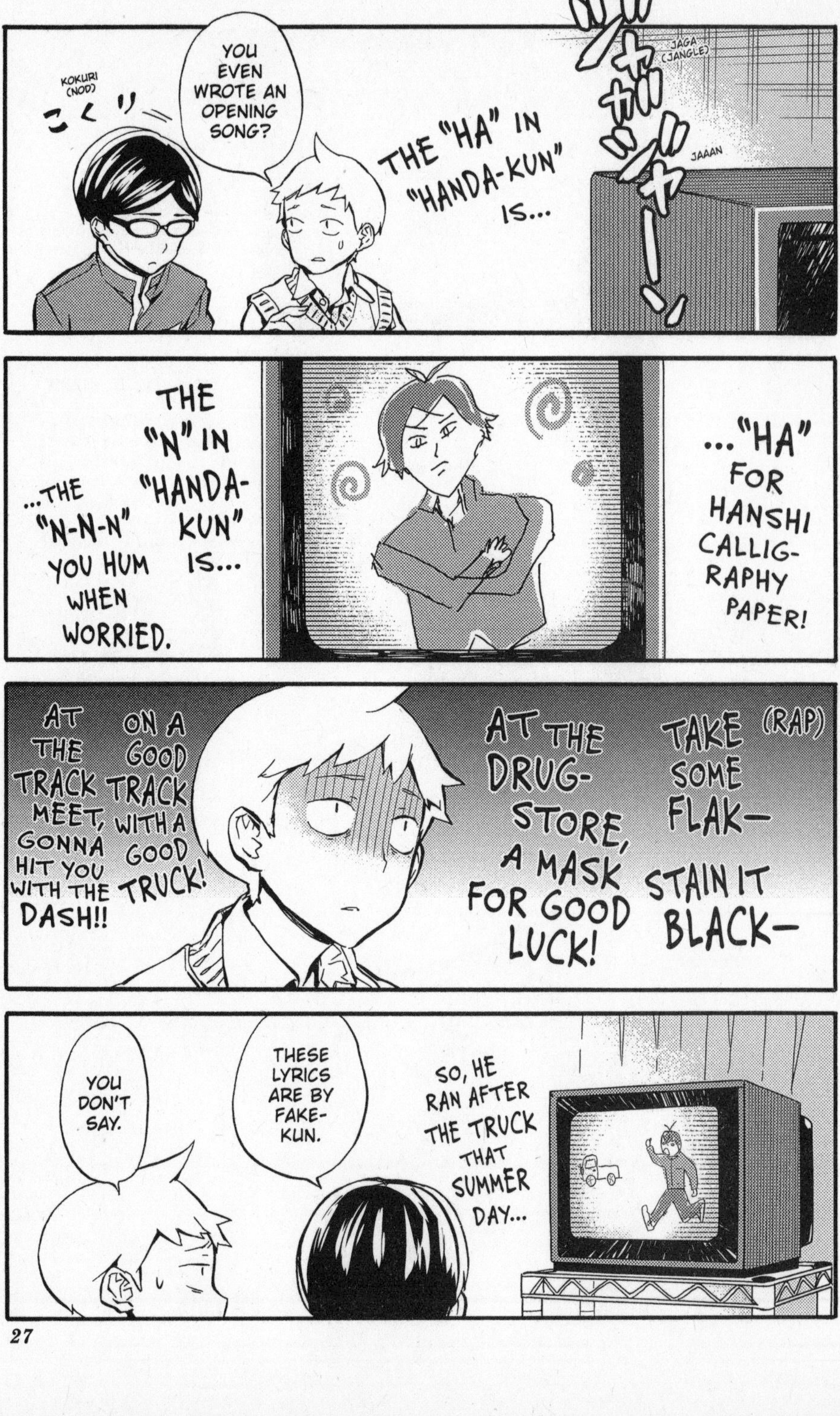
ジャガジャーン
JAGA (JANGLE)
JAAAN
THE "HA" IN "HANDA-KUN" IS...
YOU EVEN WROTE AN OPENING SONG?
こくり
KOKURI (NOD)
..."HA" FOR HANSHI CALLIGRAPHY PAPER!
THE "N" IN "HANDA-KUN" IS...
...THE "N-N-N" YOU HUM WHEN WORRIED.
(RAP)
TAKE SOME FLAK— STAIN IT BLACK—
AT THE DRUGSTORE, A MASK FOR GOOD LUCK!
ON A GOOD TRACK WITH A GOOD TRUCK!
AT THE TRACK MEET, GONNA HIT YOU WITH THE DASH!!
SO, HE RAN AFTER THE TRUCK THAT SUMMER DAY...
THESE LYRICS ARE BY FAKE-KUN.
YOU DON'T SAY.

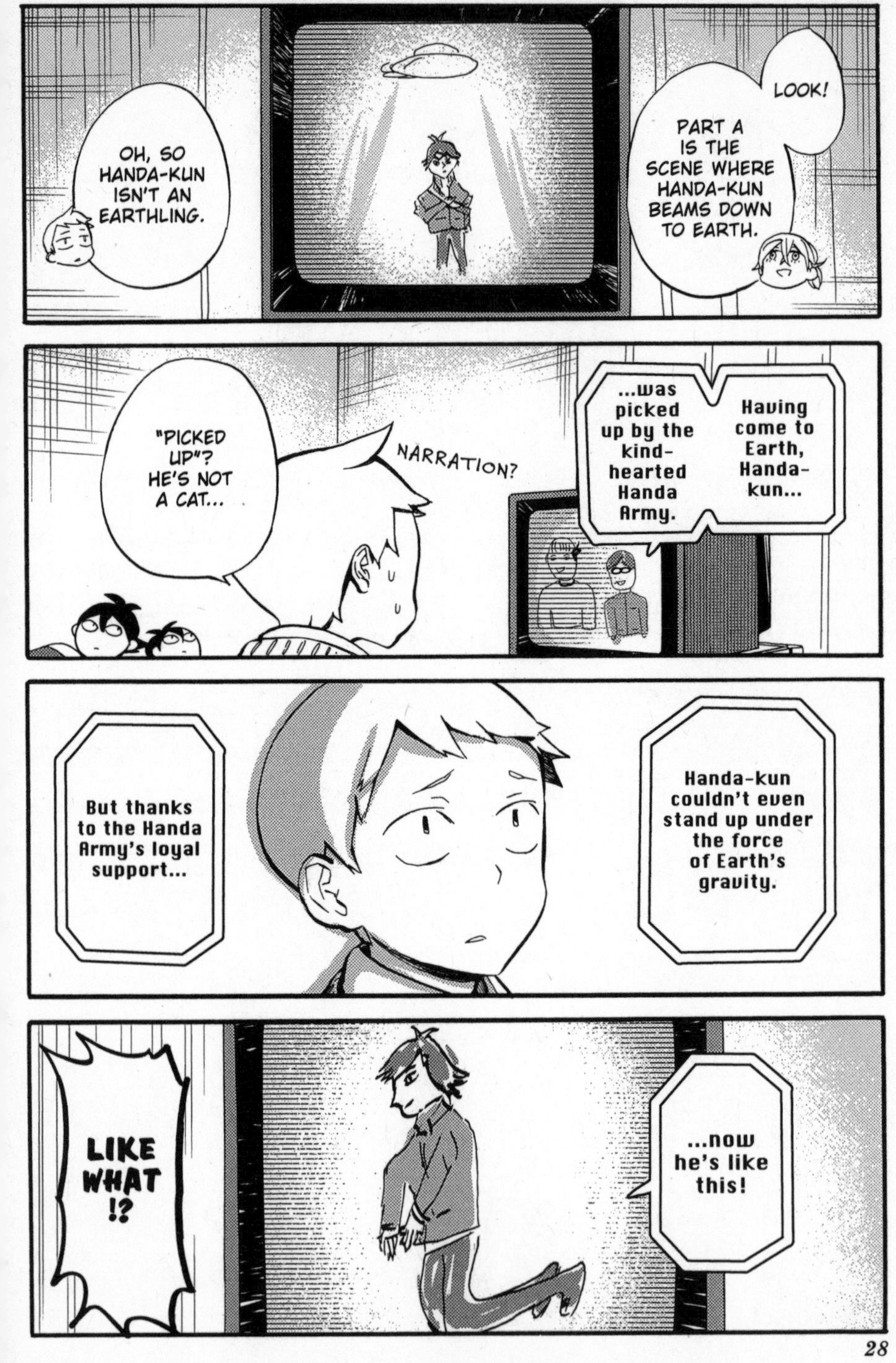
LOOK!
PART A IS THE SCENE WHERE HANDA-KUN BEAMS DOWN TO EARTH.
OH, SO HANDA-KUN ISN'T AN EARTHLING.
Having come to Earth, Handa-kun...
...was picked up by the kind-hearted Handa Army.
NARRATION?
"PICKED UP"? HE'S NOT A CAT...
Handa-kun couldn't even stand up under the force of Earth's gravity.
But thanks to the Handa Army's loyal support...
...now he's like this!
LIKE WHAT!?

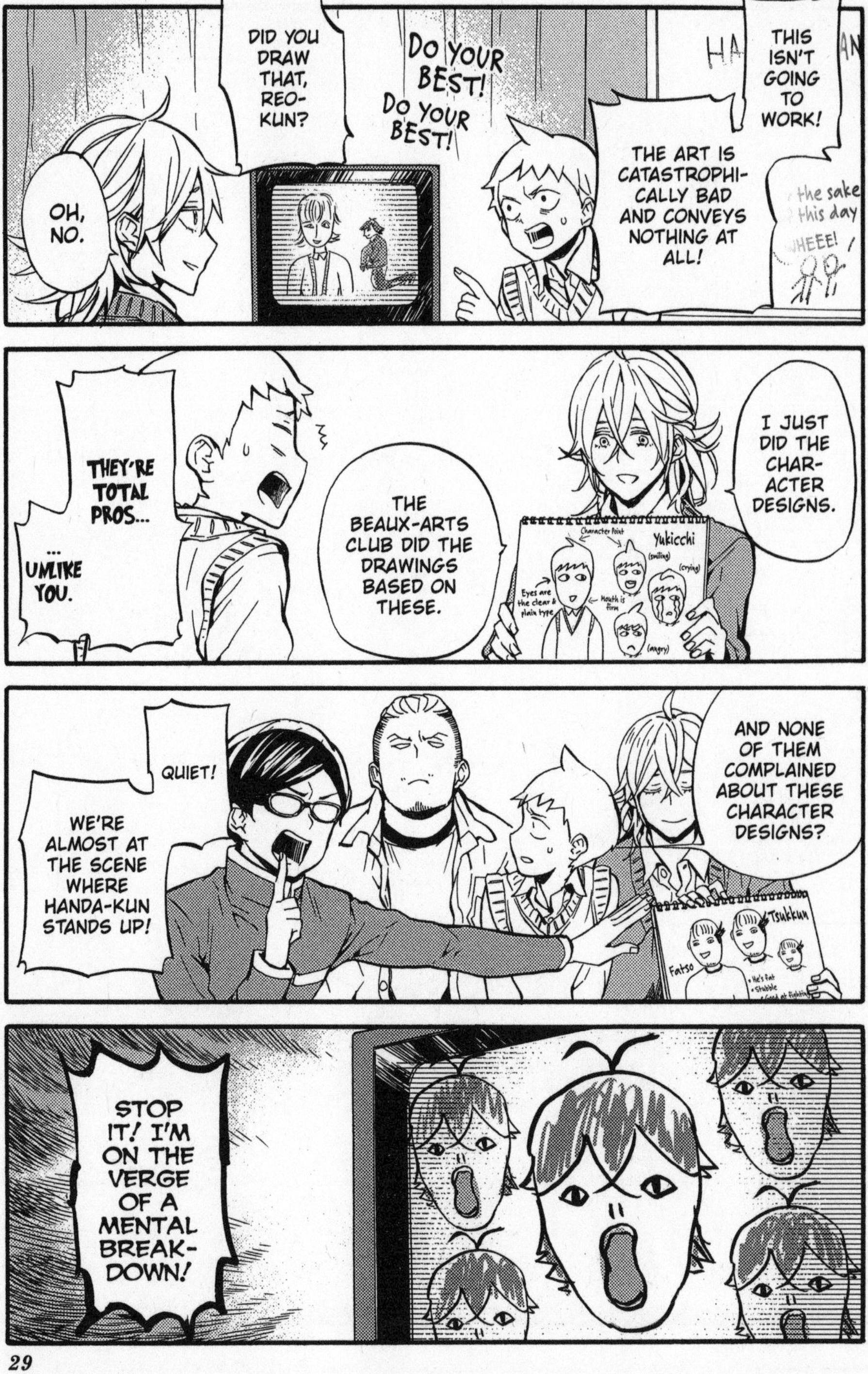
THIS ISN'T GOING TO WORK!
THE ART IS CATASTROPHICALLY BAD AND CONVEYS NOTHING AT ALL!
WHEEE!
DO YOUR BEST!
DO YOUR BEST!
DID YOU DRAW THAT, REO-KUN?
OH, NO.
I JUST DID THE CHARACTER DESIGNS.
Yukicchi
Character Point
(smiling)
(crying)
Eyes are the clear & plain type
Mouth is firm
(angry)
THE BEAUX-ARTS CLUB DID THE DRAWINGS BASED ON THESE.
THEY'RE TOTAL PROS...
...UNLIKE YOU.
AND NONE OF THEM COMPLAINED ABOUT THESE CHARACTER DESIGNS?
Tsukkun
Fatso
• He's Fat
• Stubble
QUIET!
WE'RE ALMOST AT THE SCENE WHERE HANDA-KUN STANDS UP!
STOP IT! I'M ON THE VERGE OF A MENTAL BREAKDOWN!

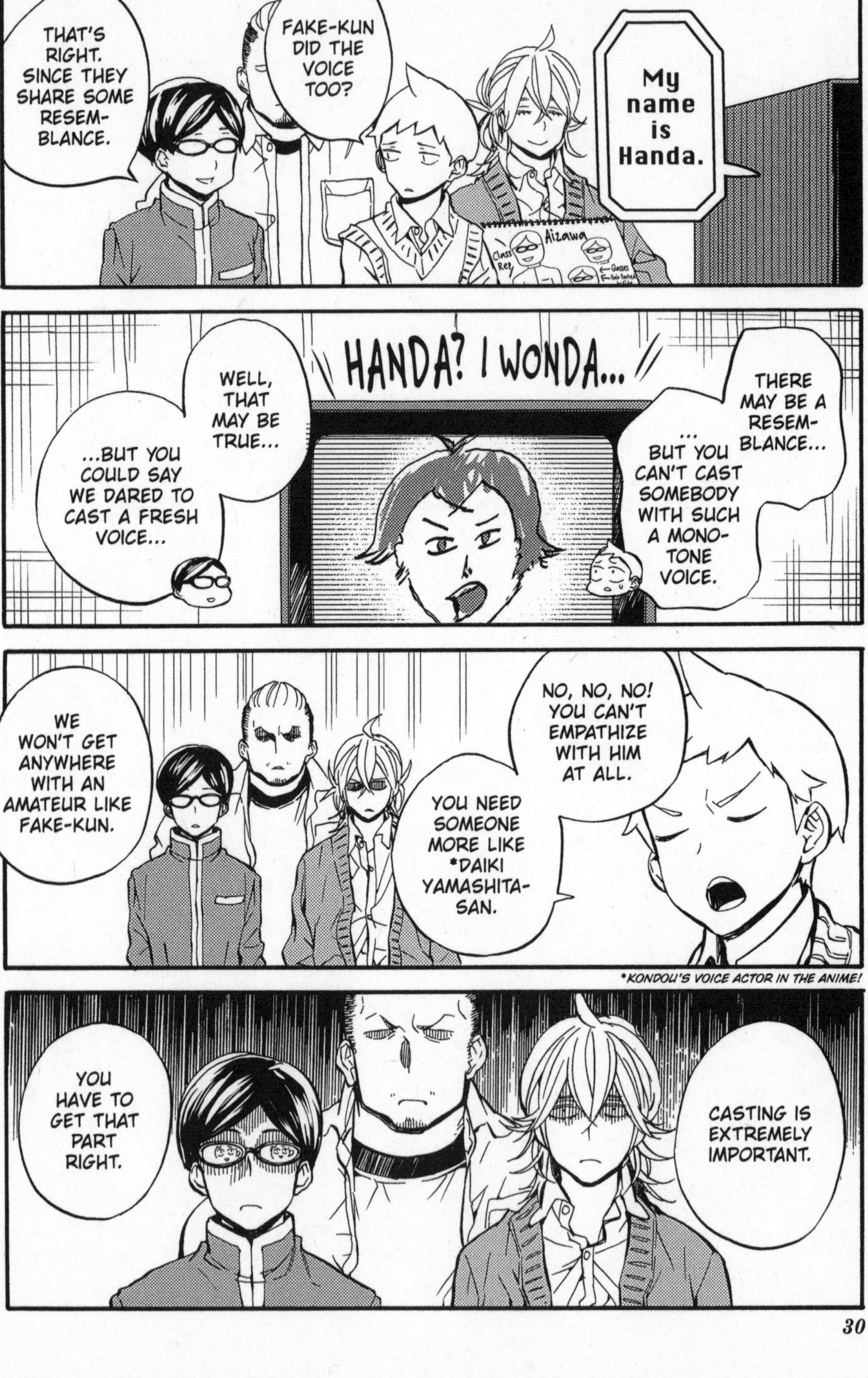
My name is Handa.
FAKE-KUN DID THE VOICE TOO?
THAT'S RIGHT. SINCE THEY SHARE SOME RESEMBLANCE.
Aizawa
Class Rep
Glasses
HANDA? I WONDA...
THERE MAY BE A RESEMBLANCE...
...BUT YOU CAN'T CAST SOMEBODY WITH SUCH A MONOTONE VOICE.
WELL, THAT MAY BE TRUE...
...BUT YOU COULD SAY WE DARED TO CAST A FRESH VOICE...
NO, NO, NO! YOU CAN'T EMPATHIZE WITH HIM AT ALL.
YOU NEED SOMEONE MORE LIKE *DAIKI YAMASHITA-SAN.
WE WON'T GET ANYWHERE WITH AN AMATEUR LIKE FAKE-KUN.
*KONDOU'S VOICE ACTOR IN THE ANIME!
CASTING IS EXTREMELY IMPORTANT.
YOU HAVE TO GET THAT PART RIGHT.

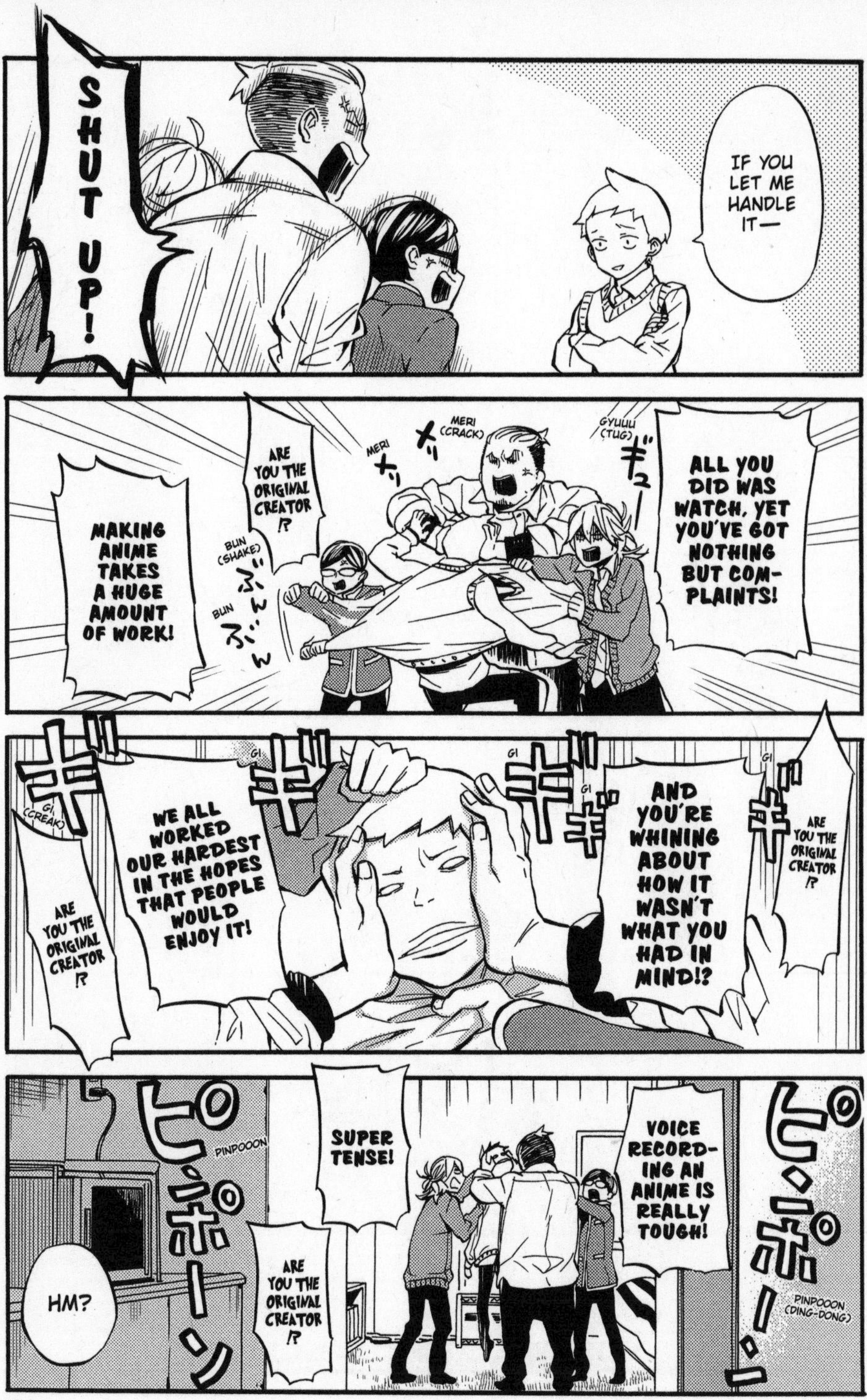
IF YOU LET ME HANDLE IT—
SHUT UP!
ALL YOU DID WAS WATCH, YET YOU'VE GOT NOTHING BUT COMPLAINTS!
GYUUU (TUG)
MERI (CRACK)
MERI
ARE YOU THE ORIGINAL CREATOR!?
BUN (SHAKE)
BUN
MAKING ANIME TAKES A HUGE AMOUNT OF WORK!
GI
ARE YOU THE ORIGINAL CREATOR!?
AND YOU'RE WHINING ABOUT HOW IT WASN'T WHAT YOU HAD IN MIND!?
GI
GI
GI
WE ALL WORKED OUR HARDEST IN THE HOPES THAT PEOPLE WOULD ENJOY IT!
GI (CREAK)
ARE YOU THE ORIGINAL CREATOR!?
PINPOOON (DING-DONG)
VOICE RECORDING AN ANIME IS REALLY TOUGH!
SUPER TENSE!
ARE YOU THE ORIGINAL CREATOR!?
PINPOOON
HM?

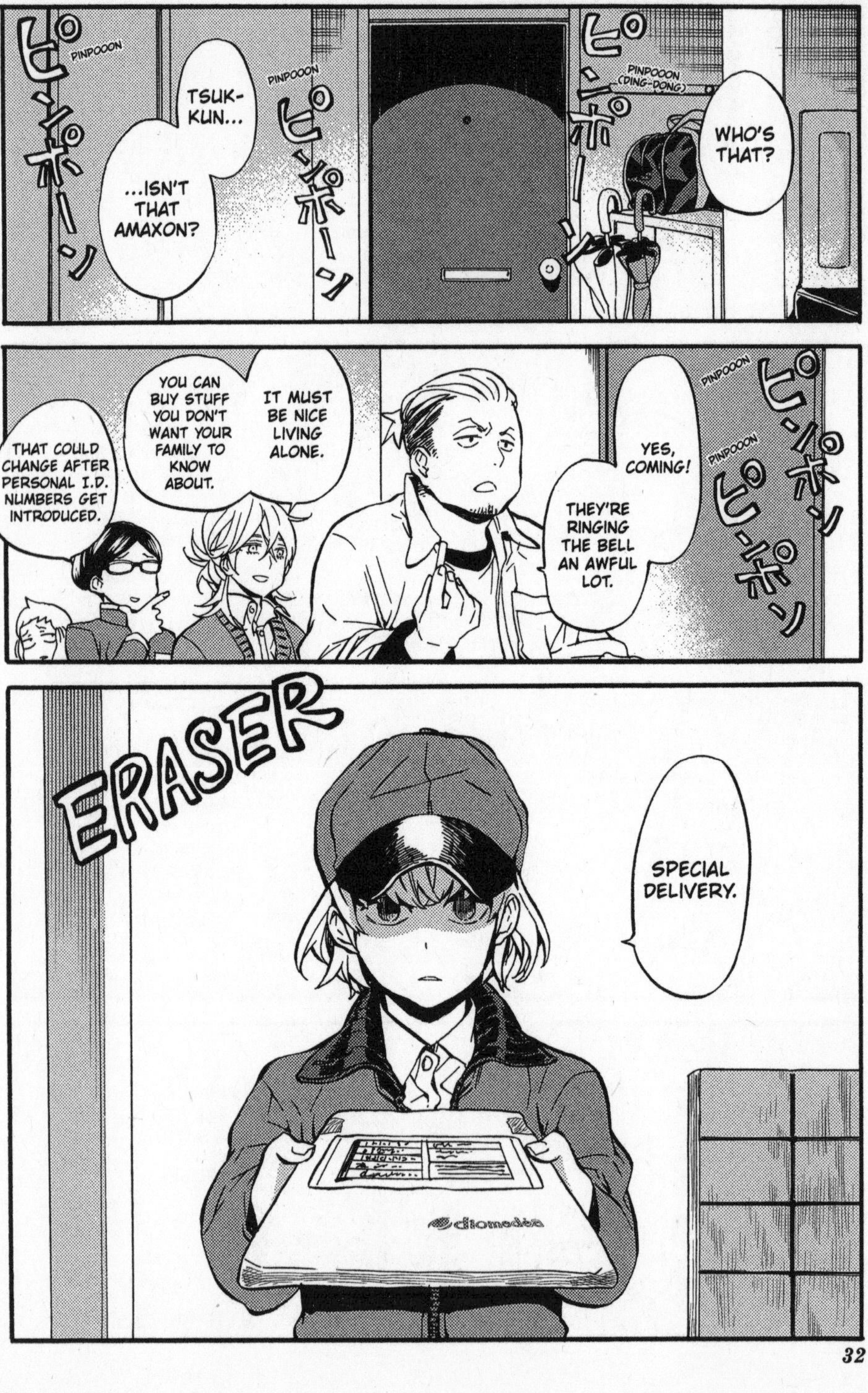
PINPOOON (DING-DONG)
WHO'S THAT?
PINPOOON
TSUK-KUN...
...ISN'T THAT AMAXON?
PINPOOON
PINPOOON
PINPOOON
YES, COMING!
THEY'RE RINGING THE BELL AN AWFUL LOT.
IT MUST BE NICE LIVING ALONE.
YOU CAN BUY STUFF YOU DON'T WANT YOUR FAMILY TO KNOW ABOUT.
THAT COULD CHANGE AFTER PERSONAL I.D. NUMBERS GET INTRODUCED.
SPECIAL DELIVERY.
ERASER

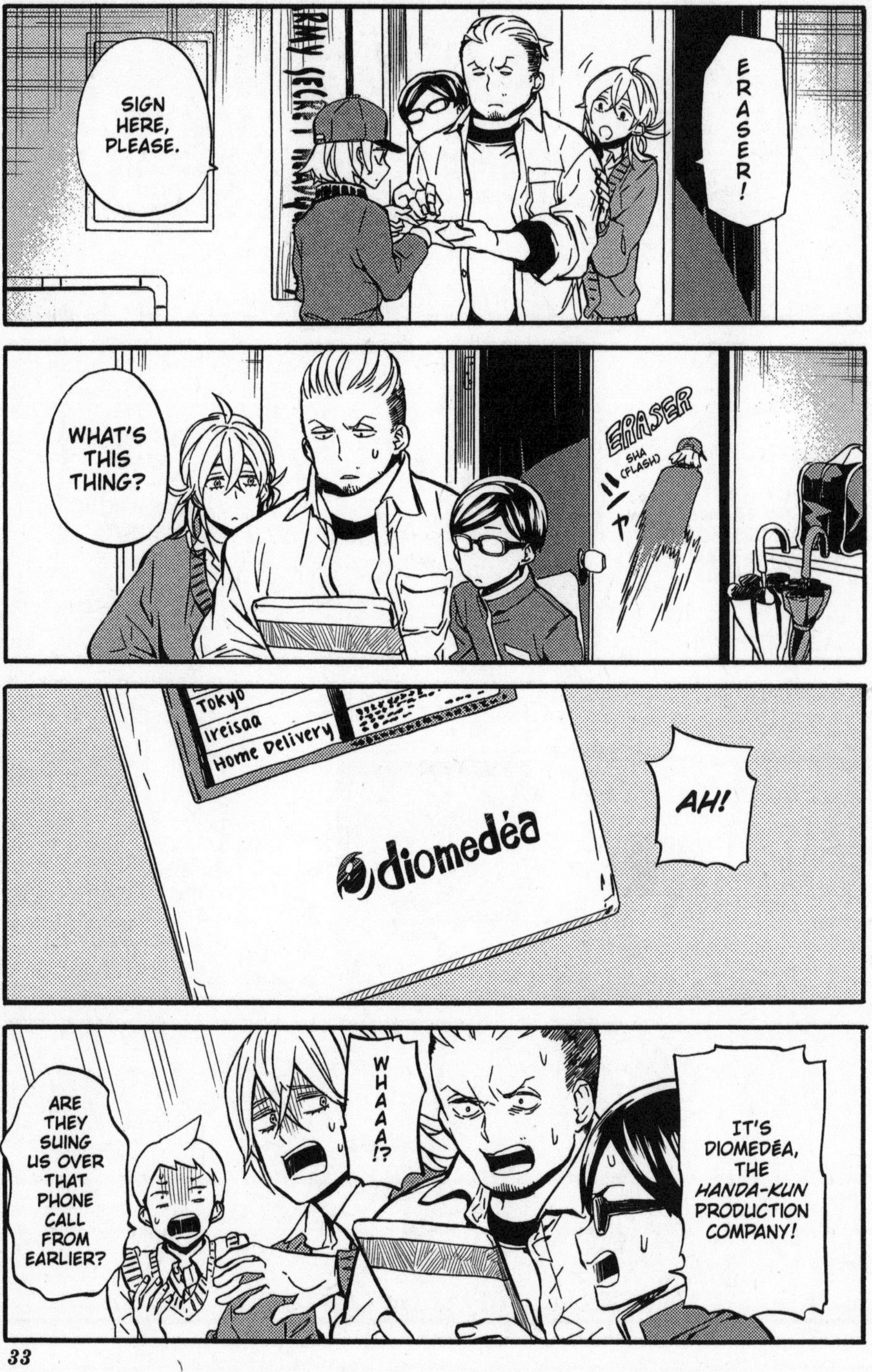
ERASER!
SIGN HERE, PLEASE.
ERASER
SHA (FLASH)
WHAT'S THIS THING?
AH!
Tokyo
Ireisaa
Home Delivery
diomedéa
IT'S DIOMEDÉA, THE *HANDA-KUN* PRODUCTION COMPANY!
WHAAAA!?
ARE THEY SUING US OVER THAT PHONE CALL FROM EARLIER?

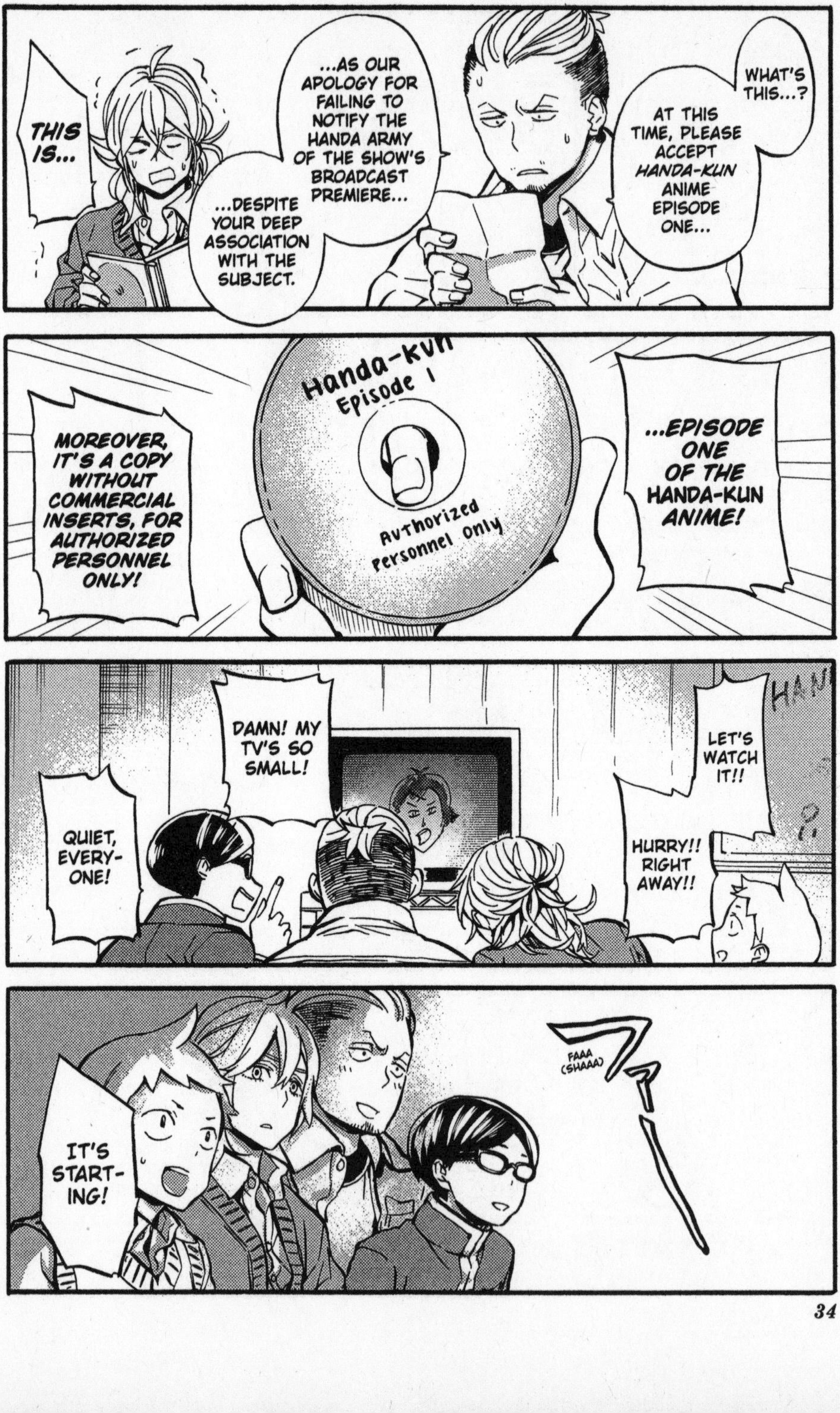
WHAT'S THIS...?
AT THIS TIME, PLEASE ACCEPT HANDA-KUN ANIME EPISODE ONE...
...AS OUR APOLOGY FOR FAILING TO NOTIFY THE HANDA ARMY OF THE SHOW'S BROADCAST PREMIERE...
...DESPITE YOUR DEEP ASSOCIATION WITH THE SUBJECT.
THIS IS...
...EPISODE ONE OF THE HANDA-KUN ANIME!
Handa-kun Episode 1
Authorized Personnel Only
MOREOVER, IT'S A COPY WITHOUT COMMERCIAL INSERTS, FOR AUTHORIZED PERSONNEL ONLY!
LET'S WATCH IT!!
HURRY!! RIGHT AWAY!!
DAMN! MY TV'S SO SMALL!
QUIET, EVERY-ONE!
FAAA (SHAAA)
IT'S STARTING-ING!

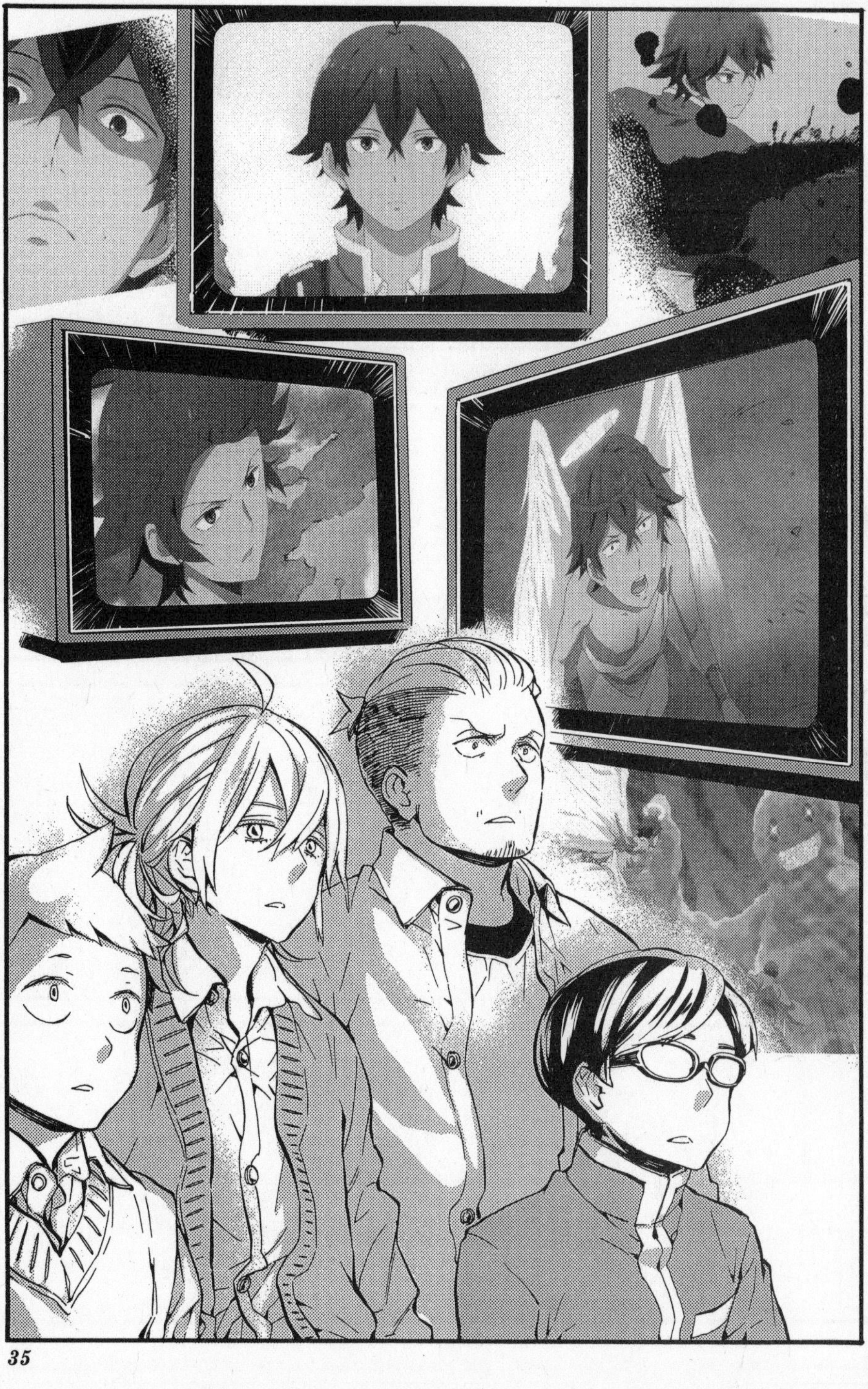

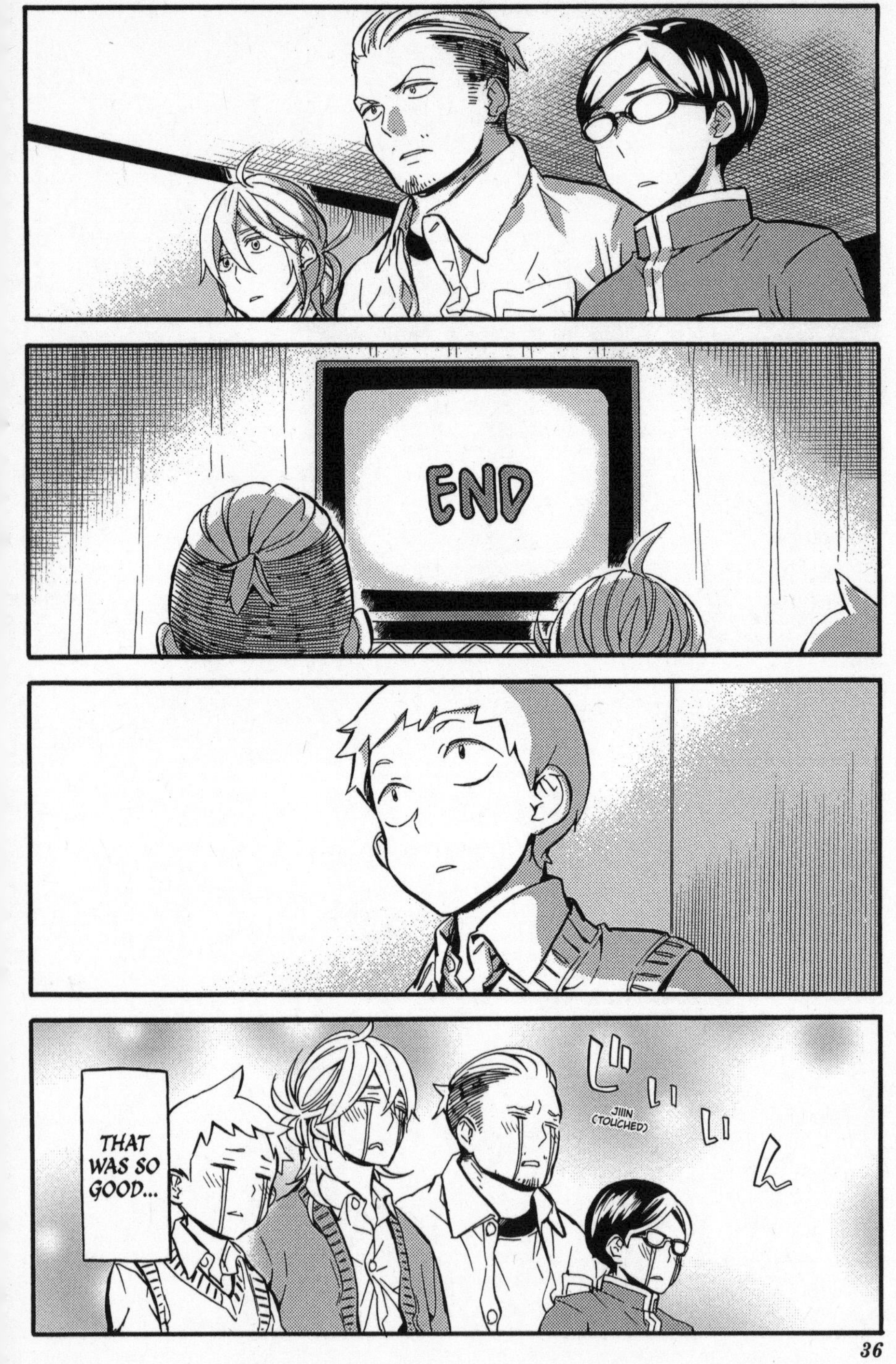
END
じぃぃぃん
JIIIN (TOUCHED)
THAT WAS SO GOOD...

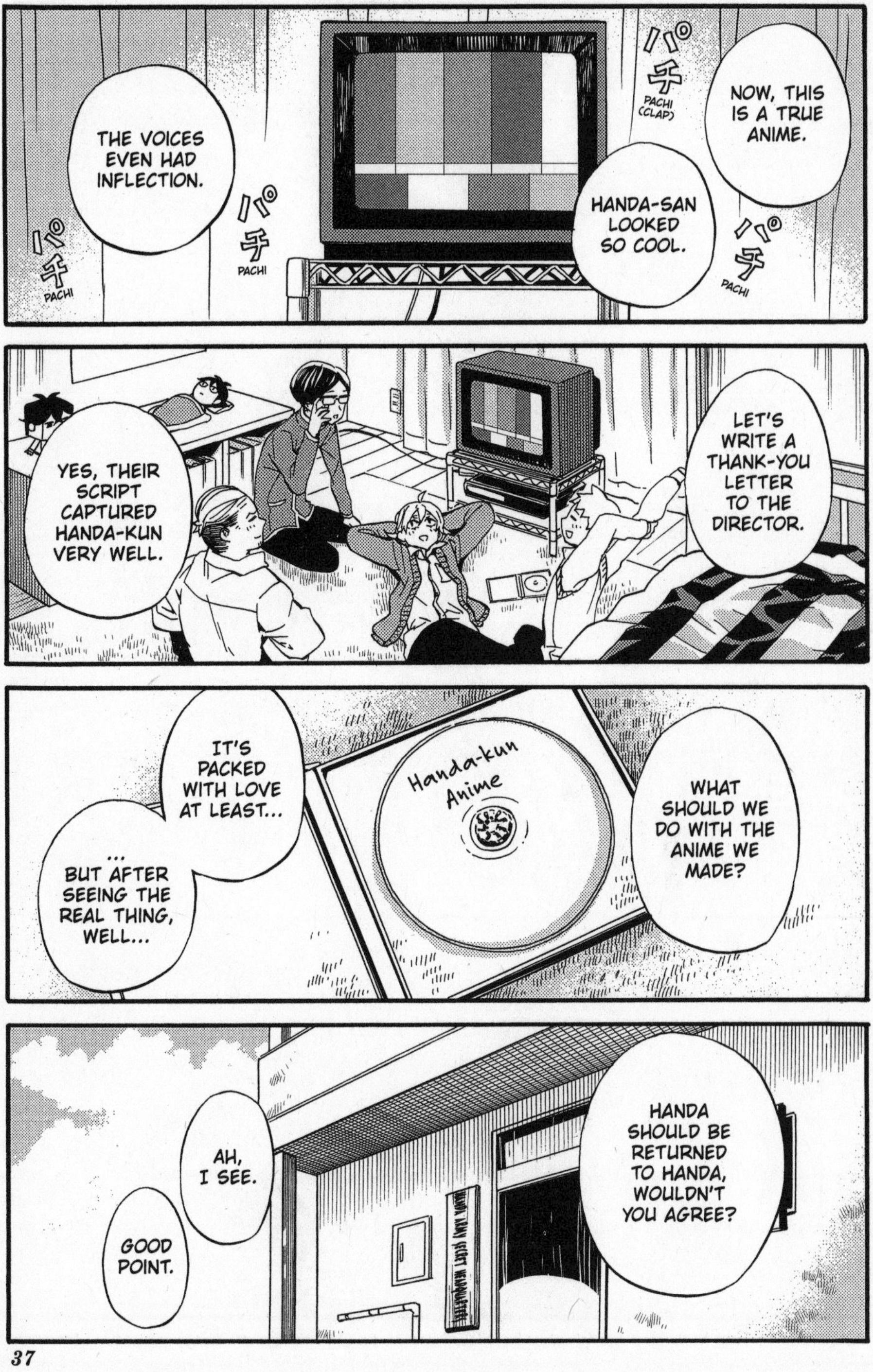
NOW, THIS IS A TRUE ANIME.
パチ
PACHI (CLAP)
HANDA-SAN LOOKED SO COOL.
パチ
PACHI
THE VOICES EVEN HAD INFLECTION.
パチ
PACHI
パチ
PACHI
LET'S WRITE A THANK-YOU LETTER TO THE DIRECTOR.
YES, THEIR SCRIPT CAPTURED HANDA-KUN VERY WELL.
WHAT SHOULD WE DO WITH THE ANIME WE MADE?
Handa-kun Anime
IT'S PACKED WITH LOVE AT LEAST...
... BUT AFTER SEEING THE REAL THING, WELL...
HANDA SHOULD BE RETURNED TO HANDA, WOULDN'T YOU AGREE?
AH, I SEE.
GOOD POINT.

SEI-SAAAN! YOU GOT A PACKAGE!
IT'S A DVD.
HM?
WHAT'S ON IT?
ERASER
JAGA (JANGLE)
JAAAN
THE "HA" IN "HANDA-KUN" IS...
PI (BEEP)
(OFF)
HE DIDN'T WATCH IT.

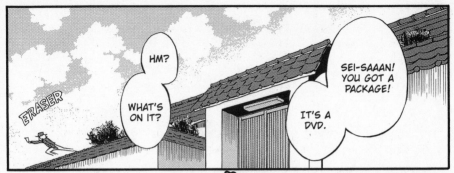

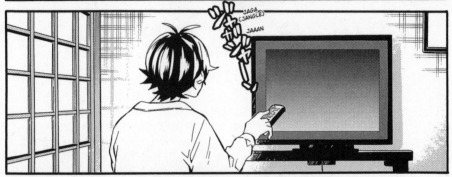

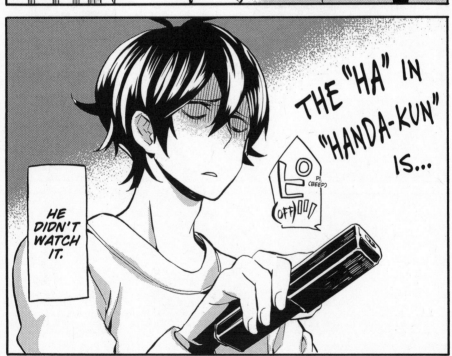

When they suggested that we do an extra arc during the three months the anime would be broadcasting, all I could think was, "NOOOO!!! I already told you I was fresh out of ideas!!"

It seemed like such a hassle that I even entertained the thought of taking a trip to someplace far away and leaving a letter reading, "I'm fine. Please don't look for me."

However, then I thought, *Since Handa-kun found out he wasn't hated in the last main chapter, couldn't we do chapters differently than before...?* Anyway, I managed to avoid resorting to a life on the run. And then, during a meeting around that time, my editor announced: "I've got a brilliant idea!" (I love the brilliant ideas my editor gets roughly three times a year.)

"How about if we have the anime do the manga material before the manga's released?"

"What!? That's a really fantastic idea!!!"

The two of us got all excited together, like we usually do, and as if my earlier desire to escape had only been a joke, I had a great time getting the chapter drawn. The anime staff also found it really funny and adapted it almost in its entirety. However...as a result, material was shoved into the first episode that left behind viewers who hadn't read the manga yet: a complaint phone call mentioning the anime company by name, the original creator getting "dissed," dialogue stating a voice actor's name (which had to be bleeped out), Fake-kun needing to impersonate a Handa-kun whose voice hadn't even been heard yet, Reo-kun's terrible drawings (nobody, not even me, knows who stipulated that), etc., etc., etc... Looking at it after regaining my sanity.........I truly apologize to the entire anime staff for how we got so carried away.

Where the *Handa-kun* anime was concerned, because I'd already been granted my selfish request that it not be turned into *Barakamon* Season 2, I wanted to use this manga chapter to give the staff something to work with. But since we got carried away, the episode material ended up only being tailored to the manga.

However, I'm sure that after watching the anime through to the last episode, you'll want to rewatch the first episode again.

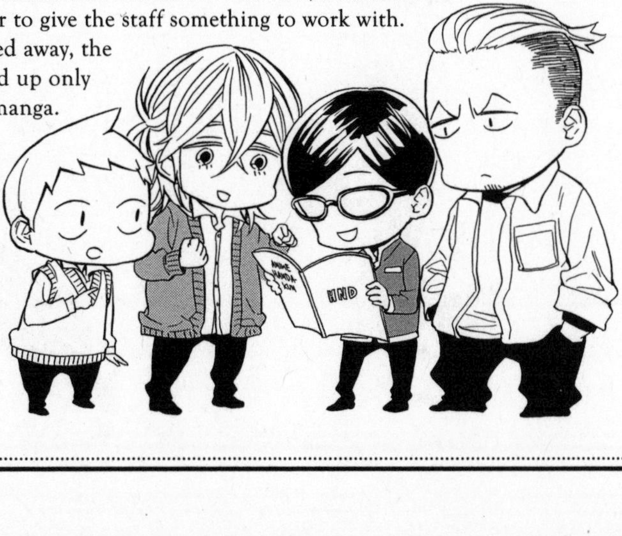
HND

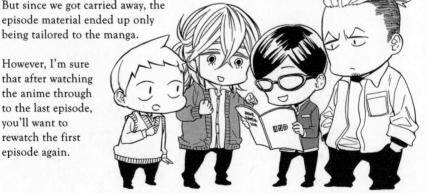

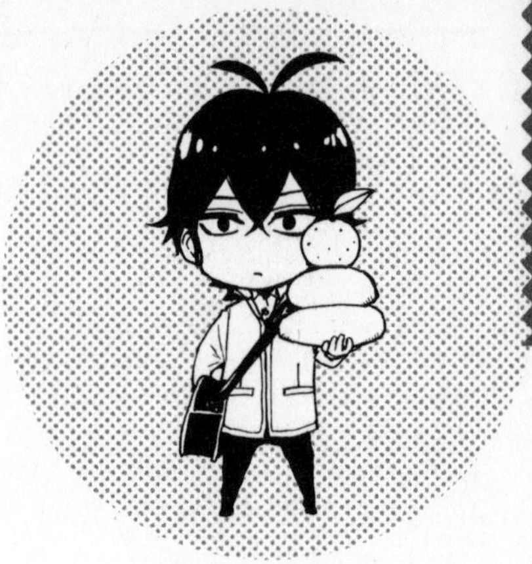

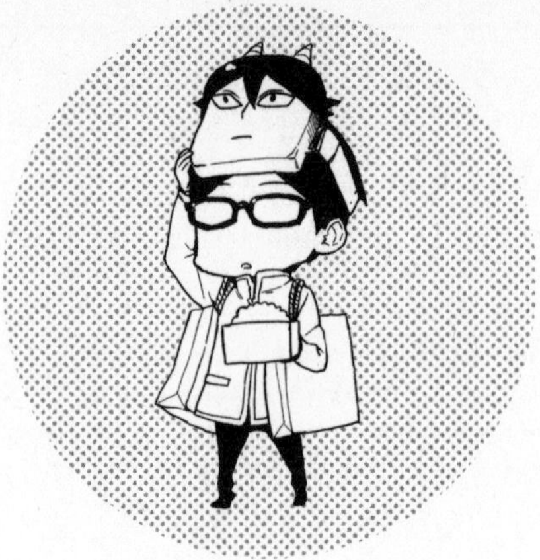

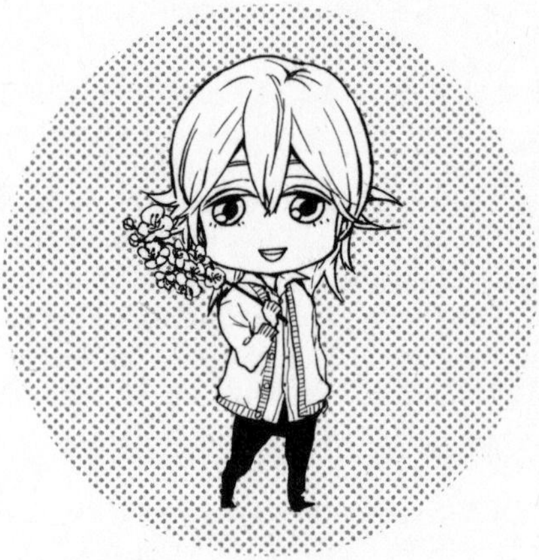

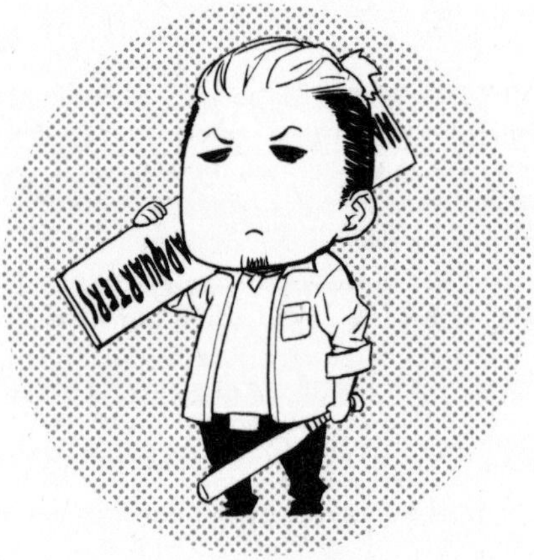
ADQUARTERS

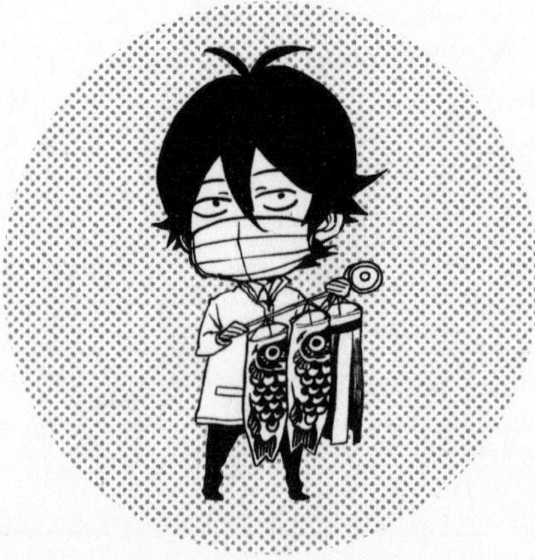

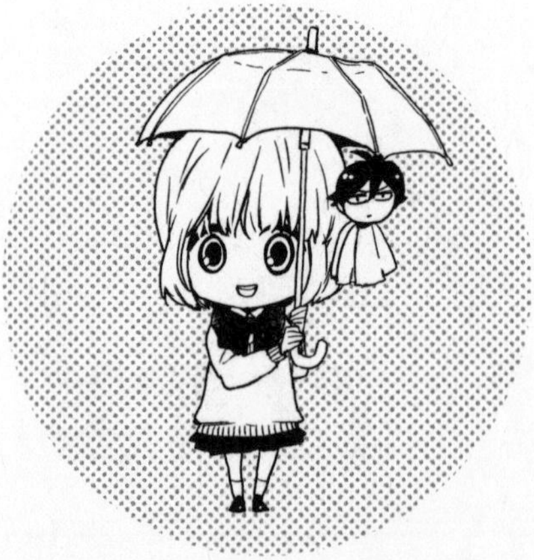

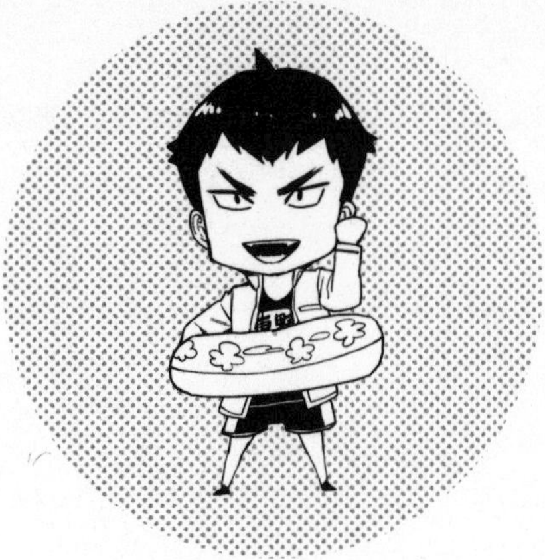
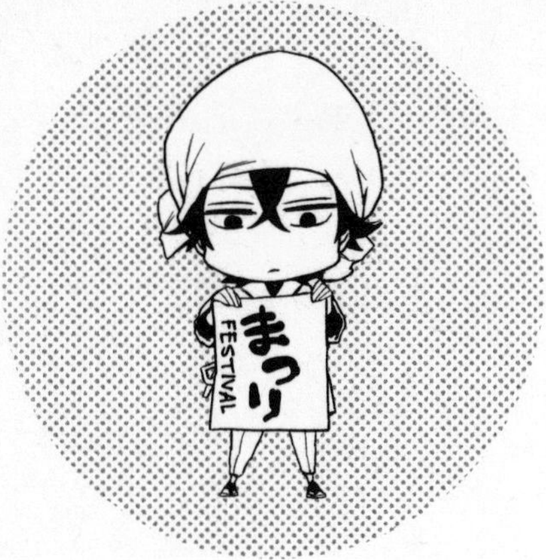
まつり
FESTIVAL
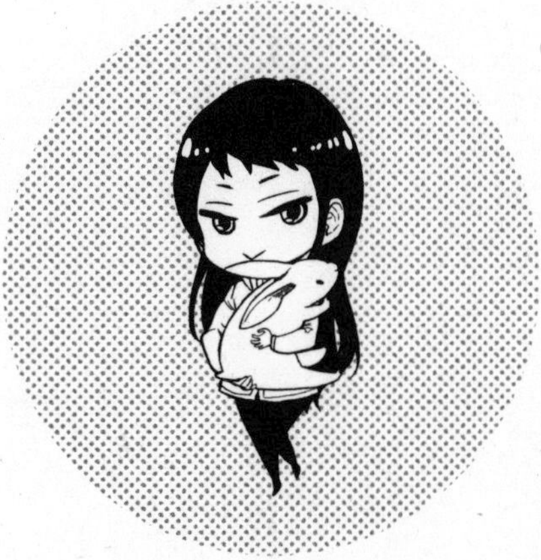
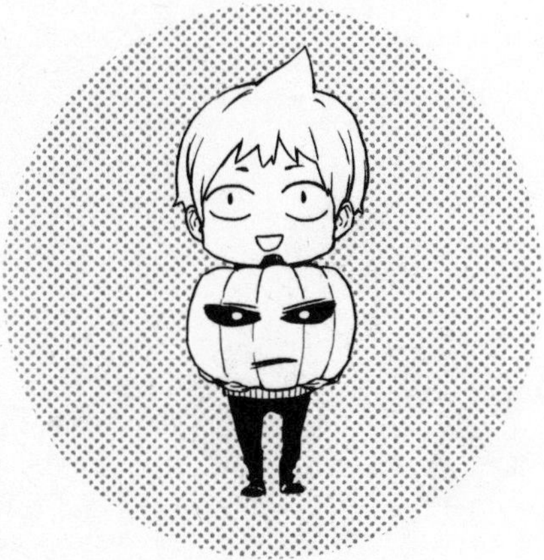
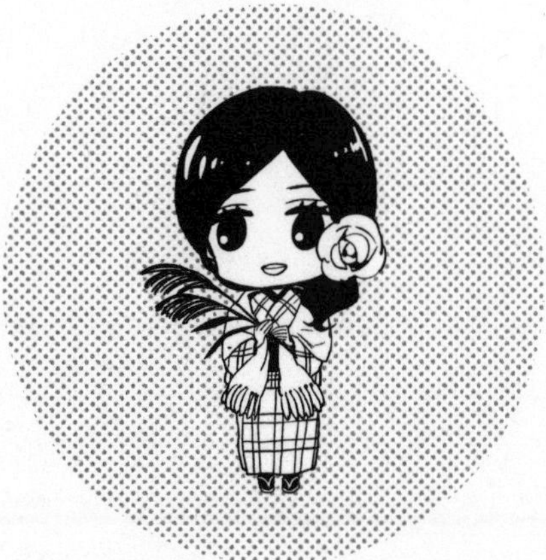
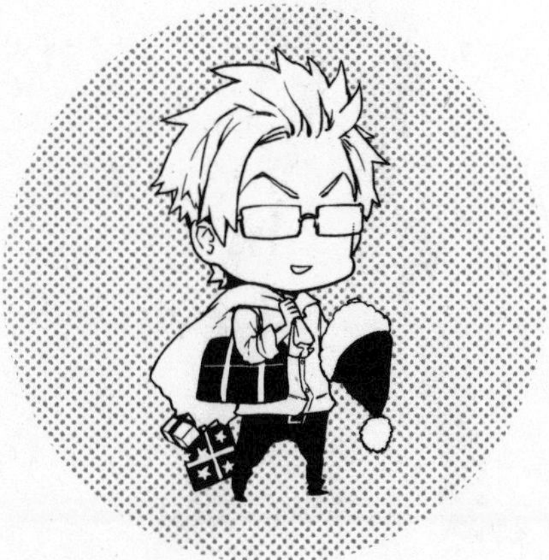

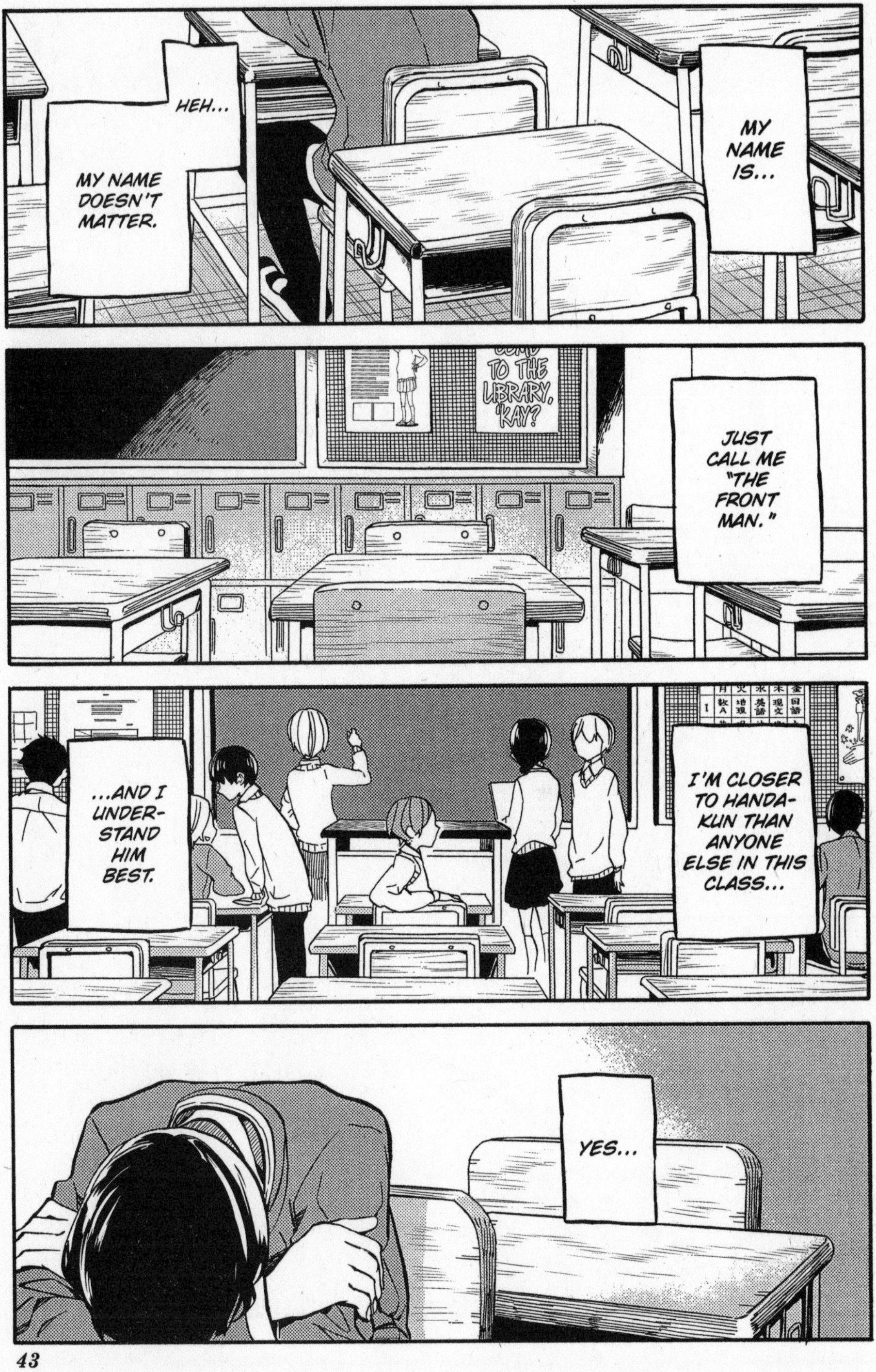
MY NAME IS...
HEH...
MY NAME DOESN'T MATTER.
TO THE LIBRARY, 'KAY?
JUST CALL ME "THE FRONT MAN."
I'M CLOSER TO HANDA-KUN THAN ANYONE ELSE IN THIS CLASS...
...AND I UNDER-STAND HIM BEST.
YES...

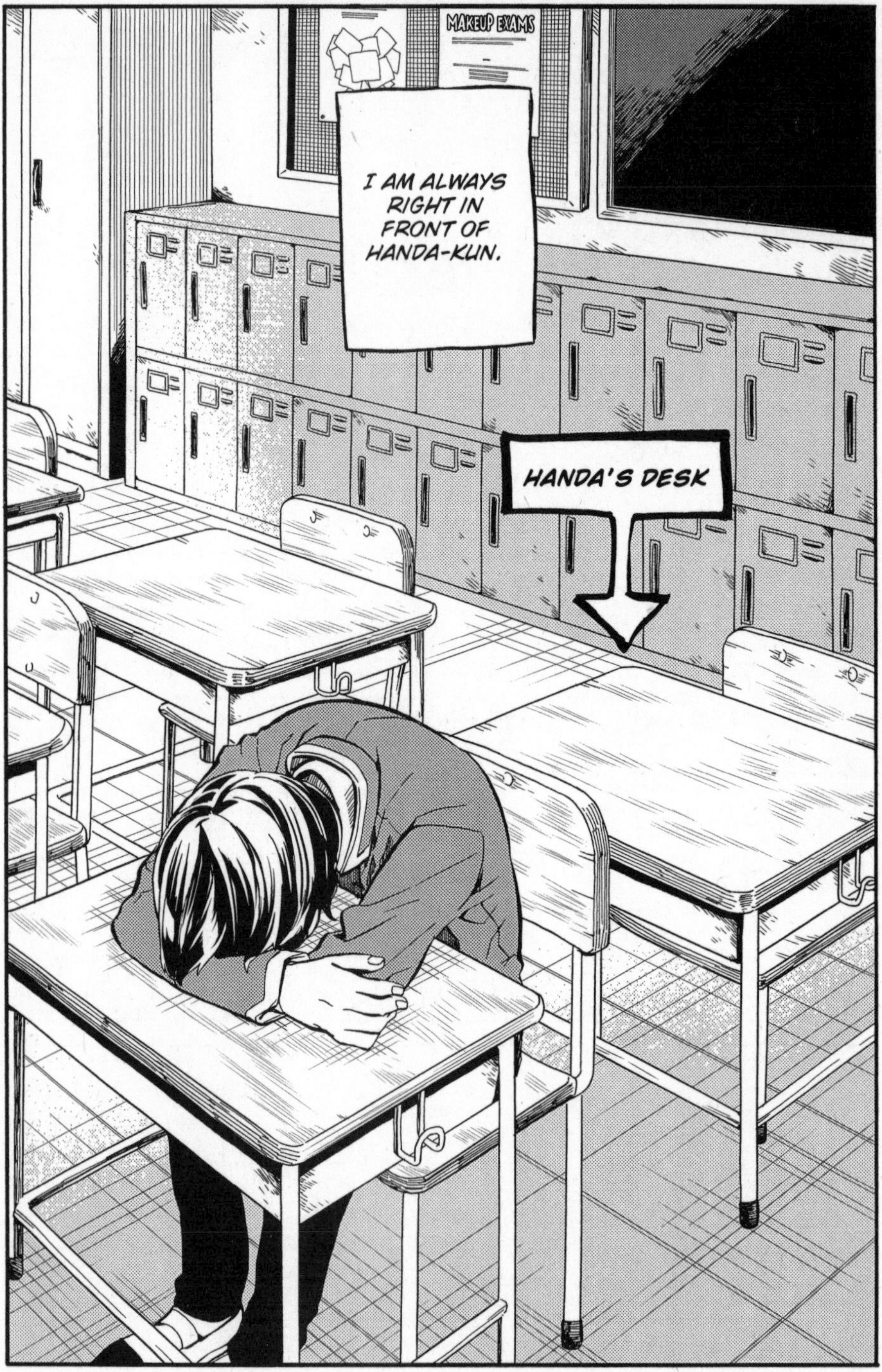
MAKEUP EXAMS
I AM ALWAYS RIGHT IN FRONT OF HANDA-KUN.
HANDA'S DESK

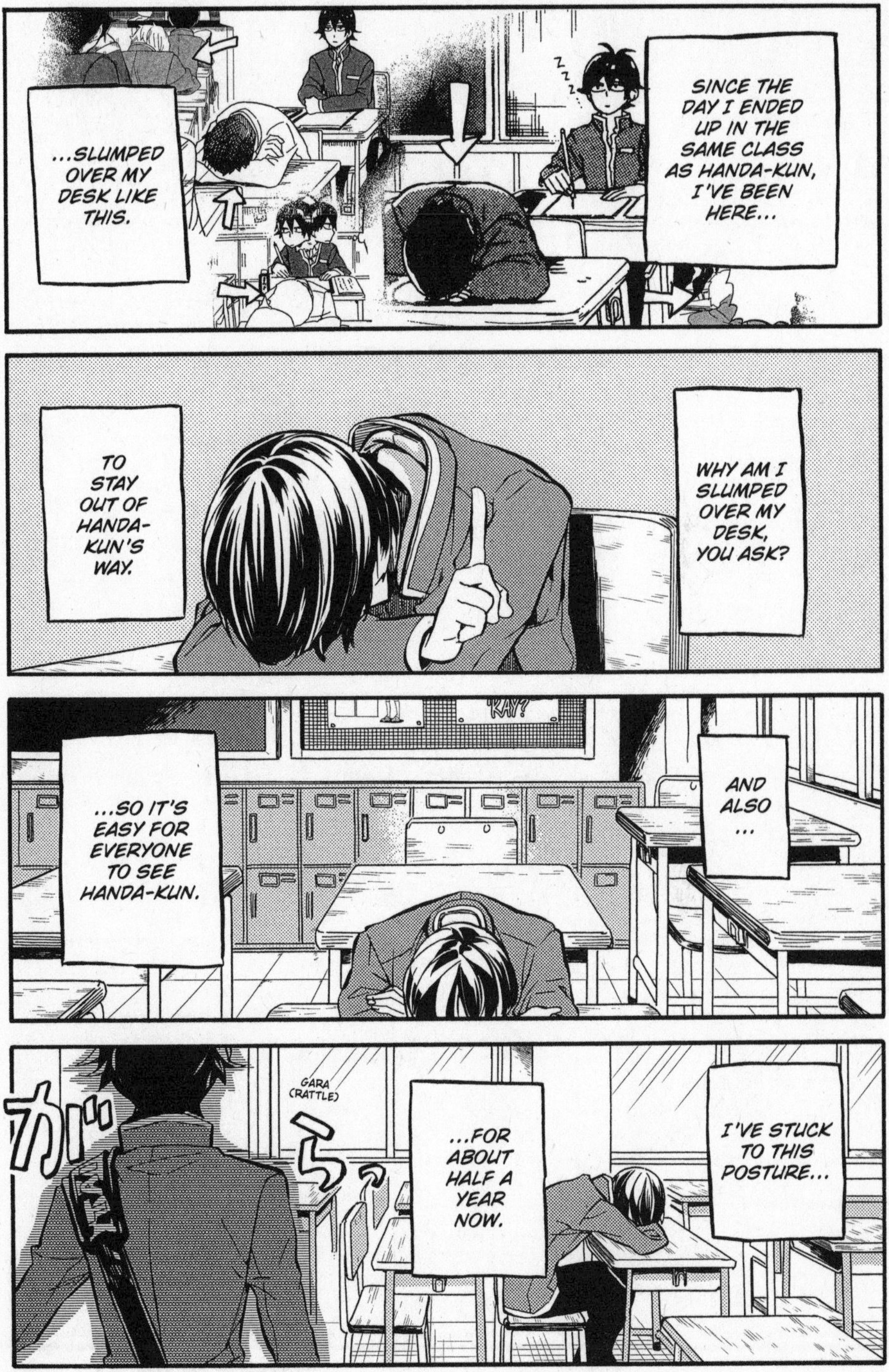

SINCE THE DAY I ENDED UP IN THE SAME CLASS AS HANDA-KUN, I'VE BEEN HERE...
...SLUMPED OVER MY DESK LIKE THIS.
WHY AM I SLUMPED OVER MY DESK, YOU ASK?
TO STAY OUT OF HANDA-KUN'S WAY.
AND ALSO ...
...SO IT'S EASY FOR EVERYONE TO SEE HANDA-KUN.
I'VE STUCK TO THIS POSTURE...
...FOR ABOUT HALF A YEAR NOW.
GARA (RATTLE)
がらっ

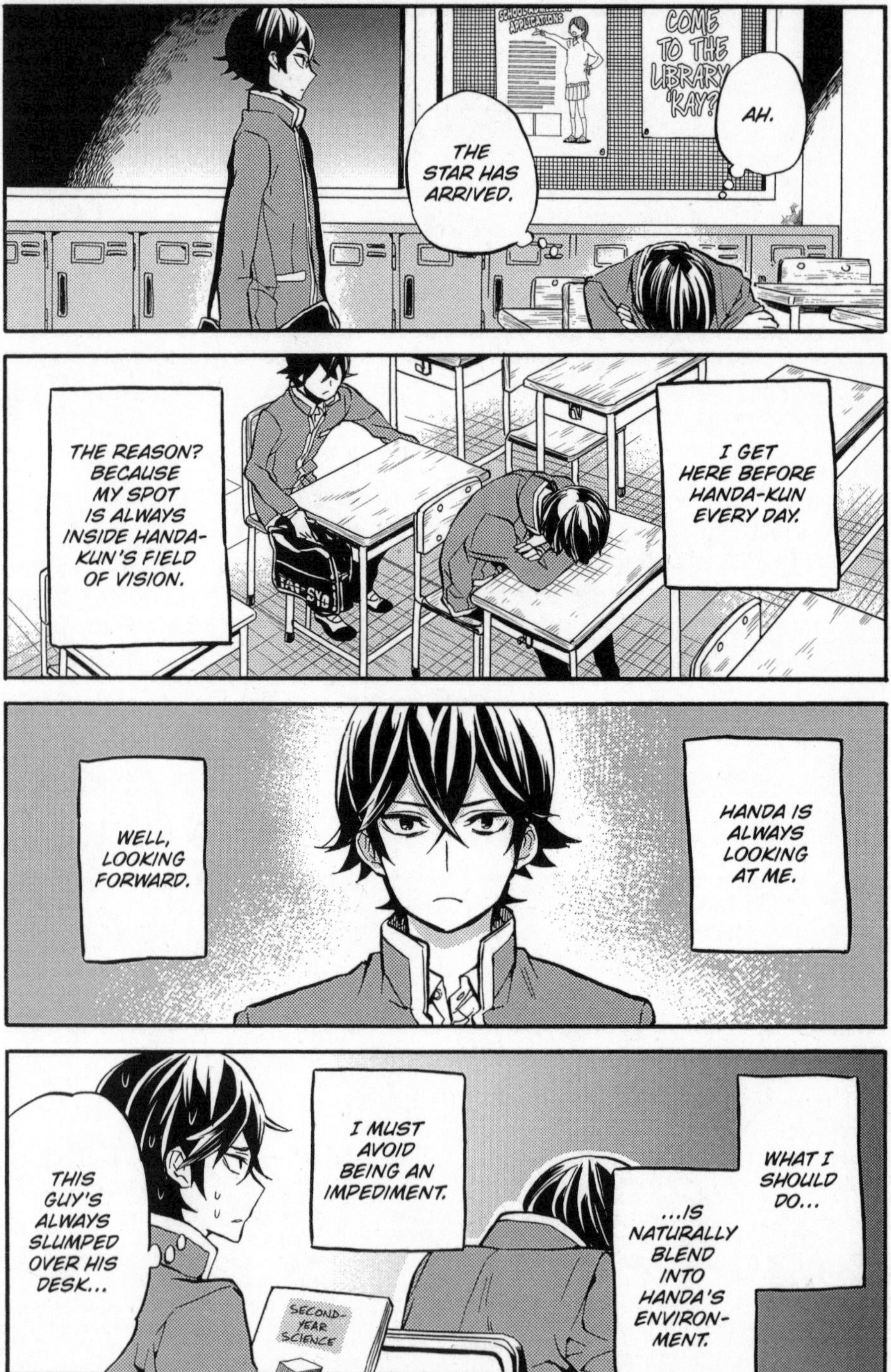
COME TO THE LIBRARY 'KAY?
AH.
THE STAR HAS ARRIVED.
I GET HERE BEFORE HANDA-KUN EVERY DAY.
THE REASON? BECAUSE MY SPOT IS ALWAYS INSIDE HANDA-KUN'S FIELD OF VISION.
TAI-SYO
HANDA IS ALWAYS LOOKING AT ME.
WELL, LOOKING FORWARD.
WHAT I SHOULD DO...
...IS NATURALLY BLEND INTO HANDA'S ENVIRONMENT.
I MUST AVOID BEING AN IMPEDIMENT.
THIS GUY'S ALWAYS SLUMPED OVER HIS DESK...
SECOND-YEAR SCIENCE

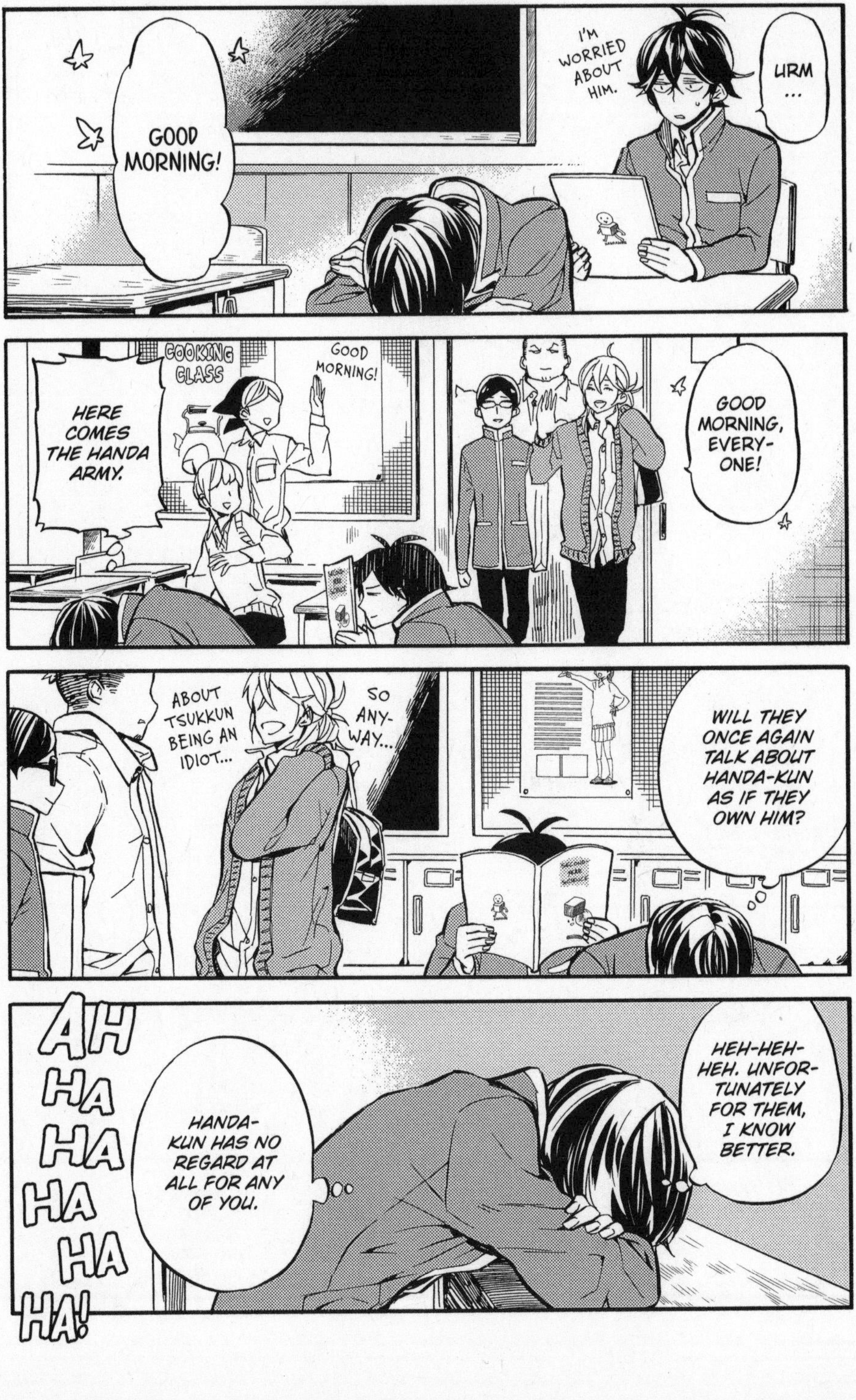
URM ...
I'M WORRIED ABOUT HIM.
GOOD MORNING!
GOOD MORNING, EVERY-ONE!
GOOD MORNING!
COOKING CLASS
HERE COMES THE HANDA ARMY.
WILL THEY ONCE AGAIN TALK ABOUT HANDA-KUN AS IF THEY OWN HIM?
SO ANY-WAY...
ABOUT TSUKKUN BEING AN IDIOT...
HEH-HEH-HEH. UNFOR-TUNATELY FOR THEM, I KNOW BETTER.
HANDA-KUN HAS NO REGARD AT ALL FOR ANY OF YOU.
AH HA HA HA HA HA HA!

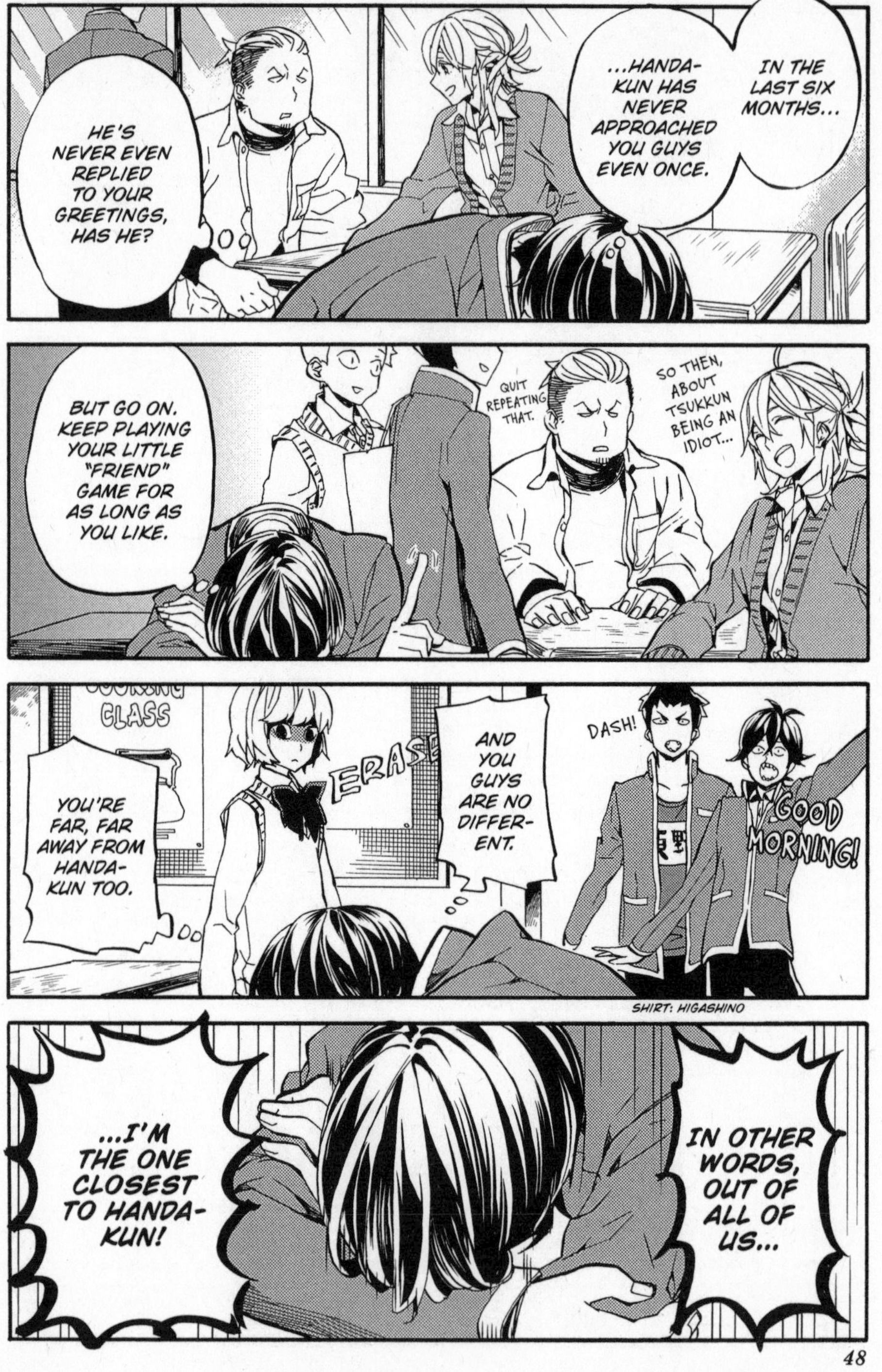
IN THE LAST SIX MONTHS...
...HANDA-KUN HAS NEVER APPROACHED YOU GUYS EVEN ONCE.
HE'S NEVER EVEN REPLIED TO YOUR GREETINGS, HAS HE?
SO THEN, ABOUT TSUKKUN BEING AN IDIOT...
QUIT REPEATING THAT.
BUT GO ON. KEEP PLAYING YOUR LITTLE "FRIEND" GAME FOR AS LONG AS YOU LIKE.
GOOD MORNING!
DASH!
AND YOU GUYS ARE NO DIFFERENT.
ERASE
YOU'RE FAR, FAR AWAY FROM HANDA-KUN TOO.
SHIRT: HIGASHINO
IN OTHER WORDS, OUT OF ALL OF US...
...I'M THE ONE CLOSEST TO HANDA-KUN!

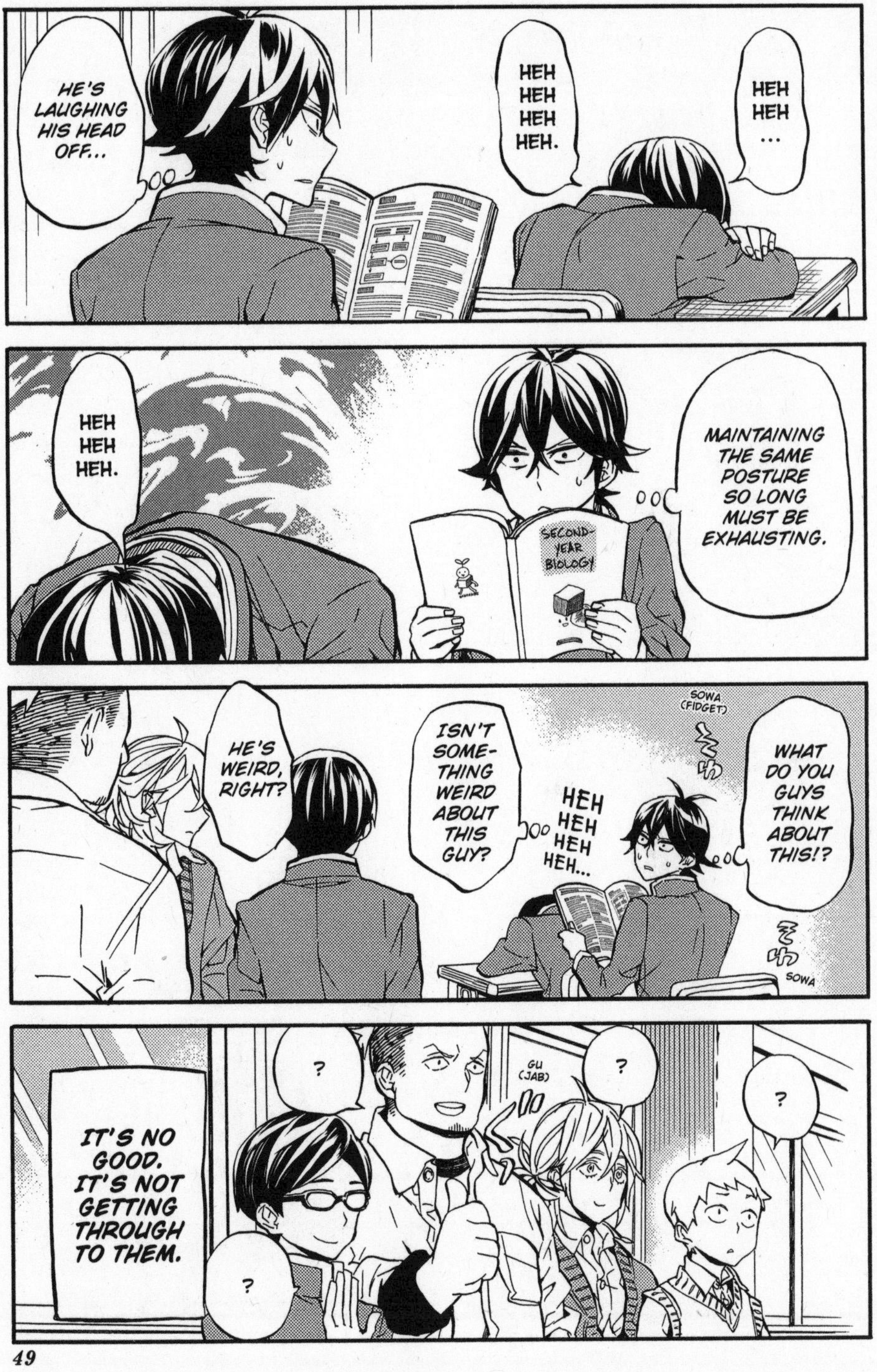
HEH HEH ...
HEH HEH HEH HEH.
HE'S LAUGHING HIS HEAD OFF...
MAINTAINING THE SAME POSTURE SO LONG MUST BE EXHAUSTING.
SECOND-YEAR BIOLOGY
HEH HEH HEH.
SOWA (FIDGET)
WHAT DO YOU GUYS THINK ABOUT THIS!?
SOWA
HEH HEH HEH HEH...
ISN'T SOMETHING WEIRD ABOUT THIS GUY?
HE'S WEIRD, RIGHT?
?
?
GU (JAB)
?
?
IT'S NO GOOD. IT'S NOT GETTING THROUGH TO THEM.

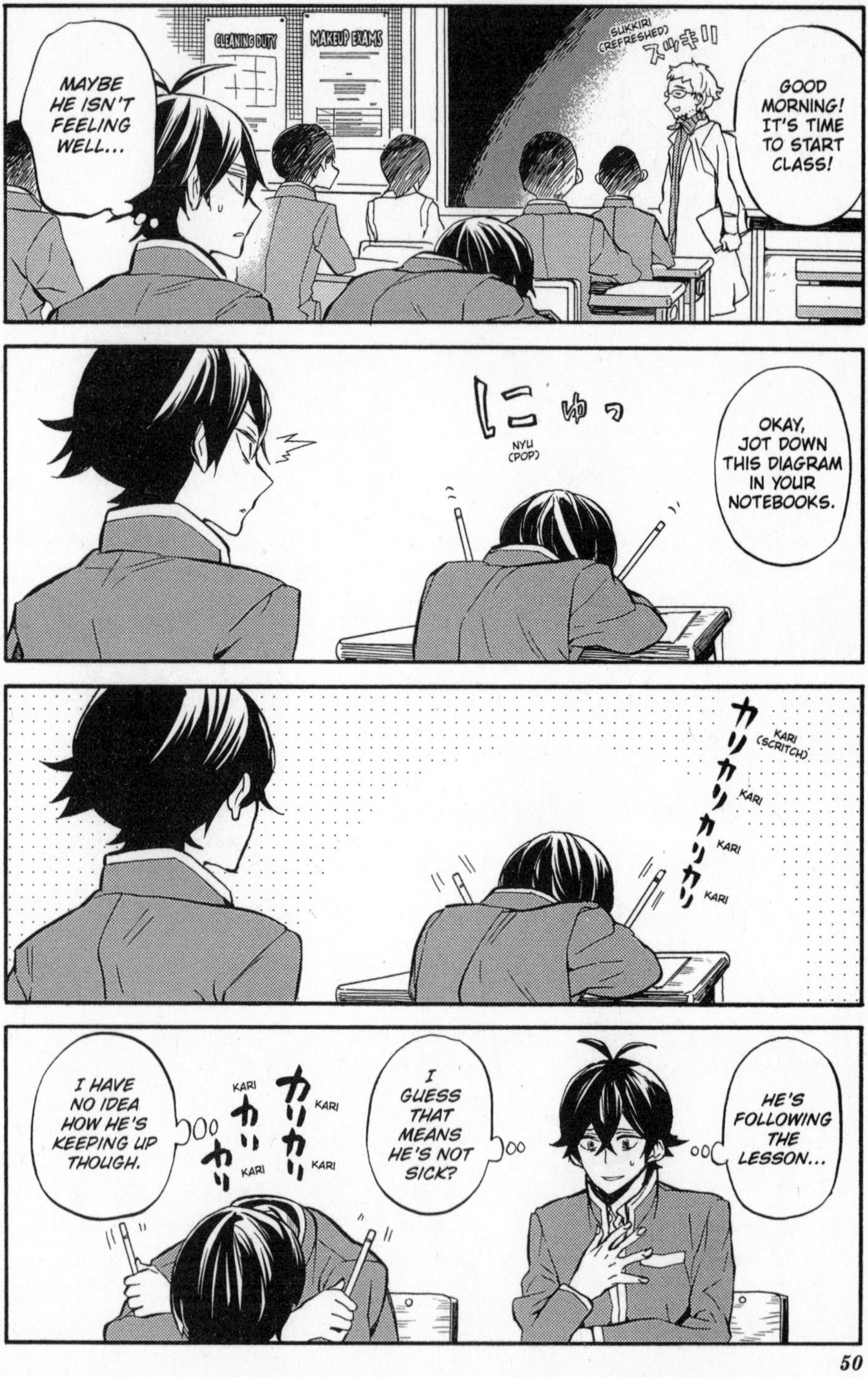
GOOD MORNING! IT'S TIME TO START CLASS!
SUKKIRI (REFRESHED)
スッキリ
CLEANING DUTY
MAKEUP EXAMS
MAYBE HE ISN'T FEELING WELL...
OKAY, JOT DOWN THIS DIAGRAM IN YOUR NOTEBOOKS.
にゅっ
NYU (POP)
カリカリカリカリ
KARI (SCRITCH)
KARI
KARI
KARI
HE'S FOLLOWING THE LESSON...
I GUESS THAT MEANS HE'S NOT SICK?
カリカリカリ
KARI
KARI
KARI
I HAVE NO IDEA HOW HE'S KEEPING UP THOUGH.

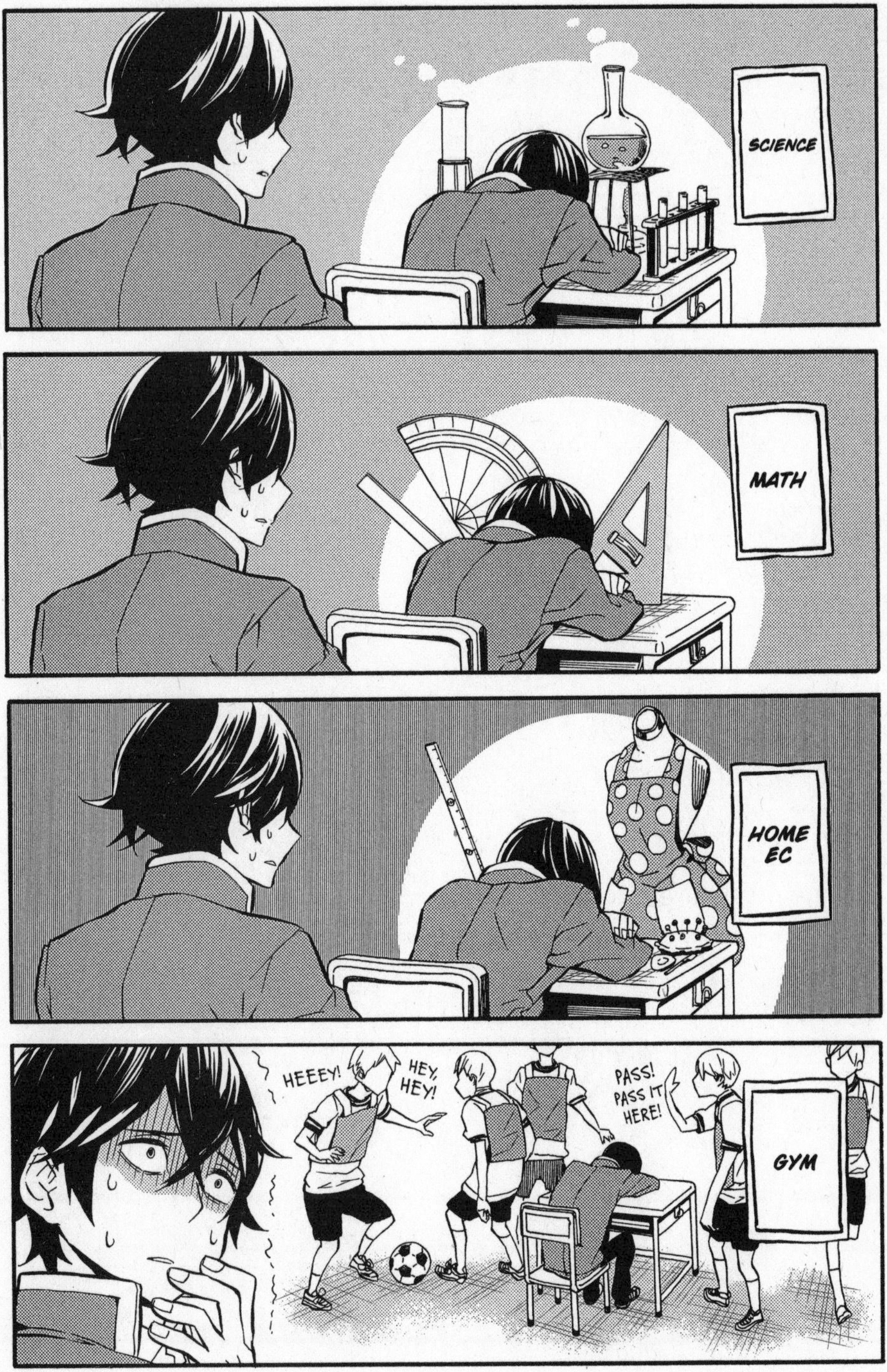
SCIENCE
MATH
HOME EC
GYM
PASS! PASS IT HERE!
HEY, HEY!
HEEEY!

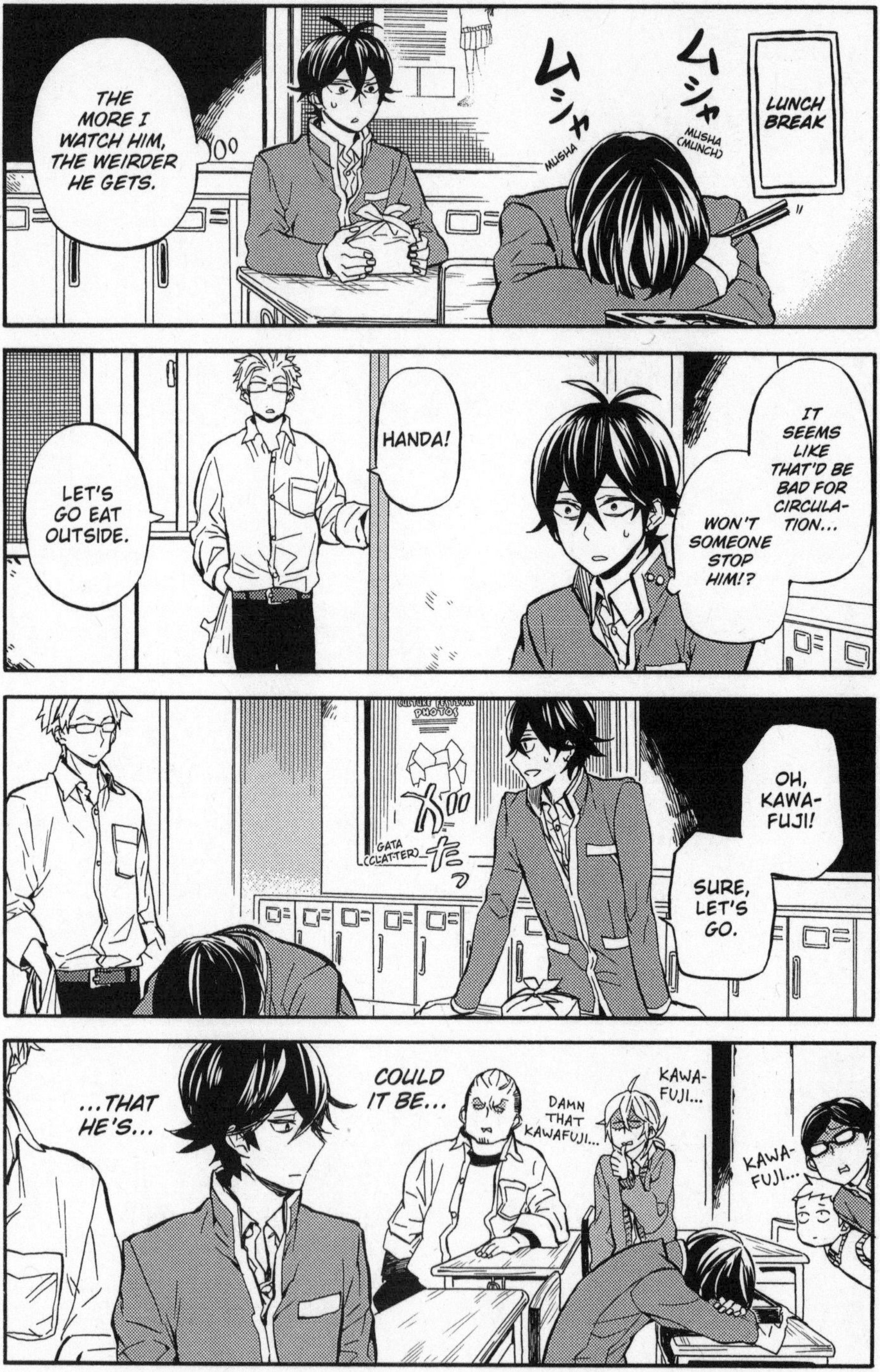
LUNCH BREAK
ムシャ
MUSHA (MUNCH)
ムシャ
MUSHA
THE MORE I WATCH HIM, THE WEIRDER HE GETS.
IT SEEMS LIKE THAT'D BE BAD FOR CIRCULATION...
WON'T SOMEONE STOP HIM!?
HANDA!
LET'S GO EAT OUTSIDE.
OH, KAWA-FUJI!
SURE, LET'S GO.
CULTURE FESTIVAL PHOTOS
GATA (CLATTER)
KAWA-FUJI...
KAWA-FUJI...
DAMN THAT KAWAFUJI...
COULD IT BE...
...THAT HE'S...

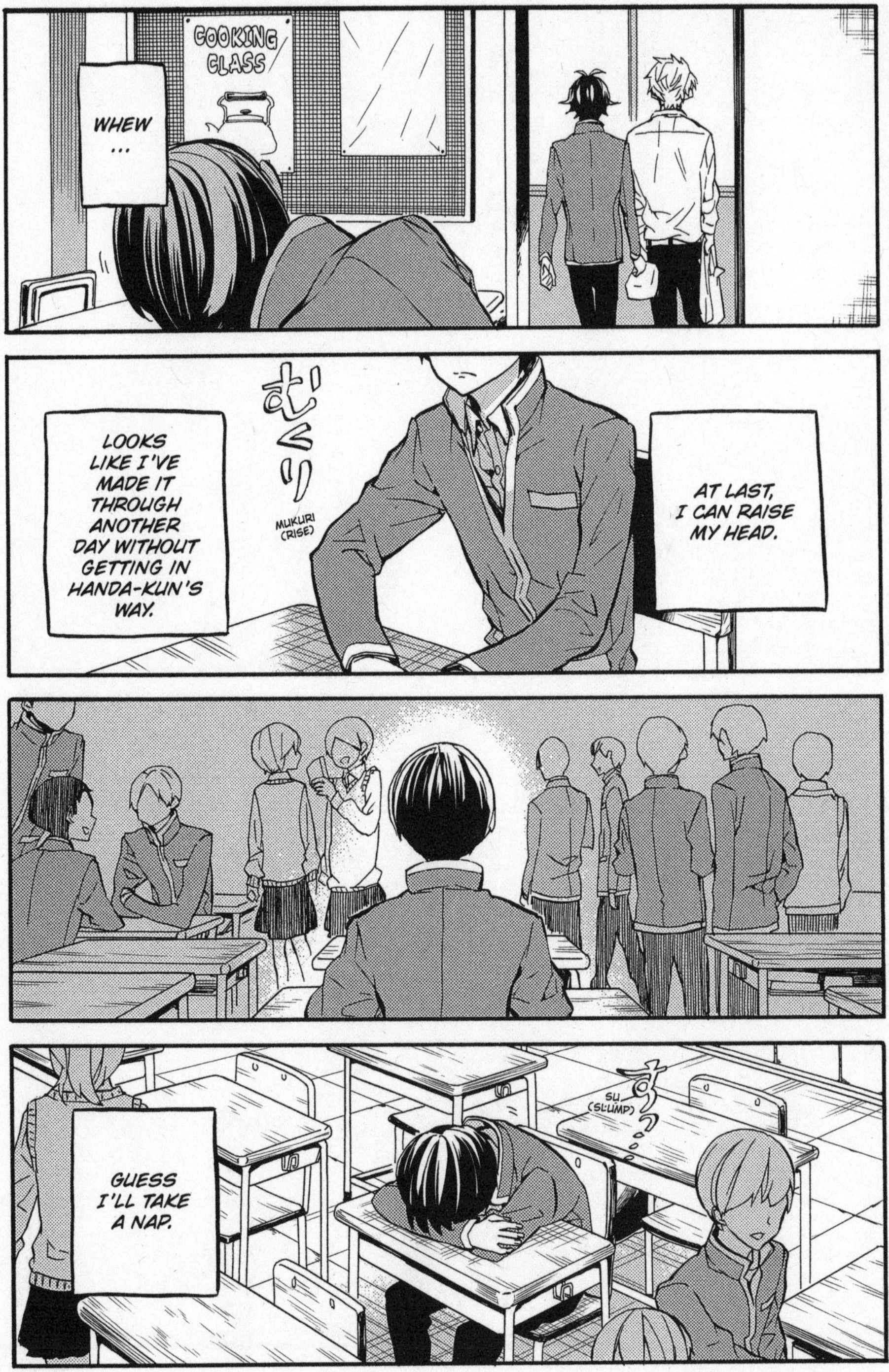
COOKING CLASS
WHEW ...
AT LAST, I CAN RAISE MY HEAD.
むくり
MUKURI (RISE)
LOOKS LIKE I'VE MADE IT THROUGH ANOTHER DAY WITHOUT GETTING IN HANDA-KUN'S WAY.
すっ
SU (SLUMP)
GUESS I'LL TAKE A NAP.

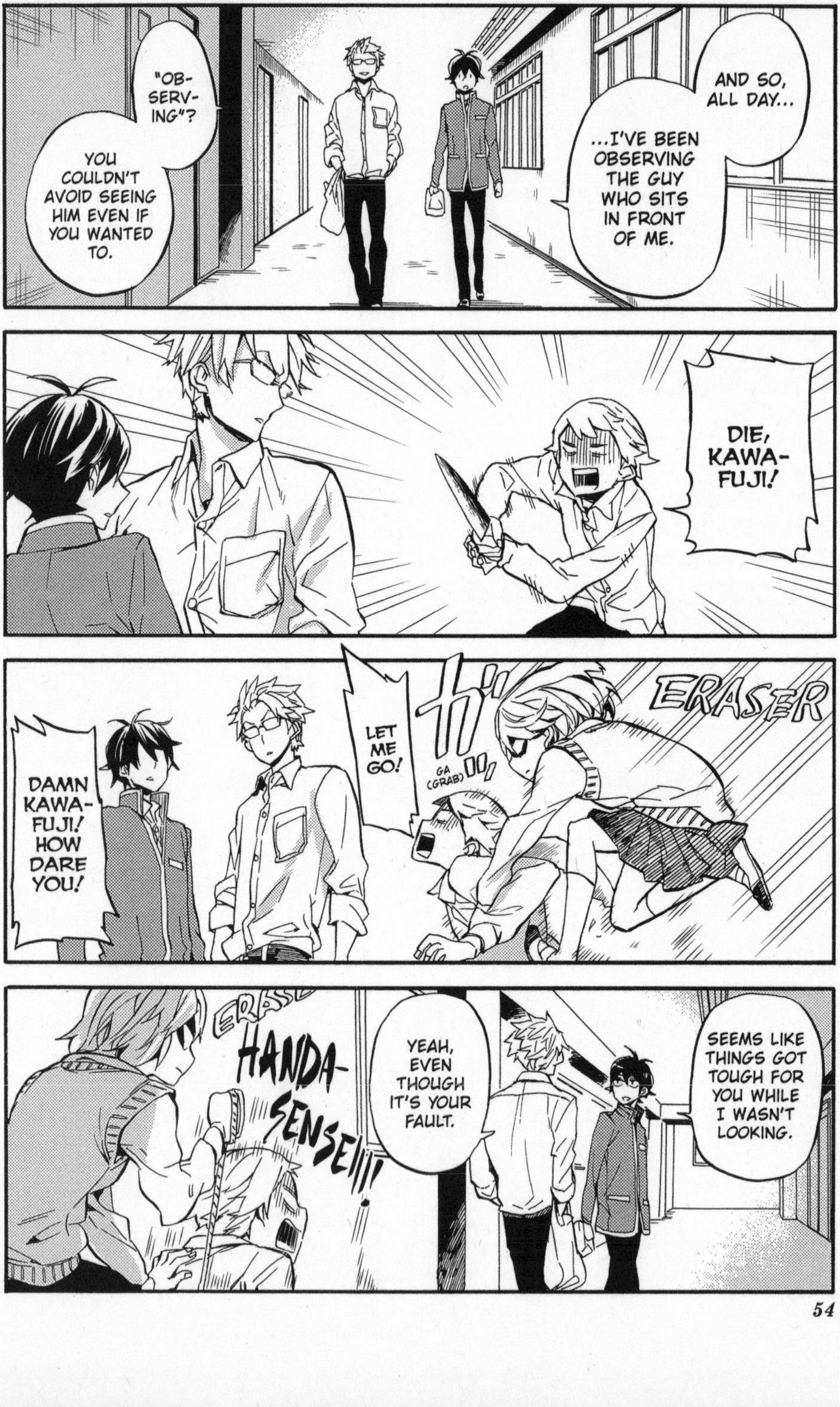
AND SO, ALL DAY...
...I'VE BEEN OBSERVING THE GUY WHO SITS IN FRONT OF ME.
"OB-SERV-ING"?
YOU COULDN'T AVOID SEEING HIM EVEN IF YOU WANTED TO.
DIE, KAWA-FUJI!
ERASER
LET ME GO!
GA (GRAB)
DAMN KAWA-FUJI! HOW DARE YOU!
SEEMS LIKE THINGS GOT TOUGH FOR YOU WHILE I WASN'T LOOKING.
YEAH, EVEN THOUGH IT'S YOUR FAULT.
HANDA-SENSEI!!!!

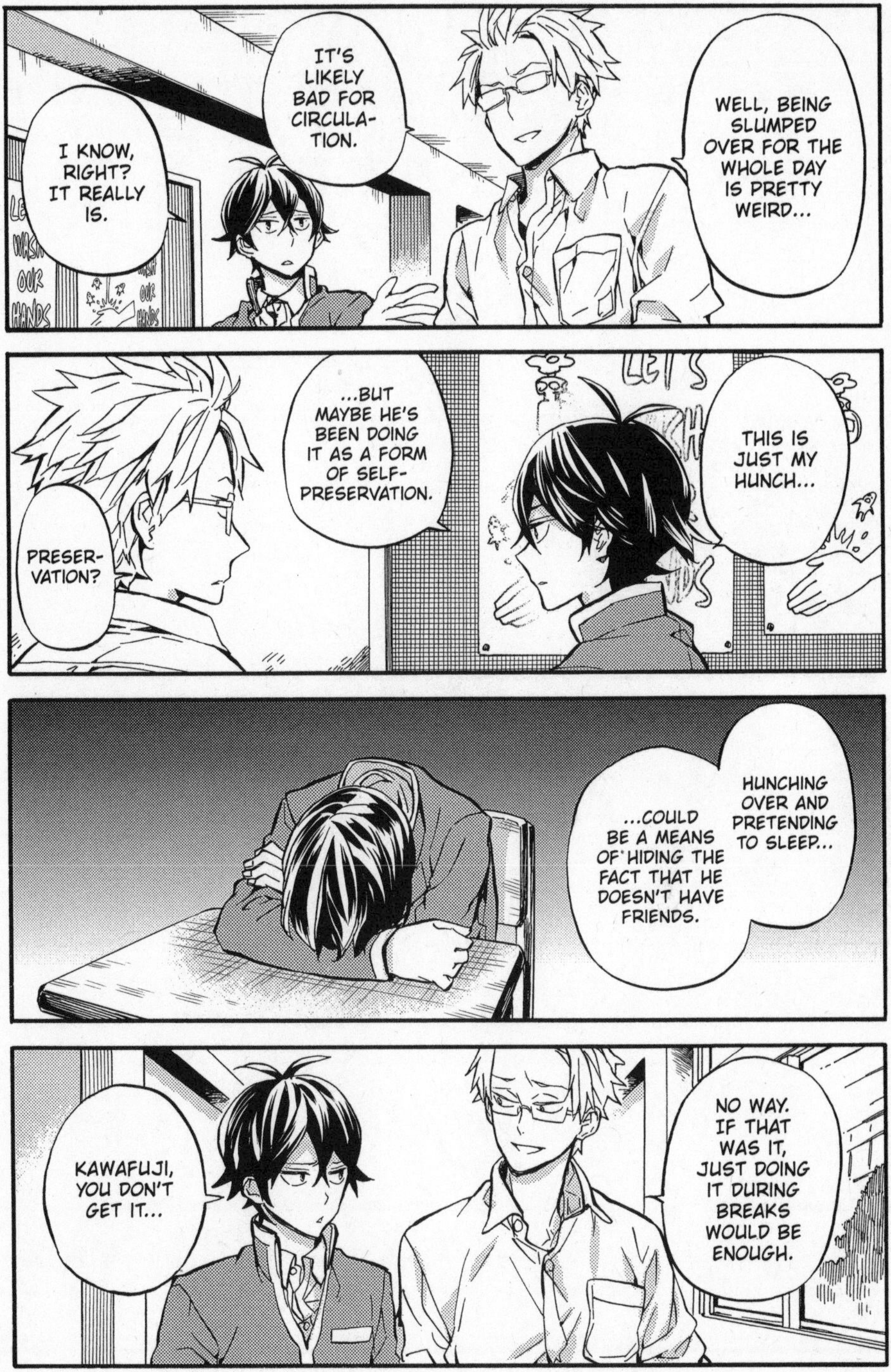
WELL, BEING SLUMPED OVER FOR THE WHOLE DAY IS PRETTY WEIRD...
IT'S LIKELY BAD FOR CIRCULATION.
I KNOW, RIGHT? IT REALLY IS.
THIS IS JUST MY HUNCH...
...BUT MAYBE HE'S BEEN DOING IT AS A FORM OF SELF-PRESERVATION.
PRESERVATION?
HUNCHING OVER AND PRETENDING TO SLEEP...
...COULD BE A MEANS OF HIDING THE FACT THAT HE DOESN'T HAVE FRIENDS.
NO WAY. IF THAT WAS IT, JUST DOING IT DURING BREAKS WOULD BE ENOUGH.
KAWAFUJI, YOU DON'T GET IT...

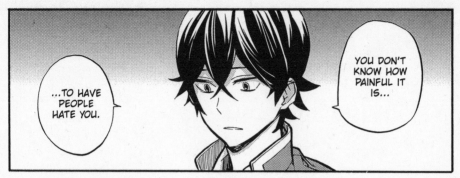

YOU DON'T KNOW HOW PAINFUL IT IS...
...TO HAVE PEOPLE HATE YOU.
DIE, KAWA-FUJI!
ERASER
AAAUGH!
WELL ...
...A POPULAR GUY LIKE ME WOULDN'T KNOW ANYTHING ABOUT THAT.

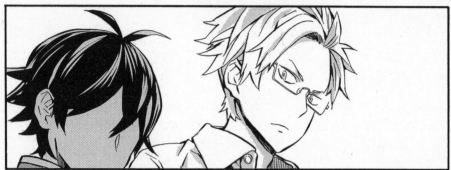

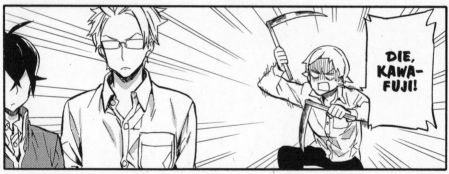

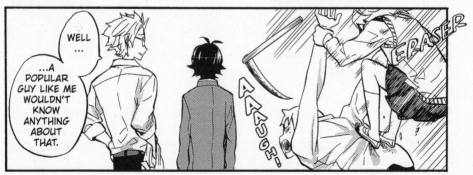

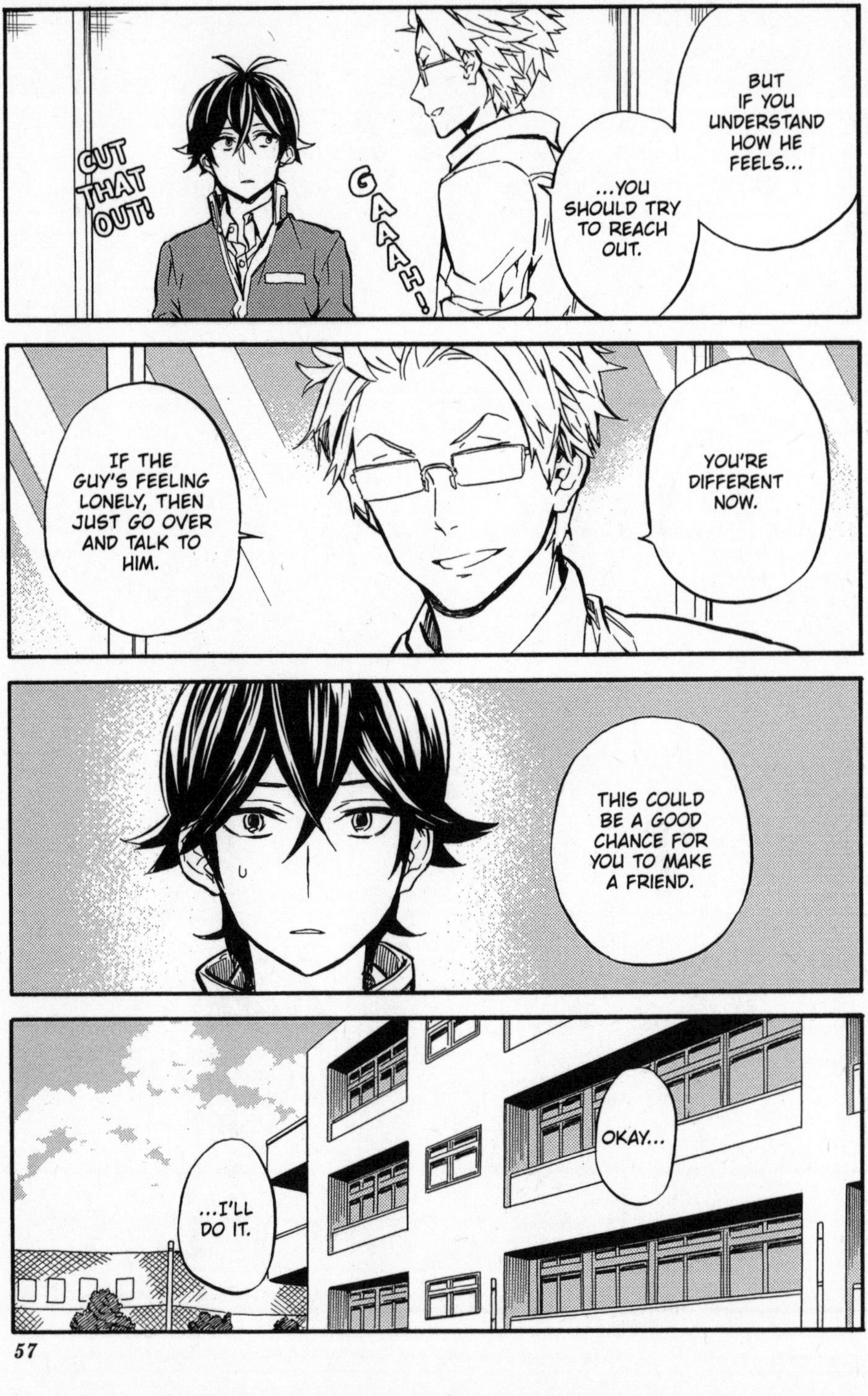
BUT IF YOU UNDERSTAND HOW HE FEELS...
...YOU SHOULD TRY TO REACH OUT.
GAAAH!
CUT THAT OUT!
YOU'RE DIFFERENT NOW.
IF THE GUY'S FEELING LONELY, THEN JUST GO OVER AND TALK TO HIM.
THIS COULD BE A GOOD CHANCE FOR YOU TO MAKE A FRIEND.
OKAY...
...I'LL DO IT.

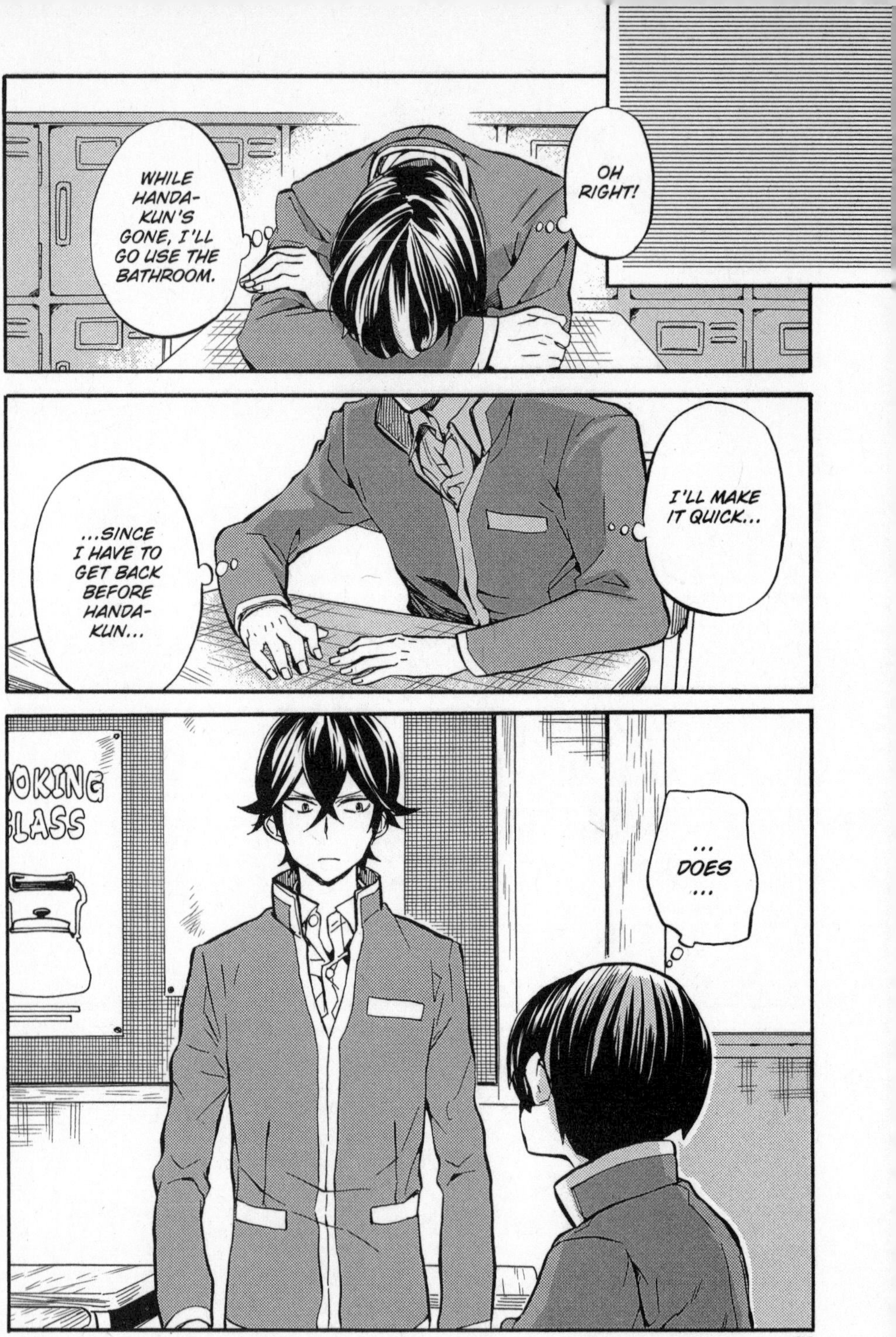
OH RIGHT!
WHILE HANDA-KUN'S GONE, I'LL GO USE THE BATHROOM.
I'LL MAKE IT QUICK...
...SINCE I HAVE TO GET BACK BEFORE HANDA-KUN...
... DOES ...

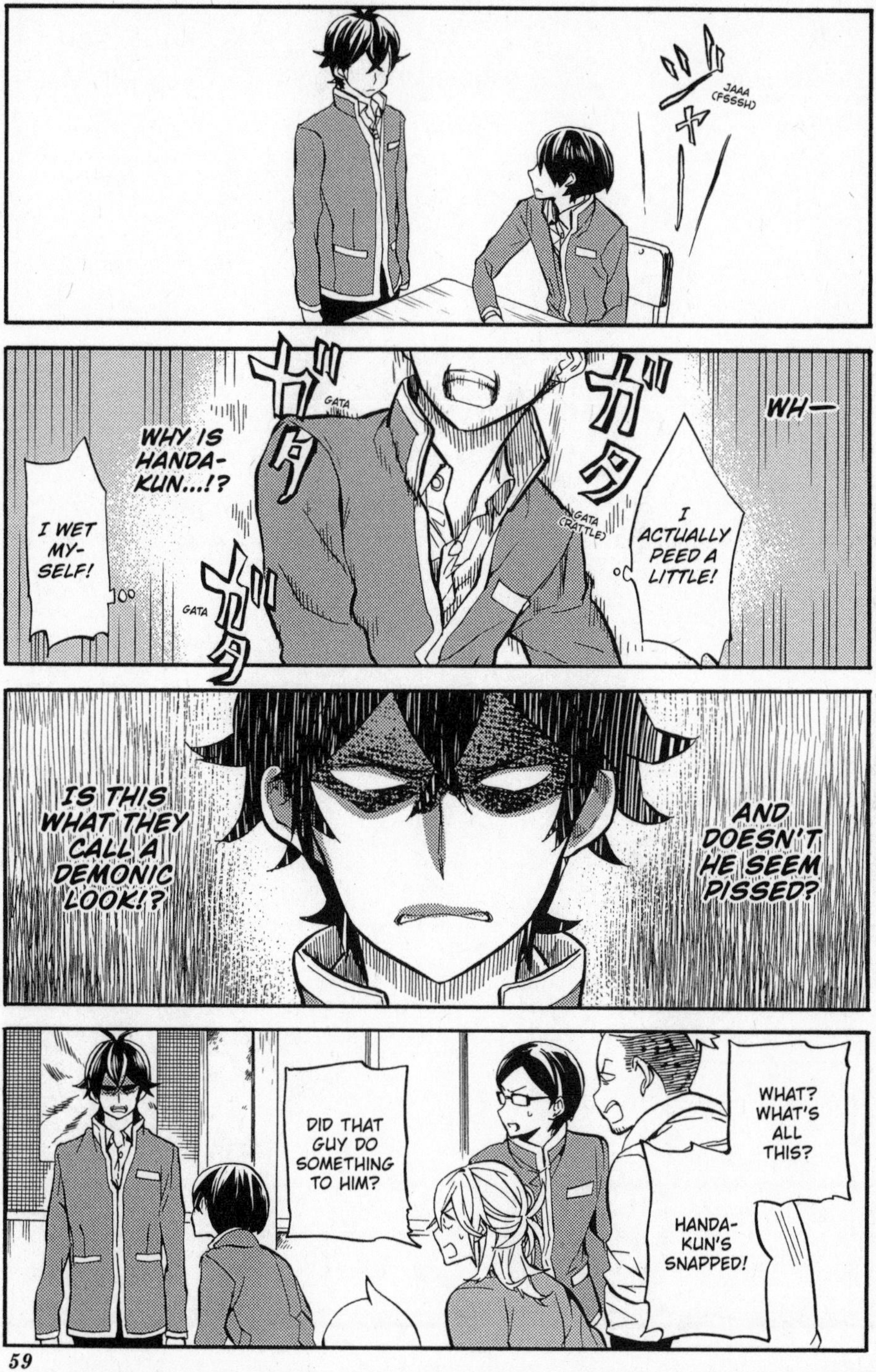
JAAA (FSSSH)
WH—
I ACTUALLY PEED A LITTLE!
GATA (RATTLE)
GATA
WHY IS HANDA-KUN...!?
I WET MYSELF!
GATA
AND DOESN'T HE SEEM PISSED?
IS THIS WHAT THEY CALL A DEMONIC LOOK!?
WHAT? WHAT'S ALL THIS?
HANDA-KUN'S SNAPPED!
DID THAT GUY DO SOMETHING TO HIM?

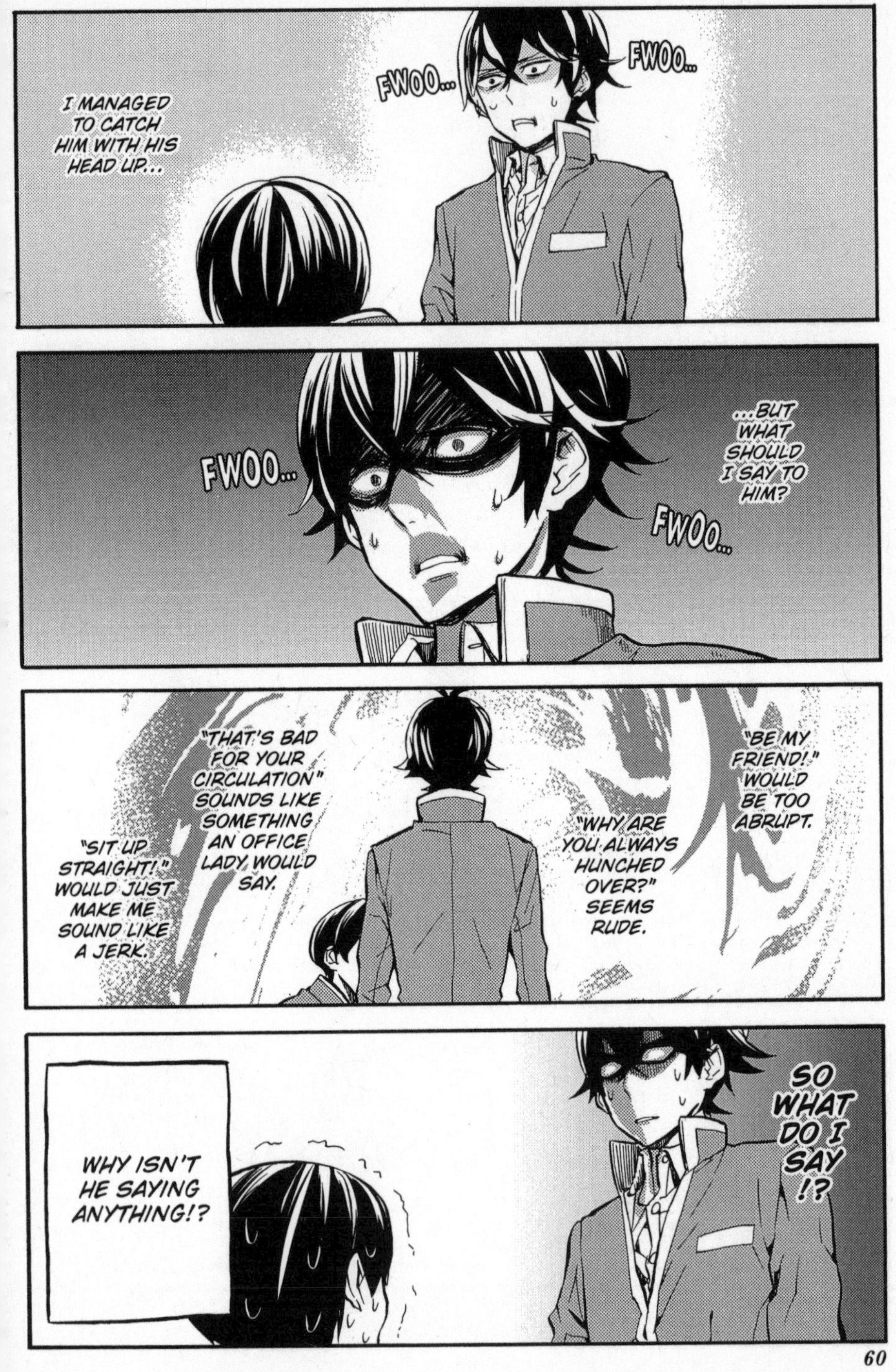
FWOO...
FWOO...
I MANAGED TO CATCH HIM WITH HIS HEAD UP...
...BUT WHAT SHOULD I SAY TO HIM?
FWOO...
FWOO...
"BE MY FRIEND!" WOULD BE TOO ABRUPT.
"WHY ARE YOU ALWAYS HUNCHED OVER?" SEEMS RUDE.
"THAT'S BAD FOR YOUR CIRCULATION" SOUNDS LIKE SOMETHING AN OFFICE LADY WOULD SAY.
"SIT UP STRAIGHT!" WOULD JUST MAKE ME SOUND LIKE A JERK.
SO WHAT DO I SAY !?
WHY ISN'T HE SAYING ANYTHING!?

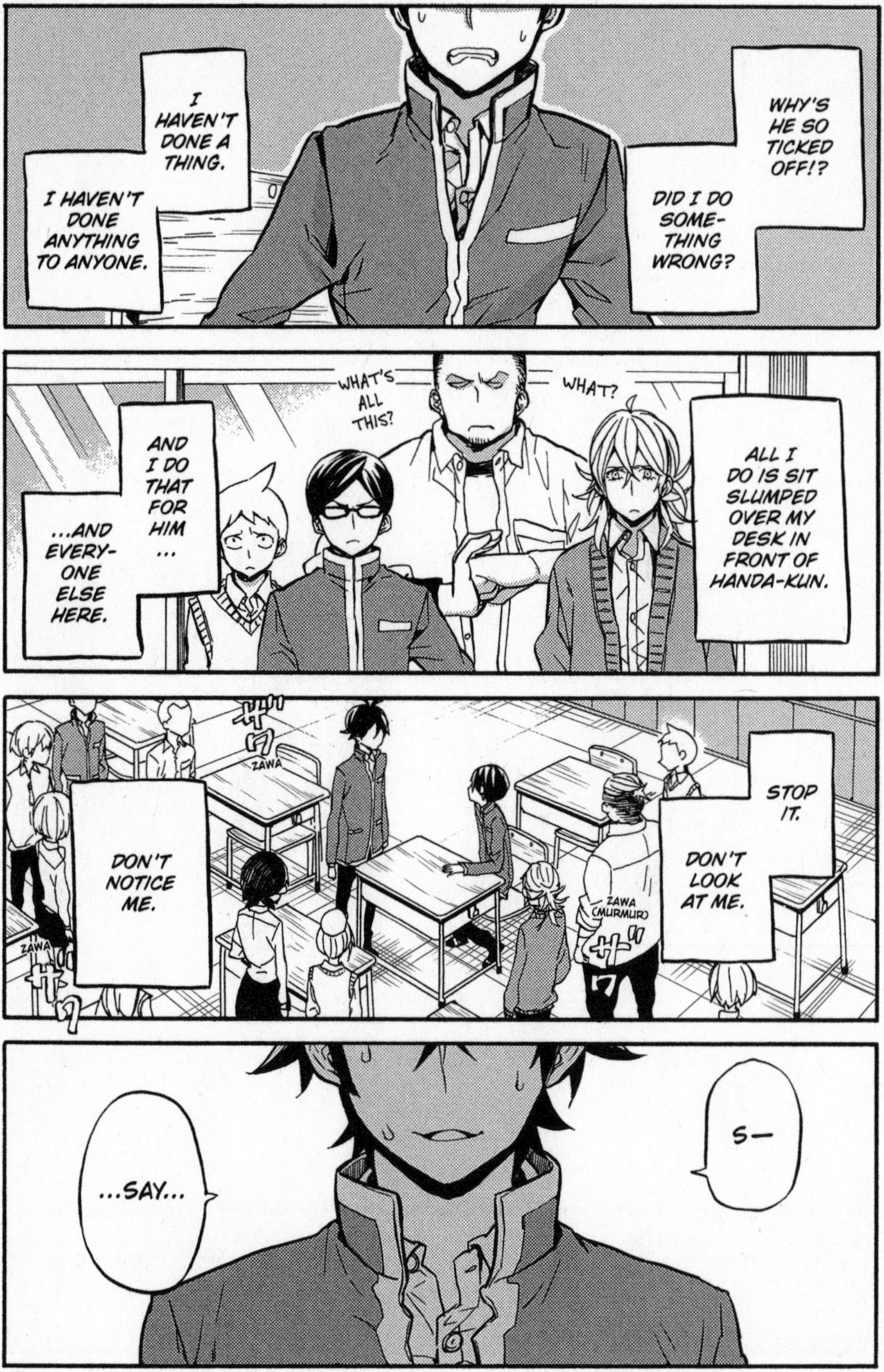
WHY'S HE SO TICKED OFF!?
DID I DO SOME-THING WRONG?
I HAVEN'T DONE A THING.
I HAVEN'T DONE ANYTHING TO ANYONE.
ALL I DO IS SIT SLUMPED OVER MY DESK IN FRONT OF HANDA-KUN.
WHAT?
WHAT'S ALL THIS?
AND I DO THAT FOR HIM ...
...AND EVERY-ONE ELSE HERE.
STOP IT.
DON'T LOOK AT ME.
ZAWA (MURMUR)
ZAWA
DON'T NOTICE ME.
ZAWA
S—
...SAY...

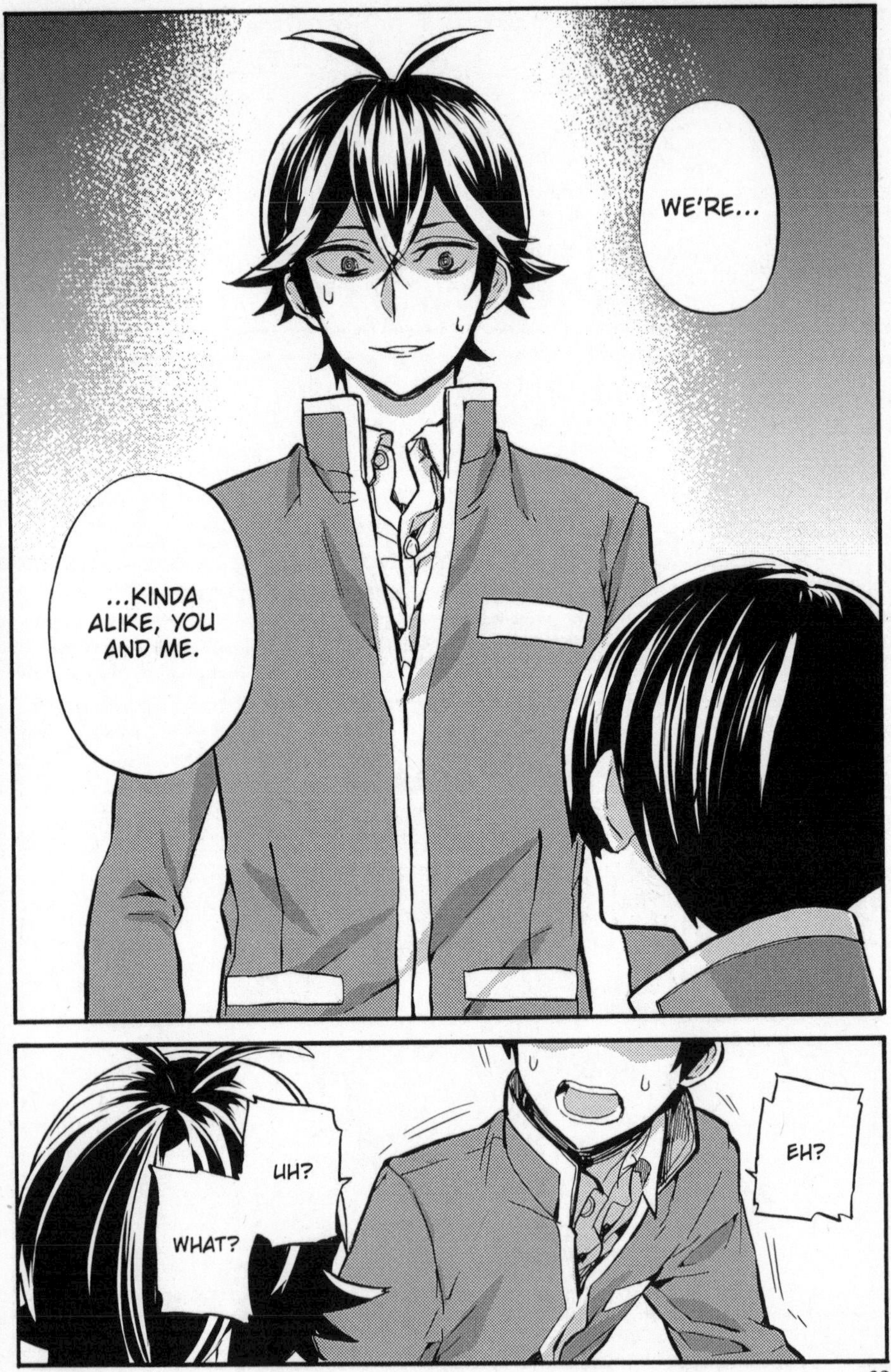
WE'RE...
...KINDA ALIKE, YOU AND ME.
EH?
UH?
WHAT?

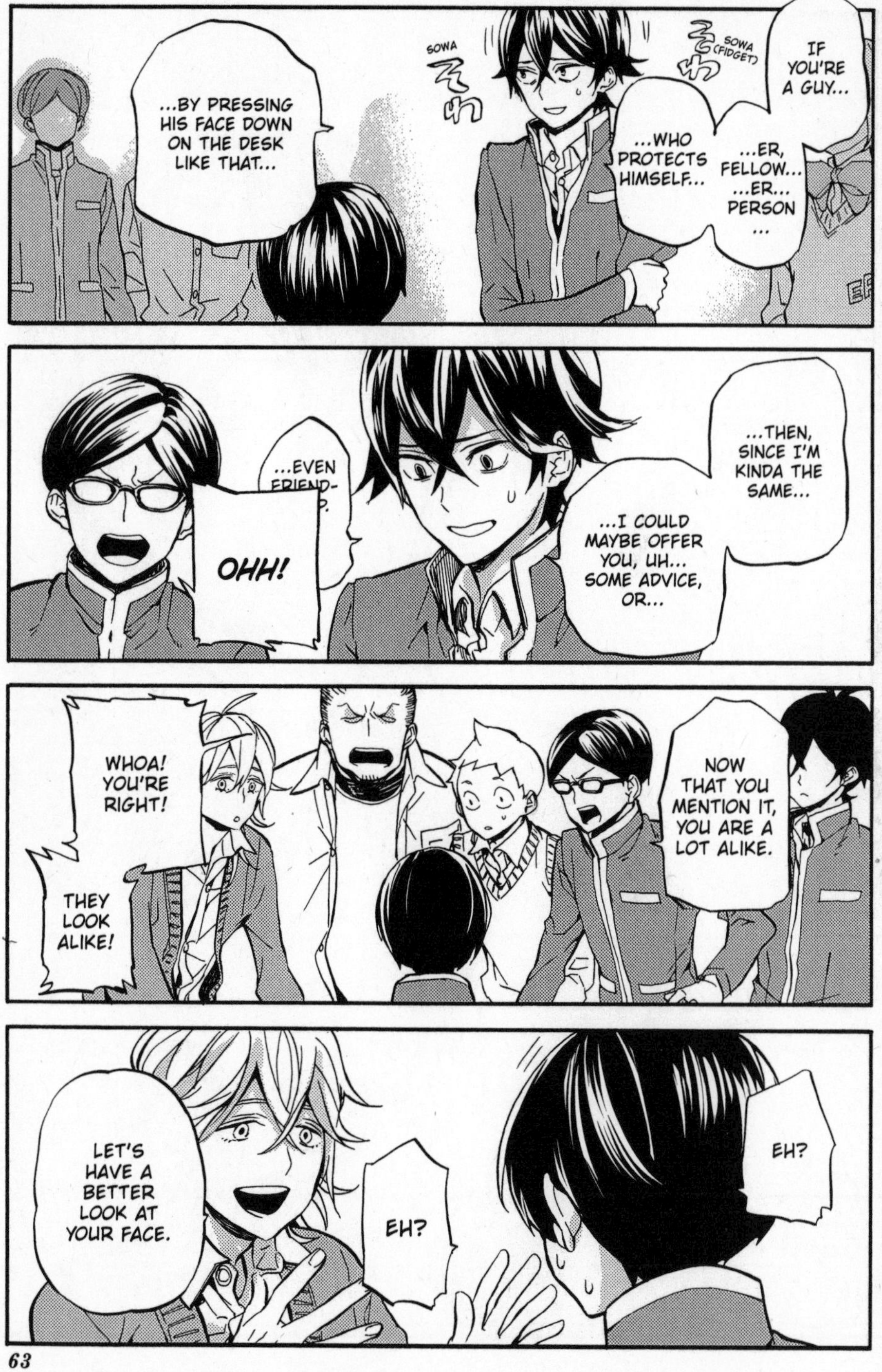
IF YOU'RE A GUY...
そわ SOWA (FIDGET)
...ER, FELLOW... ...ER... PERSON ...
...WHO PROTECTS HIMSELF...
そわ SOWA
...BY PRESSING HIS FACE DOWN ON THE DESK LIKE THAT...
...THEN, SINCE I'M KINDA THE SAME...
...I COULD MAYBE OFFER YOU, UH... SOME ADVICE, OR...
...EVEN FRIEND-
OHH!
NOW THAT YOU MENTION IT, YOU ARE A LOT ALIKE.
WHOA! YOU'RE RIGHT!
THEY LOOK ALIKE!
EH?
EH?
LET'S HAVE A BETTER LOOK AT YOUR FACE.

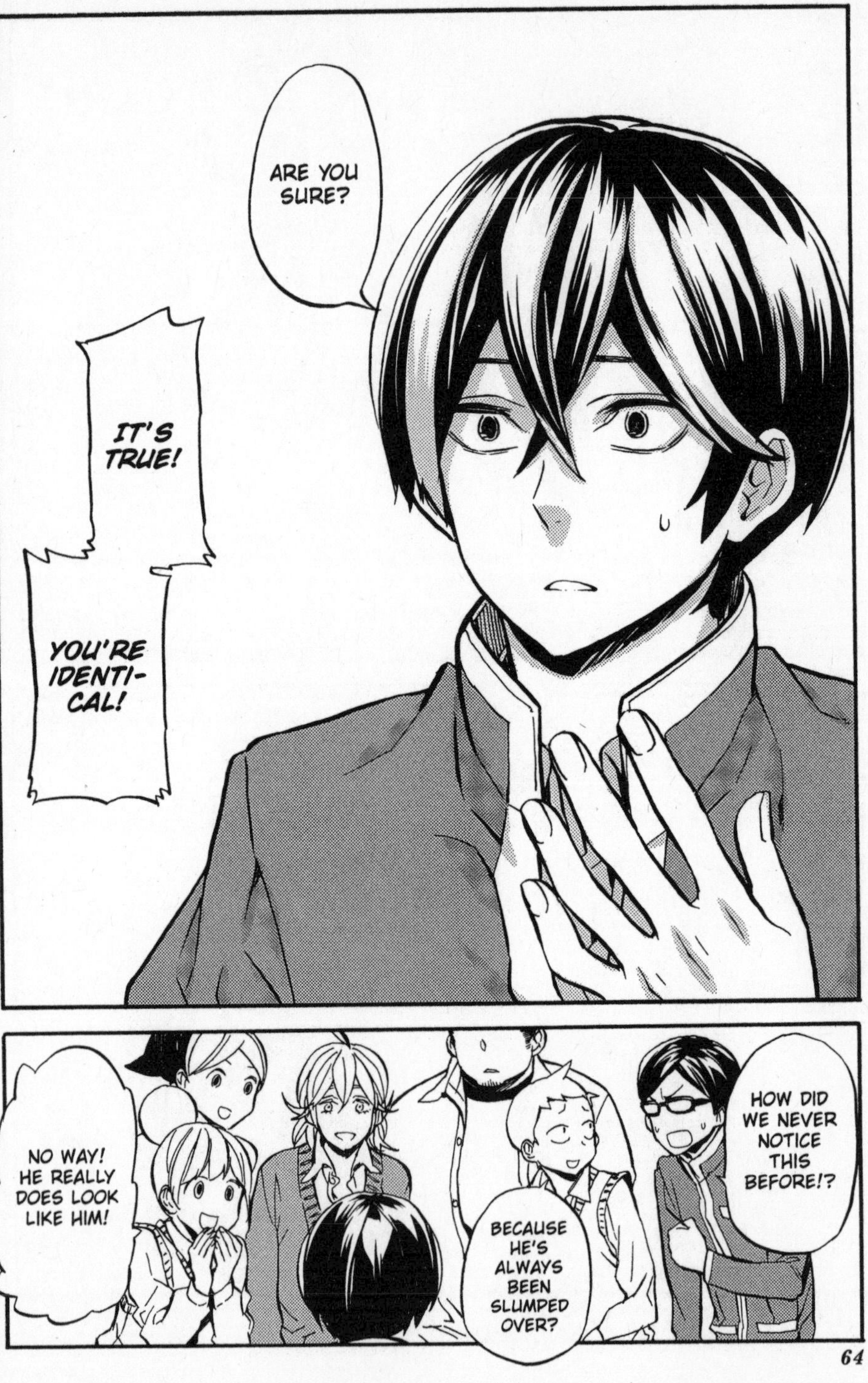
ARE YOU SURE?
IT'S TRUE!
YOU'RE IDENTI-CAL!
HOW DID WE NEVER NOTICE THIS BEFORE!?
BECAUSE HE'S ALWAYS BEEN SLUMPED OVER?
NO WAY! HE REALLY DOES LOOK LIKE HIM!

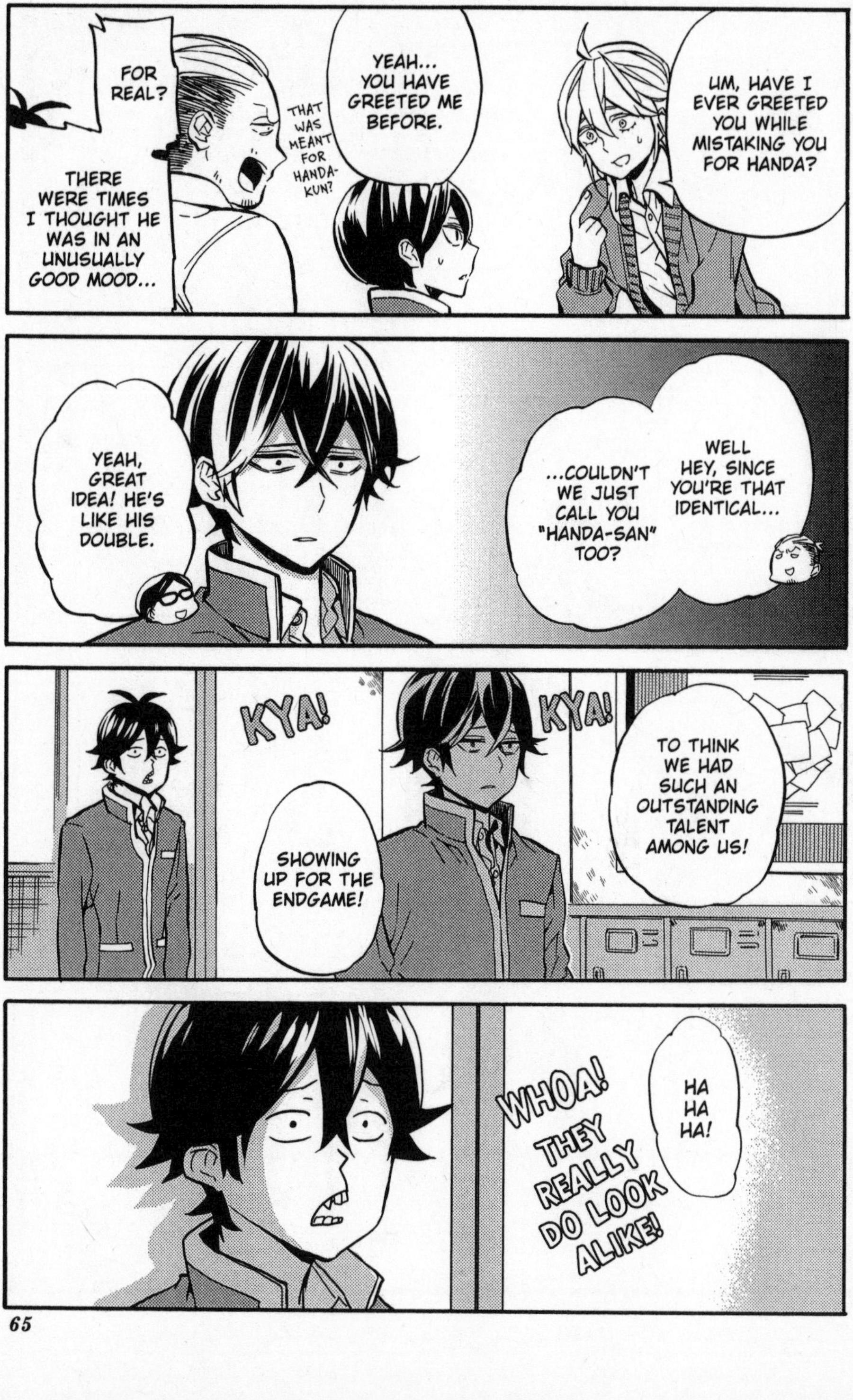
UM, HAVE I EVER GREETED YOU WHILE MISTAKING YOU FOR HANDA?
YEAH... YOU HAVE GREETED ME BEFORE.
THAT WAS MEANT FOR HANDA-KUN?
FOR REAL?
THERE WERE TIMES I THOUGHT HE WAS IN AN UNUSUALLY GOOD MOOD...
WELL HEY, SINCE YOU'RE THAT IDENTICAL...
...COULDN'T WE JUST CALL YOU "HANDA-SAN" TOO?
YEAH, GREAT IDEA! HE'S LIKE HIS DOUBLE.
TO THINK WE HAD SUCH AN OUTSTANDING TALENT AMONG US!
KYA!
SHOWING UP FOR THE ENDGAME!
KYA!
HA HA HA!
WHOA! THEY REALLY DO LOOK ALIKE!

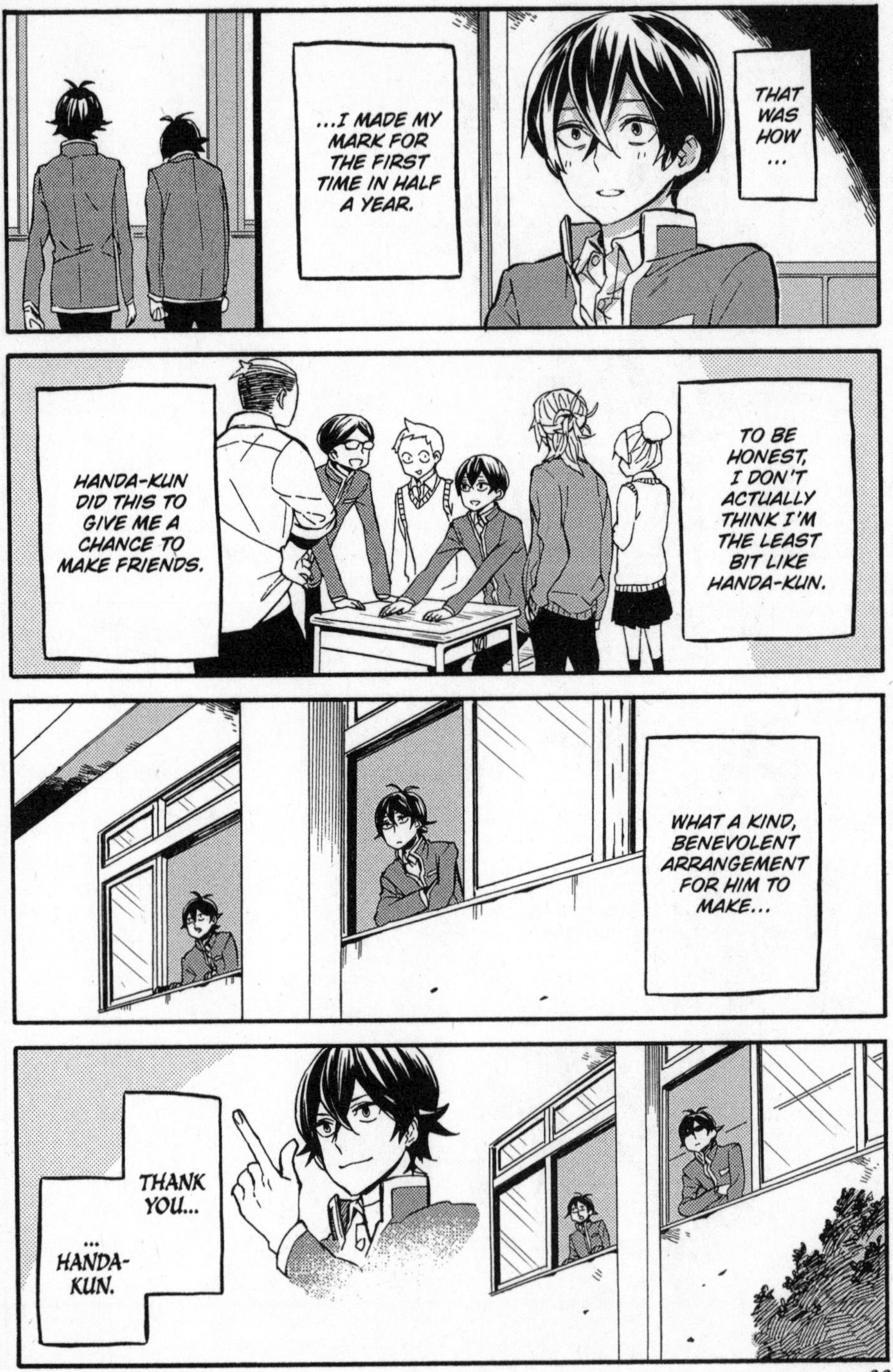
THAT WAS HOW ...
...I MADE MY MARK FOR THE FIRST TIME IN HALF A YEAR.
TO BE HONEST, I DON'T ACTUALLY THINK I'M THE LEAST BIT LIKE HANDA-KUN.
HANDA-KUN DID THIS TO GIVE ME A CHANCE TO MAKE FRIENDS.
WHAT A KIND, BENEVOLENT ARRANGEMENT FOR HIM TO MAKE...
THANK YOU...
... HANDA-KUN.

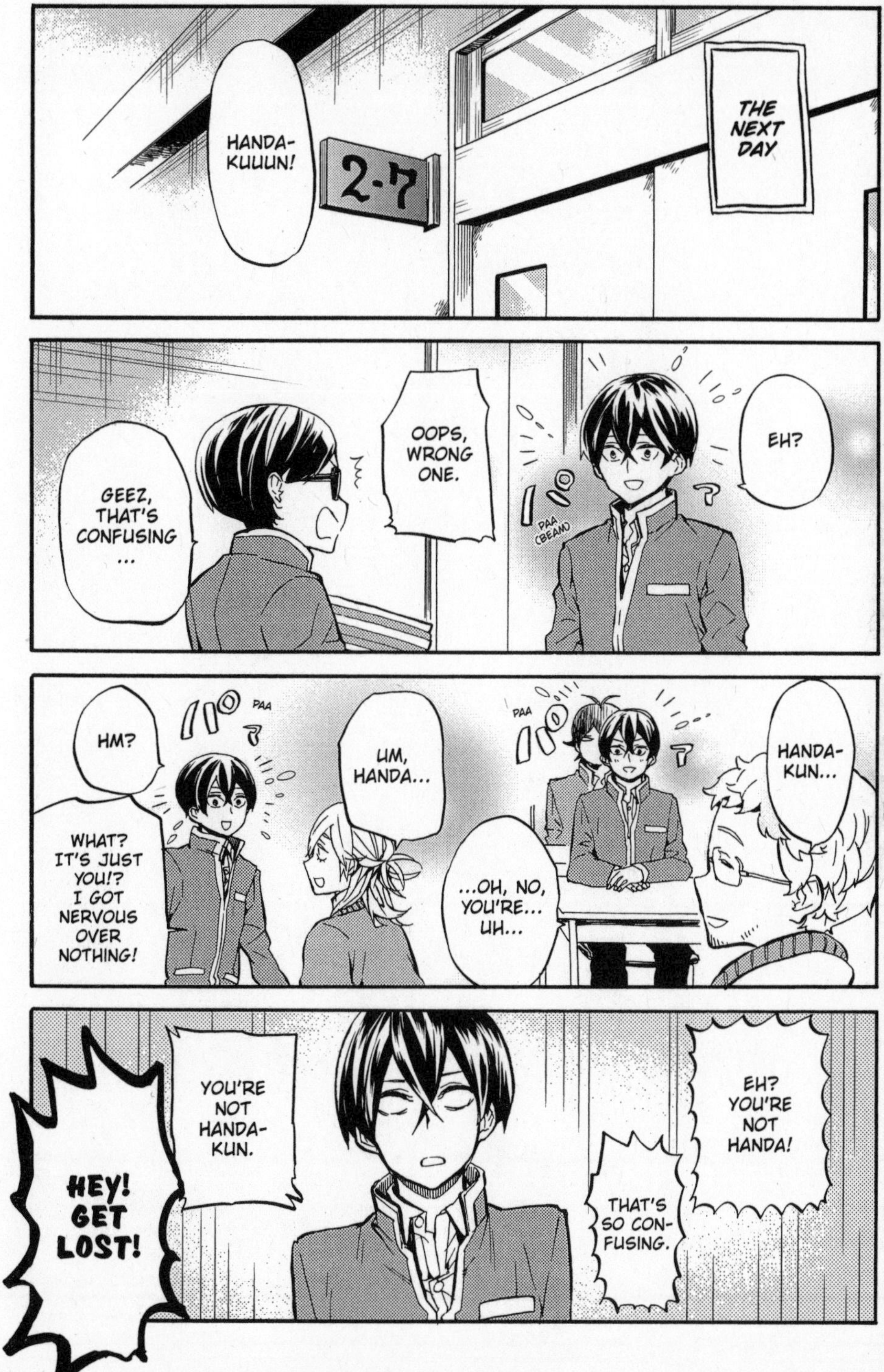
THE NEXT DAY
HANDA-KUUUN!
2-7
EH?
PAA (BEAM)
OOPS, WRONG ONE.
GEEZ, THAT'S CONFUSING...
HANDA-KUN...
PAA
...OH, NO, YOU'RE... UH...
UM, HANDA...
PAA
HM?
WHAT? IT'S JUST YOU!? I GOT NERVOUS OVER NOTHING!
EH? YOU'RE NOT HANDA!
THAT'S SO CON-FUSING.
YOU'RE NOT HANDA-KUN.
HEY! GET LOST!

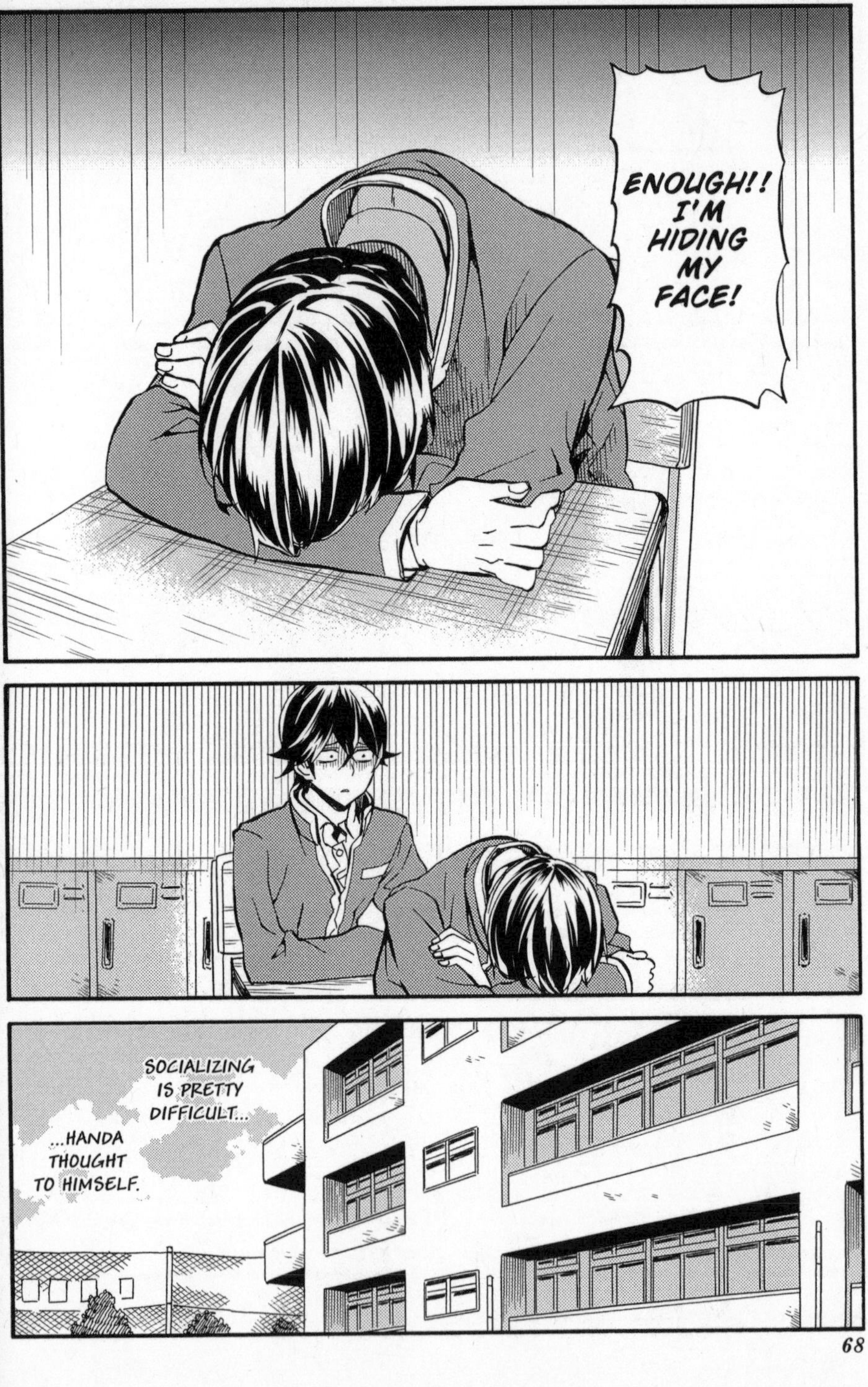
ENOUGH!! I'M HIDING MY FACE!
SOCIALIZING IS PRETTY DIFFICULT...
...HANDA THOUGHT TO HIMSELF.

After we'd finished the first extra-arc chapter that relied on the anime, we weren't sure what to do for the second extra-arc chapter. We came up with several proposals:
- a chapter where Kousuke's older sister sells a magazine about Handa-kun
- a chapter where Tsukkun returns to his earlier state (※ included in the official anthology)
- a chapter about the Ichimiya Army (※ included in the *Handa-Book*)

And lastly, there was this "kid in the seat in front" chapter.

My editor asked me, "Why won't you do a chapter about Kousuke's sister? Why not? Why not!!? WHY NOT!!!!!?" He said the readers would be thrilled with a chapter featuring Kousuke's sister from *Barakamon*, so why not!? You fool!!! YOU FOOL!! But it'd been on my mind the whole time drawing the series, how the student in front of Handa sits facedown at his desk. (Well, maybe I also thought it would be annoying to have Kousuke's sister show up...)

I began drawing with the assumption that a student who (out of consideration for Handa) always keeps his head down must have some deep feelings...This was all well and good, but he turned out to be shallower than I expected. He was the most standard of all standard Handa fans.

I didn't officially announce his name, thinking it wasn't anything that needed delving into, but his (very uncreative) family name is "Maeda" ("I'm in front."). I'd considered making his face stunningly beautiful, so that it'd draw everyone's eyes, but since the last main chapter was finished, I thought, *Why not do whatever I want?* So I made him a Handa look-alike.

And thanks to him being a look-alike, I was able to retcon away any possibility that a classmate could have greeted Handa during the year. For example, when Reo mustered the courage to greet Handa-kun, Handa would have felt an affinity for Reo ("What a great guy...!")—so I prevented that. He'd meant to greet Handa-kun, but he greeted Maeda instead! This way, Handa is left eternally unawares. *Yes! This solves everything!!*

In each chapter, I'd forcibly distort matters to make Handa isolated, but I get the feeling that my forcefulness really stood out the most in this particular chapter. All along, I was torn about whether or not to show Maeda's face, but it was fun to draw a character who had remained shrouded in mystery until now.

There were questions like, "How would this person go through his daily life!?" but he just keeps his head down the whole time. Because that's the kind of character he is; that's the idea.

That's the sort of mind-set I had when drawing *Handa-kun*.

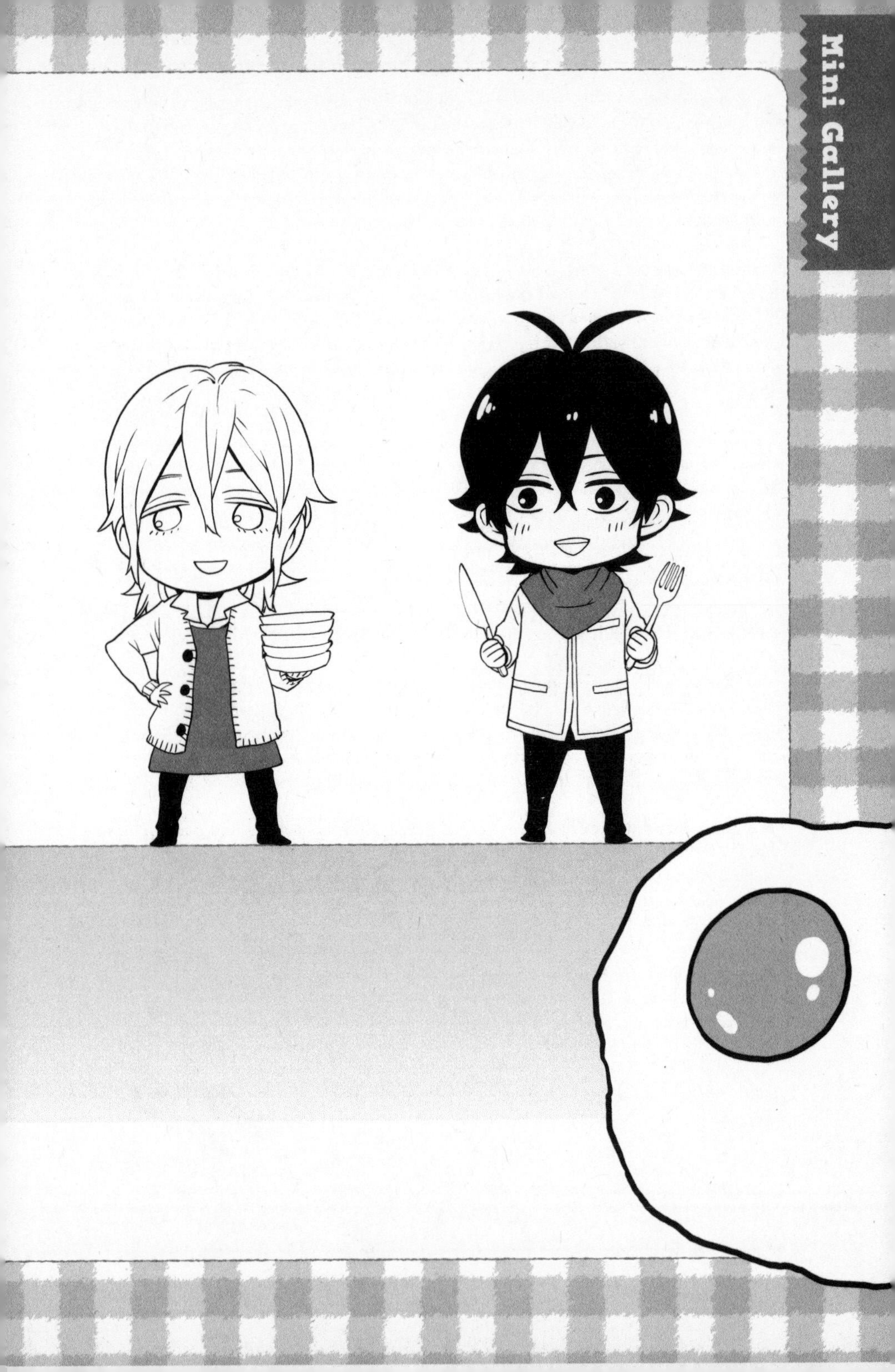
Mini Gallery

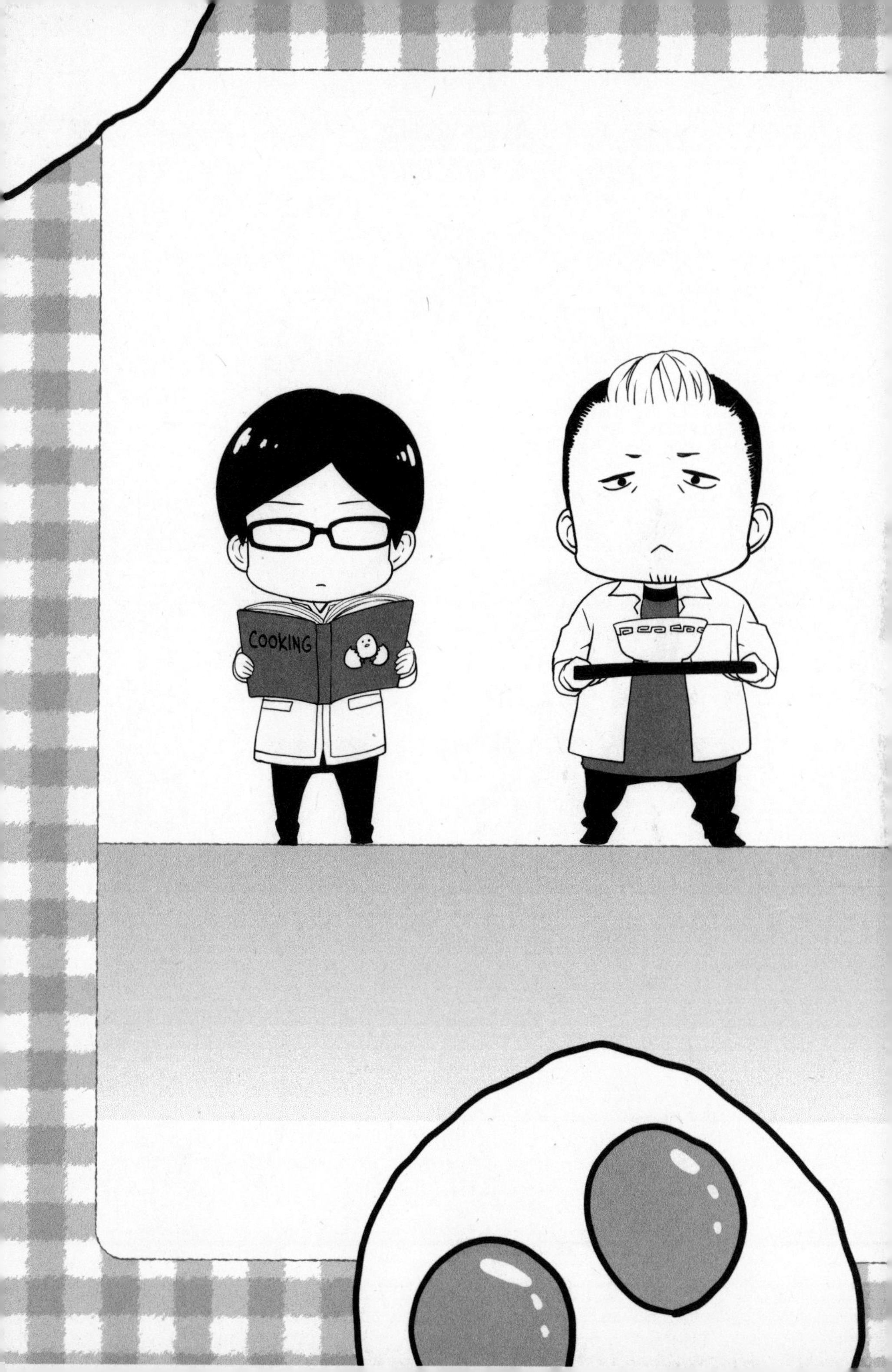
COOKING

Mini Gallery

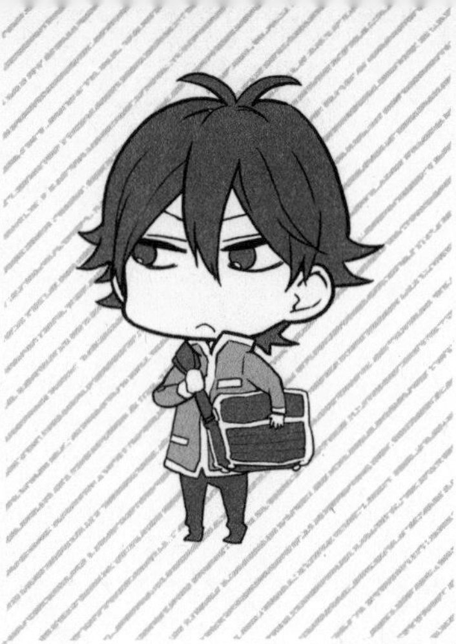

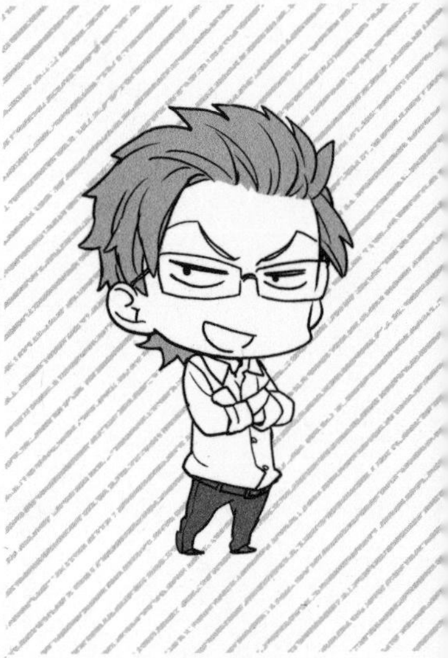

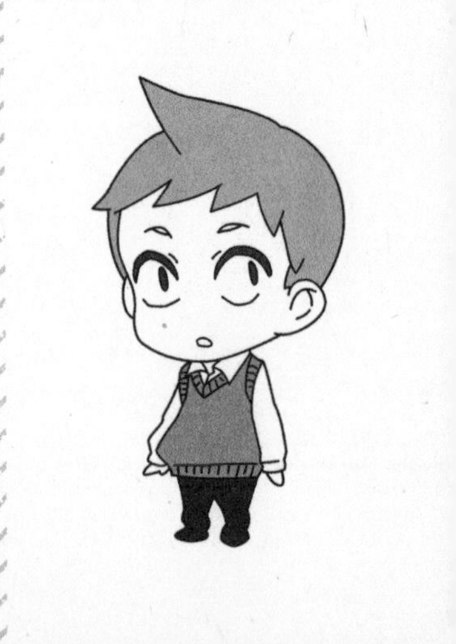

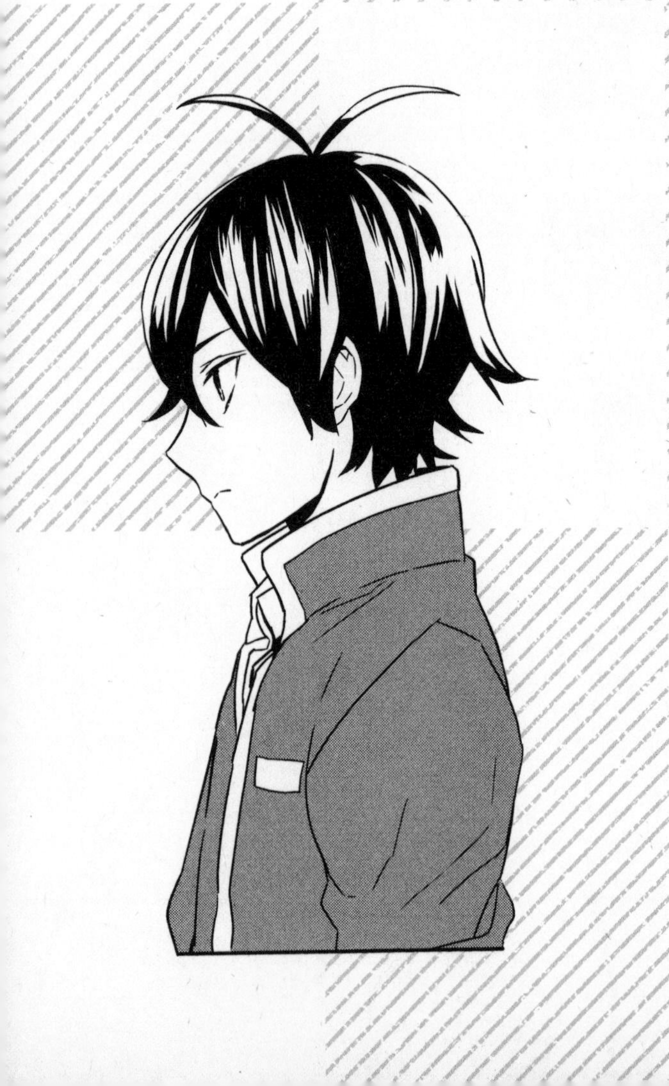

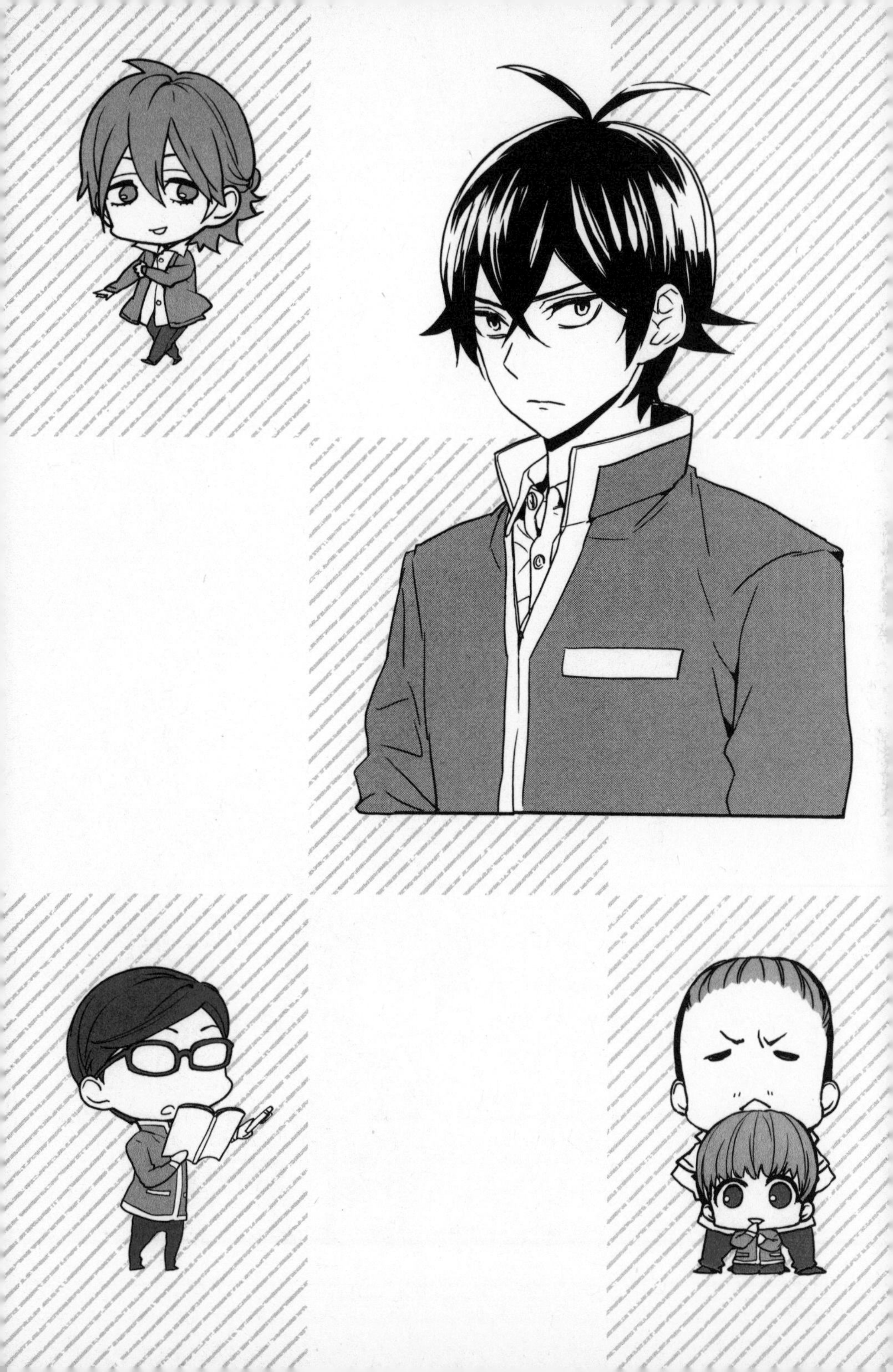

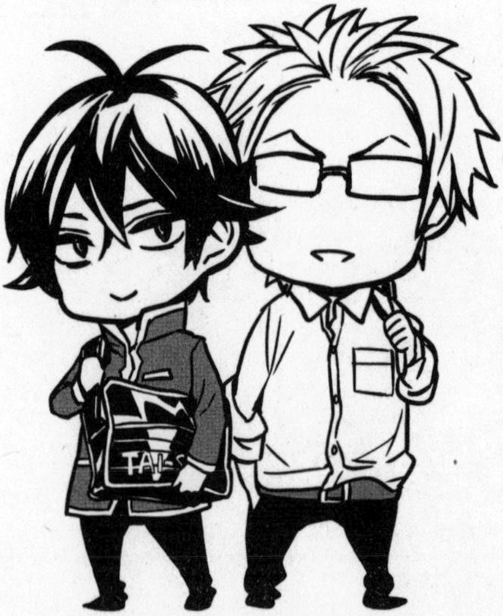
TAI-

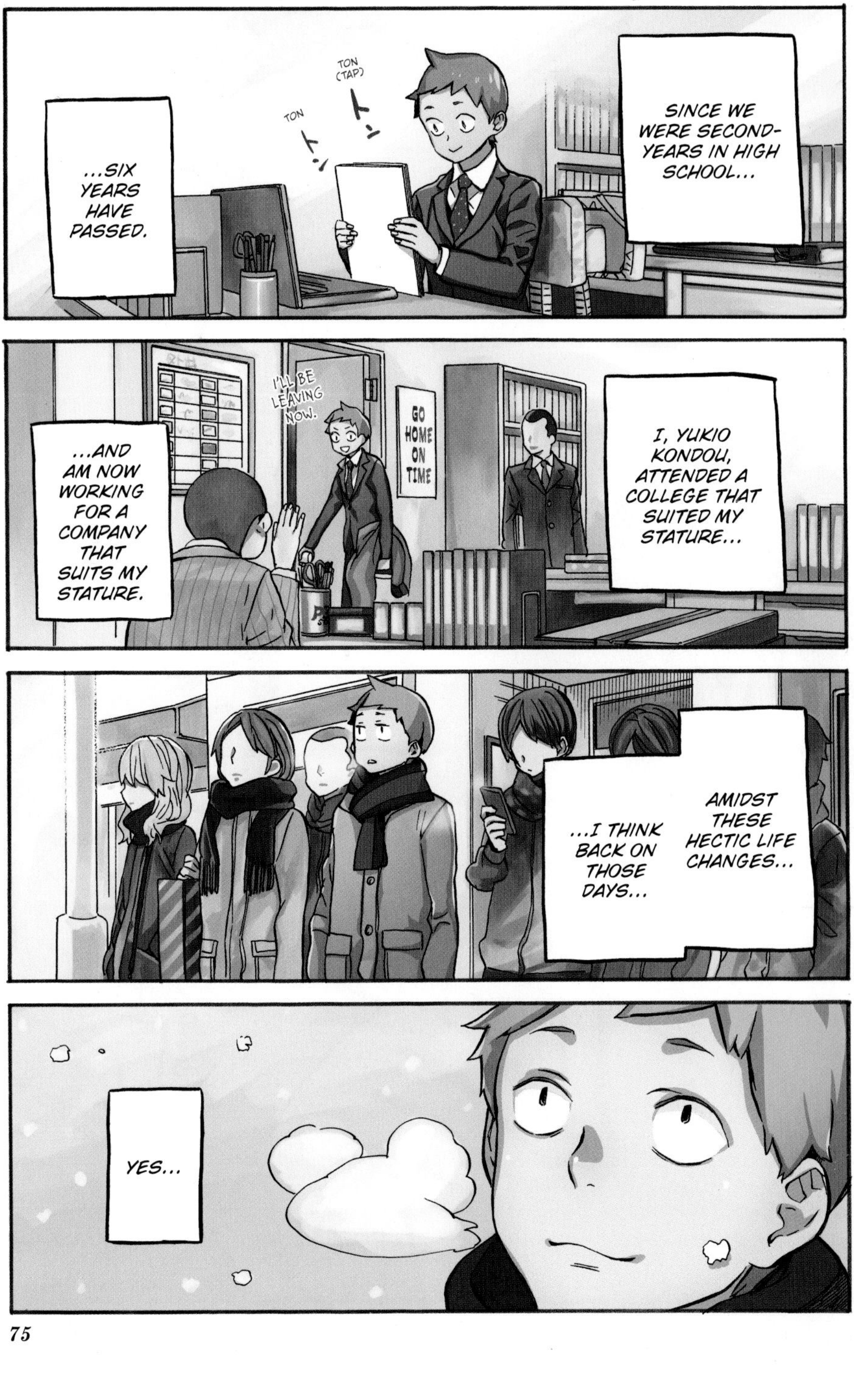
SINCE WE WERE SECOND-YEARS IN HIGH SCHOOL...
TON (TAP)
TON
...SIX YEARS HAVE PASSED.
I, YUKIO KONDOU, ATTENDED A COLLEGE THAT SUITED MY STATURE...
GO HOME ON TIME
I'LL BE LEAVING NOW.
...AND AM NOW WORKING FOR A COMPANY THAT SUITS MY STATURE.
AMIDST THESE HECTIC LIFE CHANGES...
...I THINK BACK ON THOSE DAYS...
YES...

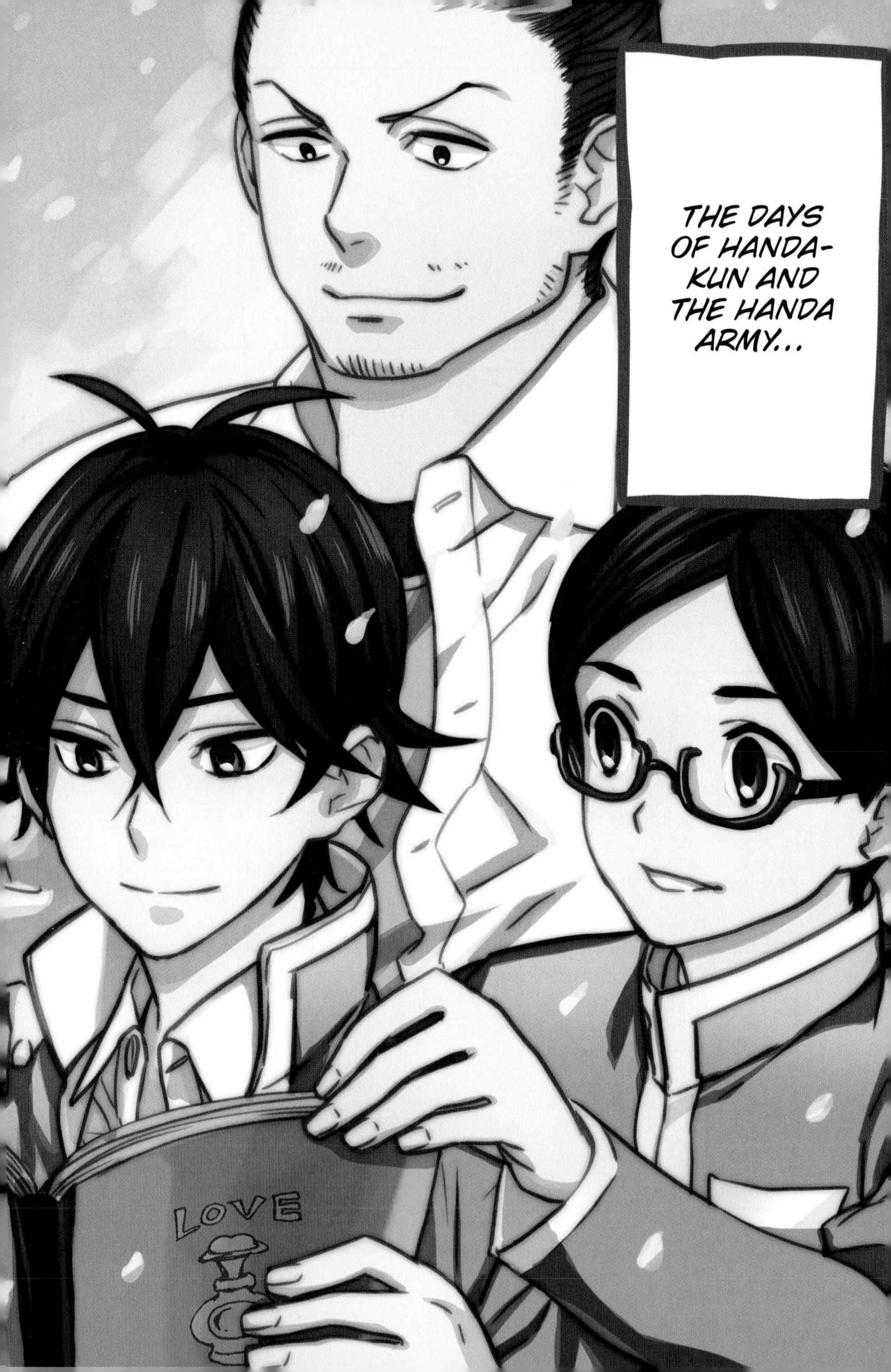
THE DAYS OF HANDA-KUN AND THE HANDA ARMY...
LOVE

ロミオ&ジュリエット
ROMEO & JULIET
2-7

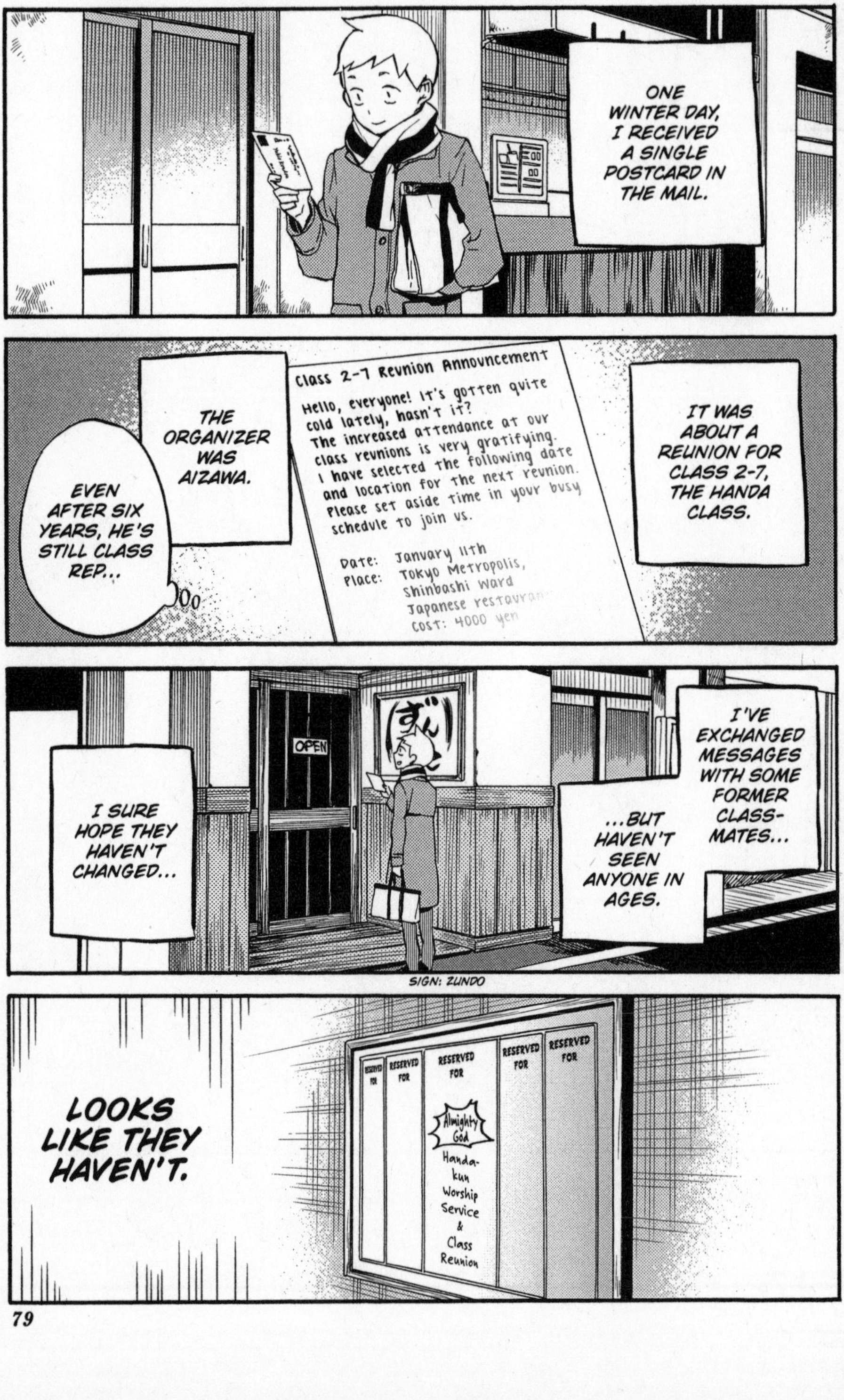
ONE WINTER DAY, I RECEIVED A SINGLE POSTCARD IN THE MAIL.
IT WAS ABOUT A REUNION FOR CLASS 2-7, THE HANDA CLASS.
Class 2-7 Reunion Announcement
Hello, everyone! It's gotten quite cold lately, hasn't it? The increased attendance at our class reunions is very gratifying. I have selected the following date and location for the next reunion. Please set aside time in your busy schedule to join us.
Date: January 11th
Place: Tokyo Metropolis, Shinbashi Ward
Japanese restaurant
Cost: 4000 yen
THE ORGANIZER WAS AIZAWA.
EVEN AFTER SIX YEARS, HE'S STILL CLASS REP...
I'VE EXCHANGED MESSAGES WITH SOME FORMER CLASS-MATES...
...BUT HAVEN'T SEEN ANYONE IN AGES.
ずん
OPEN
I SURE HOPE THEY HAVEN'T CHANGED...
SIGN: ZUNDO
RESERVED FOR
RESERVED FOR
RESERVED FOR
RESERVED FOR
RESERVED FOR
Almighty God
Handa-kun Worship Service & Class Reunion
LOOKS LIKE THEY HAVEN'T.

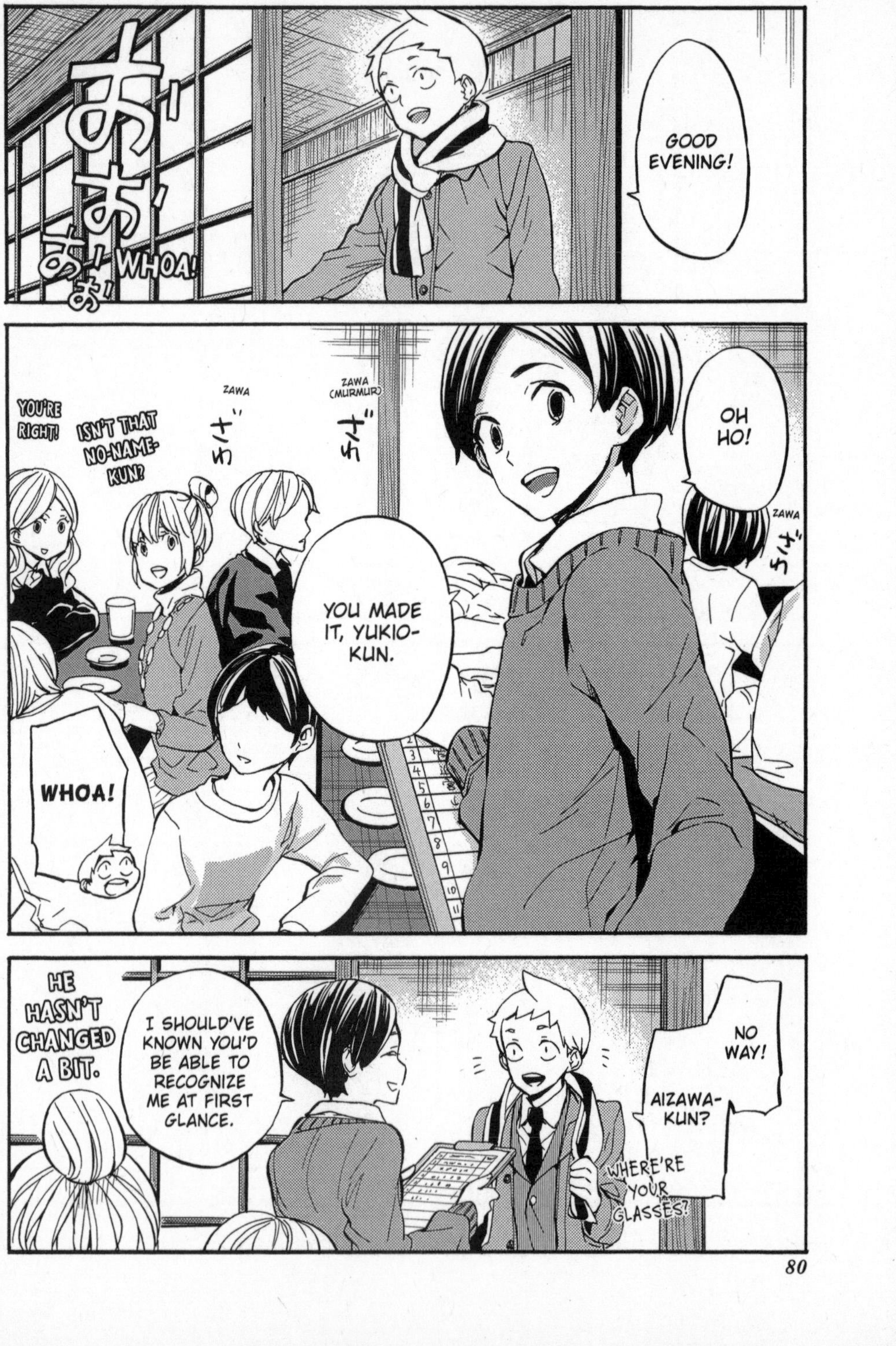
GOOD EVENING!
WHOA!
OH HO!
ZAWA
YOU MADE IT, YUKIO-KUN.
ZAWA (MURMUR)
ZAWA
ISN'T THAT NO-NAME-KUN?
YOU'RE RIGHT!
WHOA!
NO WAY!
AIZAWA-KUN?
WHERE'RE YOUR GLASSES?
I SHOULD'VE KNOWN YOU'D BE ABLE TO RECOGNIZE ME AT FIRST GLANCE.
HE HASN'T CHANGED A BIT.

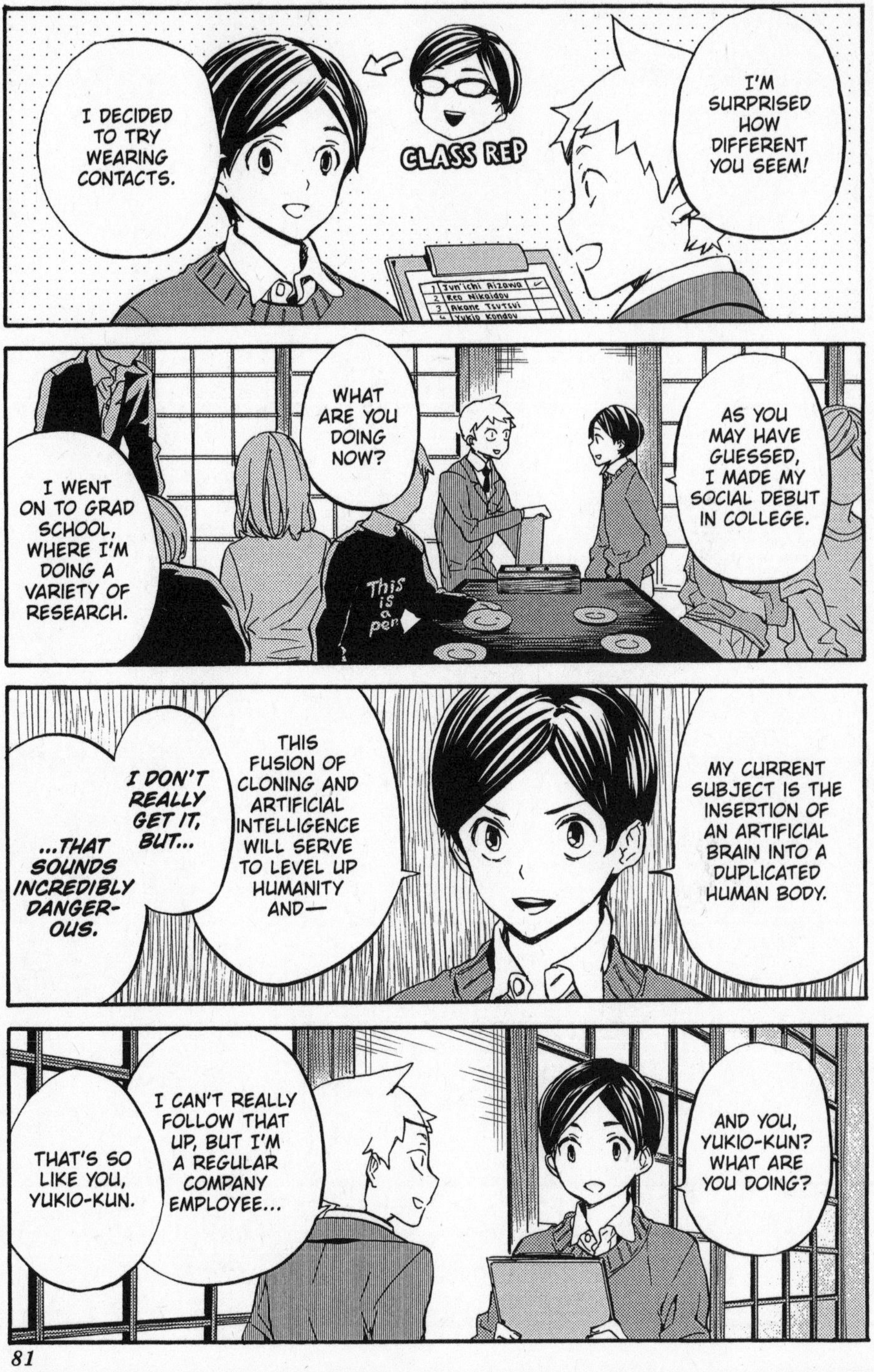
I'M SURPRISED HOW DIFFERENT YOU SEEM!
CLASS REP
I DECIDED TO TRY WEARING CONTACTS.
1 Jun'ichi Aizawa
2 Reo Nikaidou
3 Akane Tsutsui
4 Yukio Kondou
AS YOU MAY HAVE GUESSED, I MADE MY SOCIAL DEBUT IN COLLEGE.
WHAT ARE YOU DOING NOW?
I WENT ON TO GRAD SCHOOL, WHERE I'M DOING A VARIETY OF RESEARCH.
This is a pen
MY CURRENT SUBJECT IS THE INSERTION OF AN ARTIFICIAL BRAIN INTO A DUPLICATED HUMAN BODY.
THIS FUSION OF CLONING AND ARTIFICIAL INTELLIGENCE WILL SERVE TO LEVEL UP HUMANITY AND—
I DON'T REALLY GET IT, BUT...
...THAT SOUNDS INCREDIBLY DANGER-OUS.
AND YOU, YUKIO-KUN? WHAT ARE YOU DOING?
I CAN'T REALLY FOLLOW THAT UP, BUT I'M A REGULAR COMPANY EMPLOYEE...
THAT'S SO LIKE YOU, YUKIO-KUN.

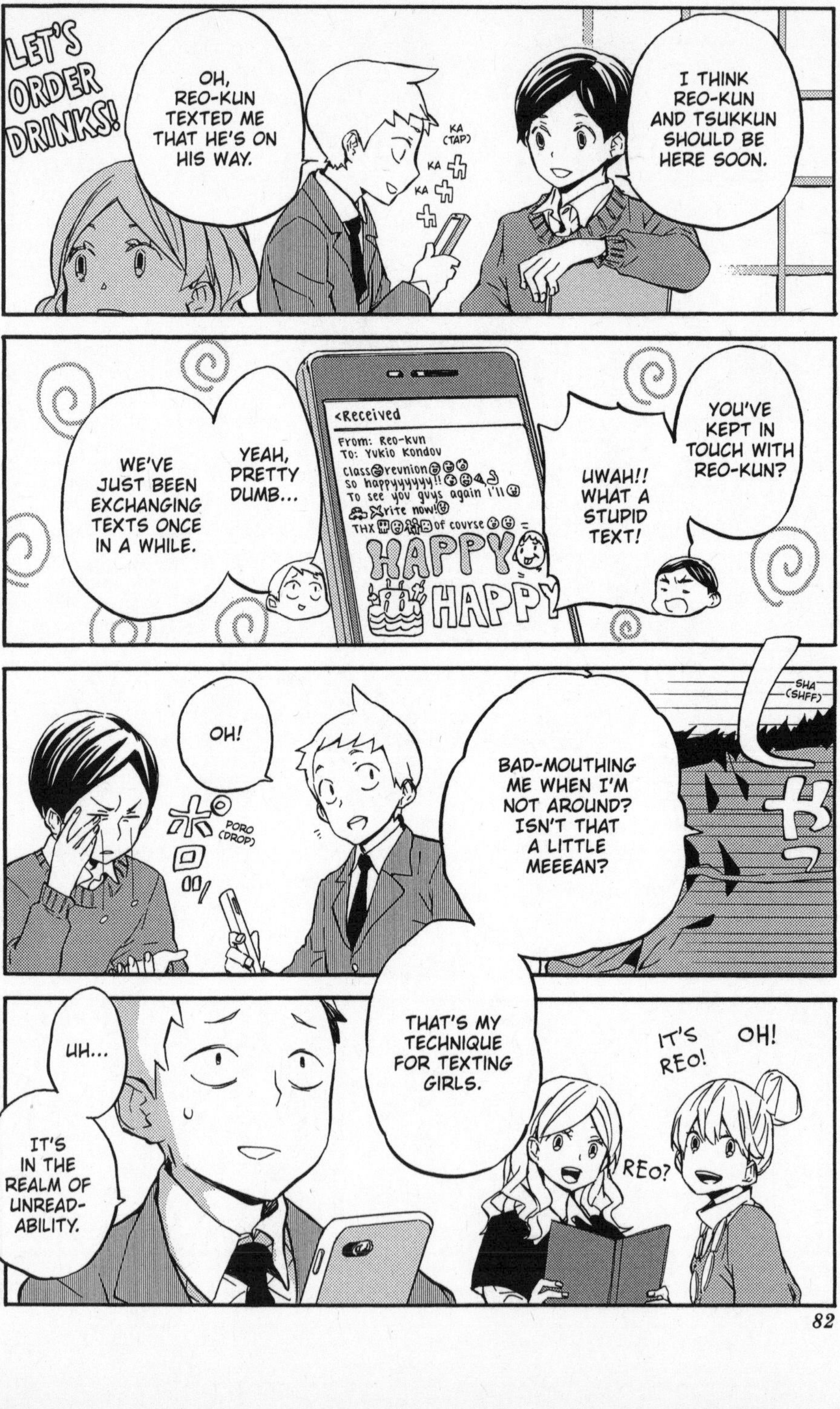
I THINK REO-KUN AND TSUKKUN SHOULD BE HERE SOON.
KA (TAP)
KA
KA
OH, REO-KUN TEXTED ME THAT HE'S ON HIS WAY.
LET'S ORDER DRINKS!
YOU'VE KEPT IN TOUCH WITH REO-KUN?
UWAH!! WHAT A STUPID TEXT!
<Received
From: Reo-kun
To: Yukio Kondou
Class reunion
so happyyyyyy!!
To see you guys again I'll
rite now!
THX of course
HAPPY
HAPPY
YEAH, PRETTY DUMB...
WE'VE JUST BEEN EXCHANGING TEXTS ONCE IN A WHILE.
SHA (SHFF)
BAD-MOUTHING ME WHEN I'M NOT AROUND? ISN'T THAT A LITTLE MEEEAN?
OH!
PORO (DROP)
OH!
IT'S REO!
REO?
THAT'S MY TECHNIQUE FOR TEXTING GIRLS.
UH...
IT'S IN THE REALM OF UNREAD-ABILITY.

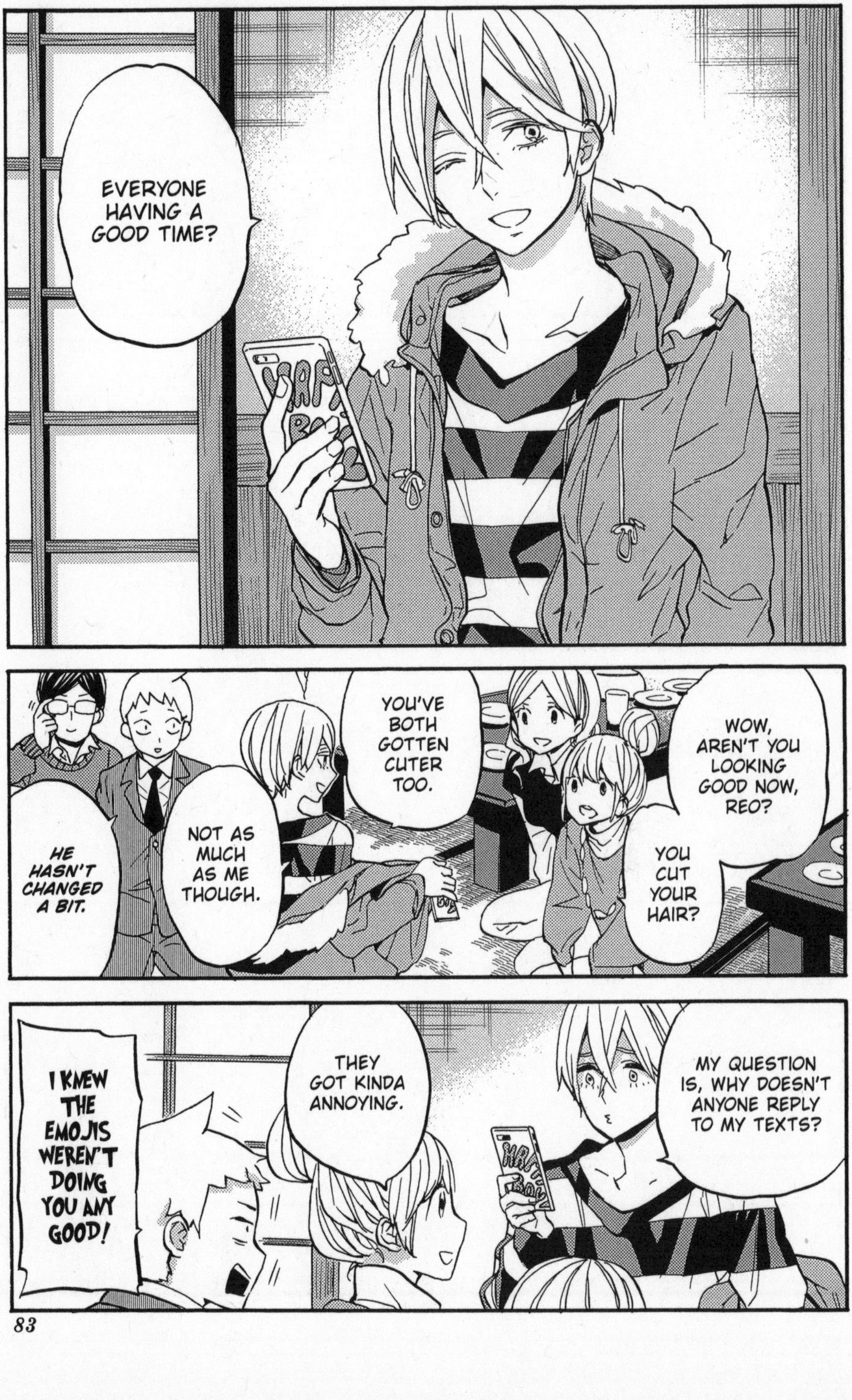
EVERYONE HAVING A GOOD TIME?
WOW, AREN'T YOU LOOKING GOOD NOW, REO?
YOU CUT YOUR HAIR?
YOU'VE BOTH GOTTEN CUTER TOO.
NOT AS MUCH AS ME THOUGH.
HE HASN'T CHANGED A BIT.
MY QUESTION IS, WHY DOESN'T ANYONE REPLY TO MY TEXTS?
THEY GOT KINDA ANNOYING.
I KNEW THE EMOJIS WEREN'T DOING YOU ANY GOOD!

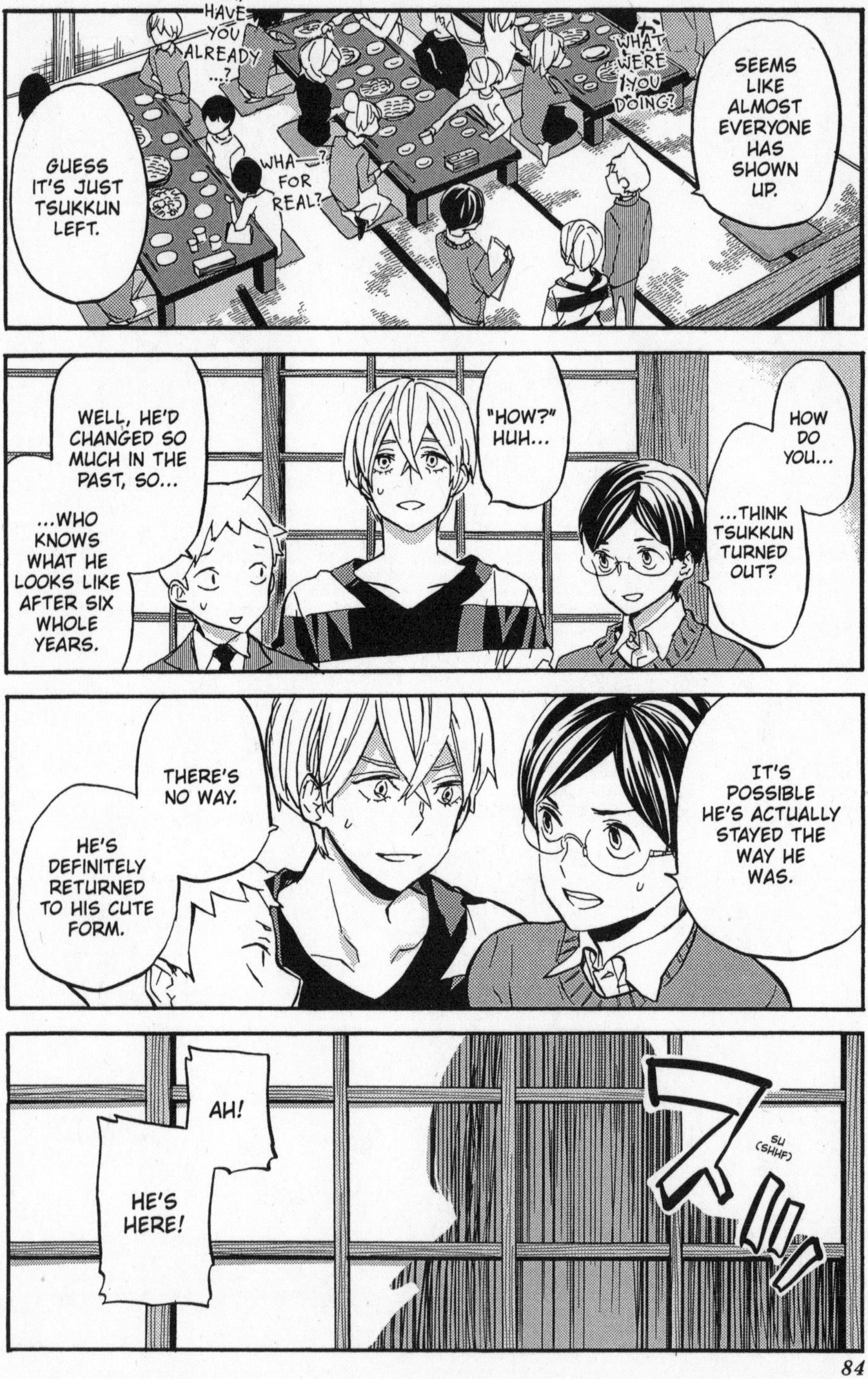
SEEMS LIKE ALMOST EVERYONE HAS SHOWN UP.
WHAT WERE YOU DOING?
HEY, HAVE YOU ALREADY ...?
WHA—? FOR REAL?
GUESS IT'S JUST TSUKKUN LEFT.
HOW DO YOU...
...THINK TSUKKUN TURNED OUT?
"HOW?" HUH...
WELL, HE'D CHANGED SO MUCH IN THE PAST, SO...
...WHO KNOWS WHAT HE LOOKS LIKE AFTER SIX WHOLE YEARS.
IT'S POSSIBLE HE'S ACTUALLY STAYED THE WAY HE WAS.
THERE'S NO WAY.
HE'S DEFINITELY RETURNED TO HIS CUTE FORM.
SU (SHHF)
AH!
HE'S HERE!

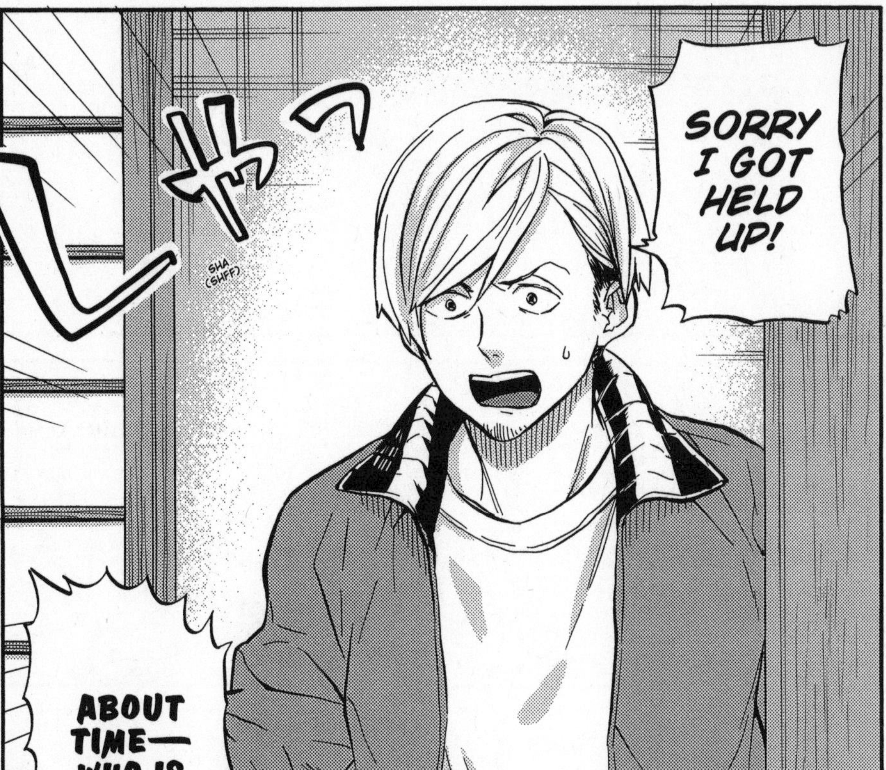
SORRY I GOT HELD UP!
SHA (SHFF)
ABOUT TIME— WHO IS THAT!?

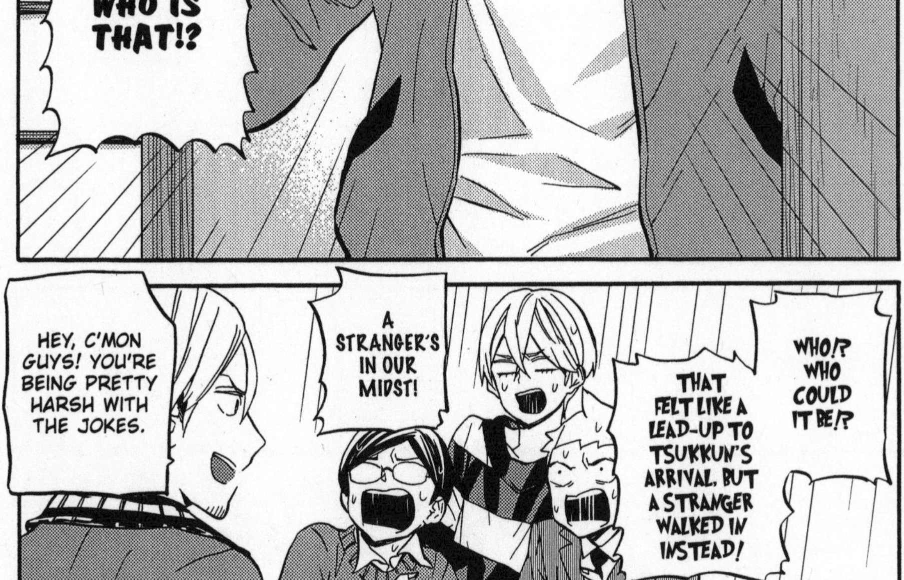
WHO!? WHO COULD IT BE!?
THAT FELT LIKE A LEAD-UP TO TSUKKUN'S ARRIVAL, BUT A STRANGER WALKED IN INSTEAD!
A STRANGER'S IN OUR MIDST!
HEY, C'MON GUYS! YOU'RE BEING PRETTY HARSH WITH THE JOKES.

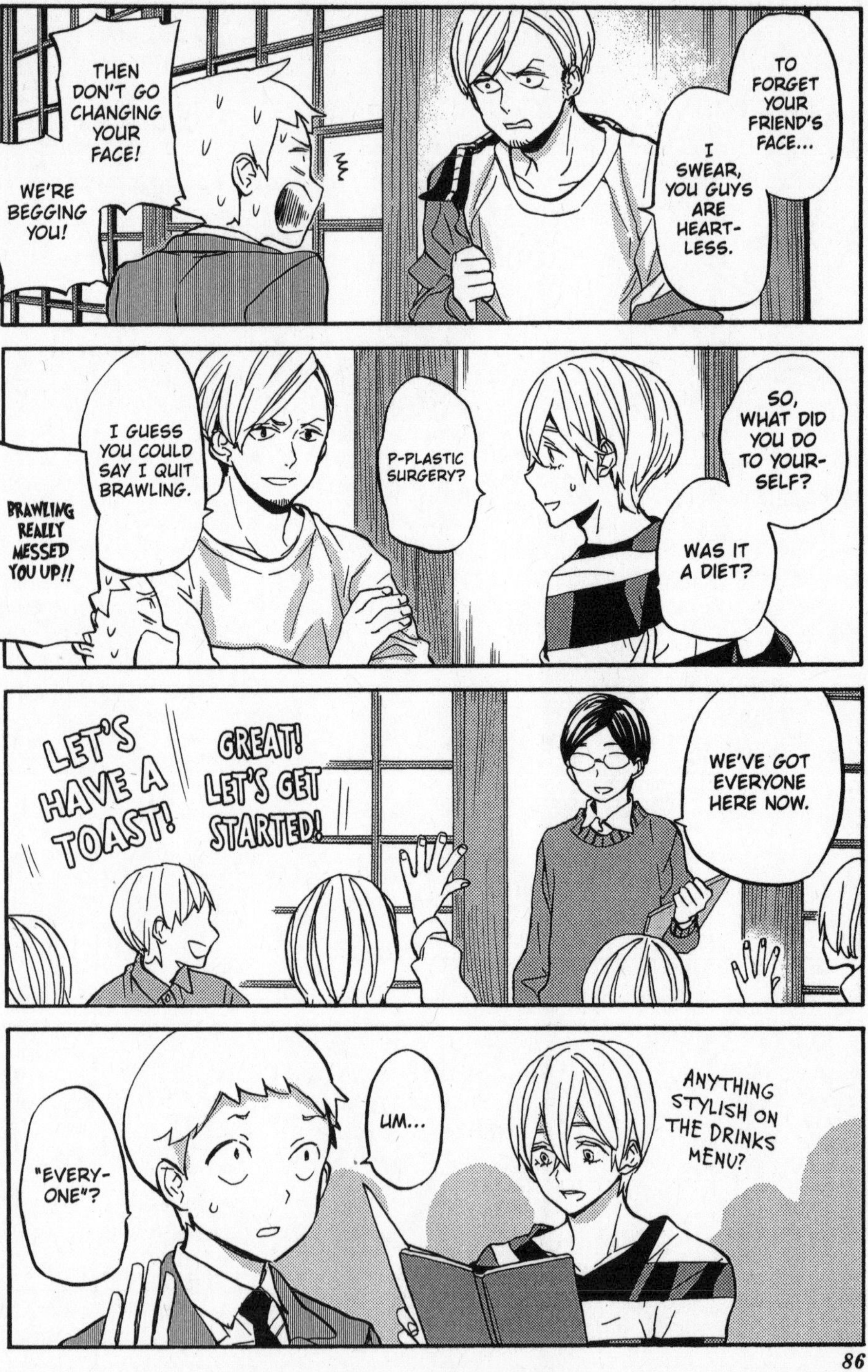
TO FORGET YOUR FRIEND'S FACE...
I SWEAR, YOU GUYS ARE HEART-LESS.
THEN DON'T GO CHANGING YOUR FACE!
WE'RE BEGGING YOU!
SO, WHAT DID YOU DO TO YOUR-SELF?
WAS IT A DIET?
P-PLASTIC SURGERY?
I GUESS YOU COULD SAY I QUIT BRAWLING.
BRAWLING REALLY MESSED YOU UP!!
WE'VE GOT EVERYONE HERE NOW.
GREAT! LET'S GET STARTED!
LET'S HAVE A TOAST!
ANYTHING STYLISH ON THE DRINKS MENU?
UM...
"EVERY-ONE"?

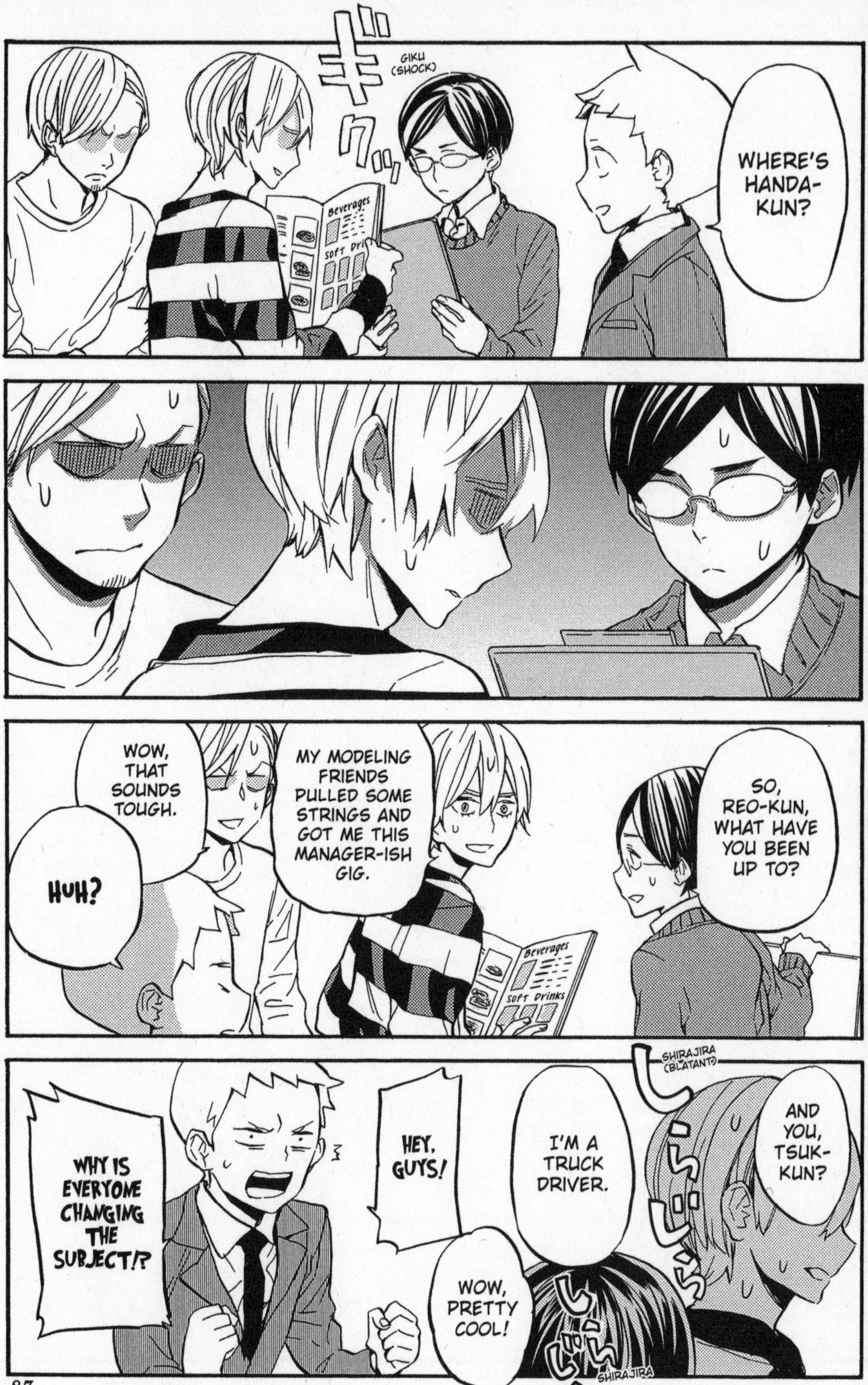
WHERE'S HANDA-KUN?
GIKU (SHOCK)
SO, REO-KUN, WHAT HAVE YOU BEEN UP TO?
MY MODELING FRIENDS PULLED SOME STRINGS AND GOT ME THIS MANAGER-ISH GIG.
WOW, THAT SOUNDS TOUGH.
HUH?
AND YOU, TSUK-KUN?
SHIRAJIRA (BLATANT)
I'M A TRUCK DRIVER.
WOW, PRETTY COOL!
SHIRAJIRA
HEY, GUYS!
WHY IS EVERYONE CHANGING THE SUBJECT!?

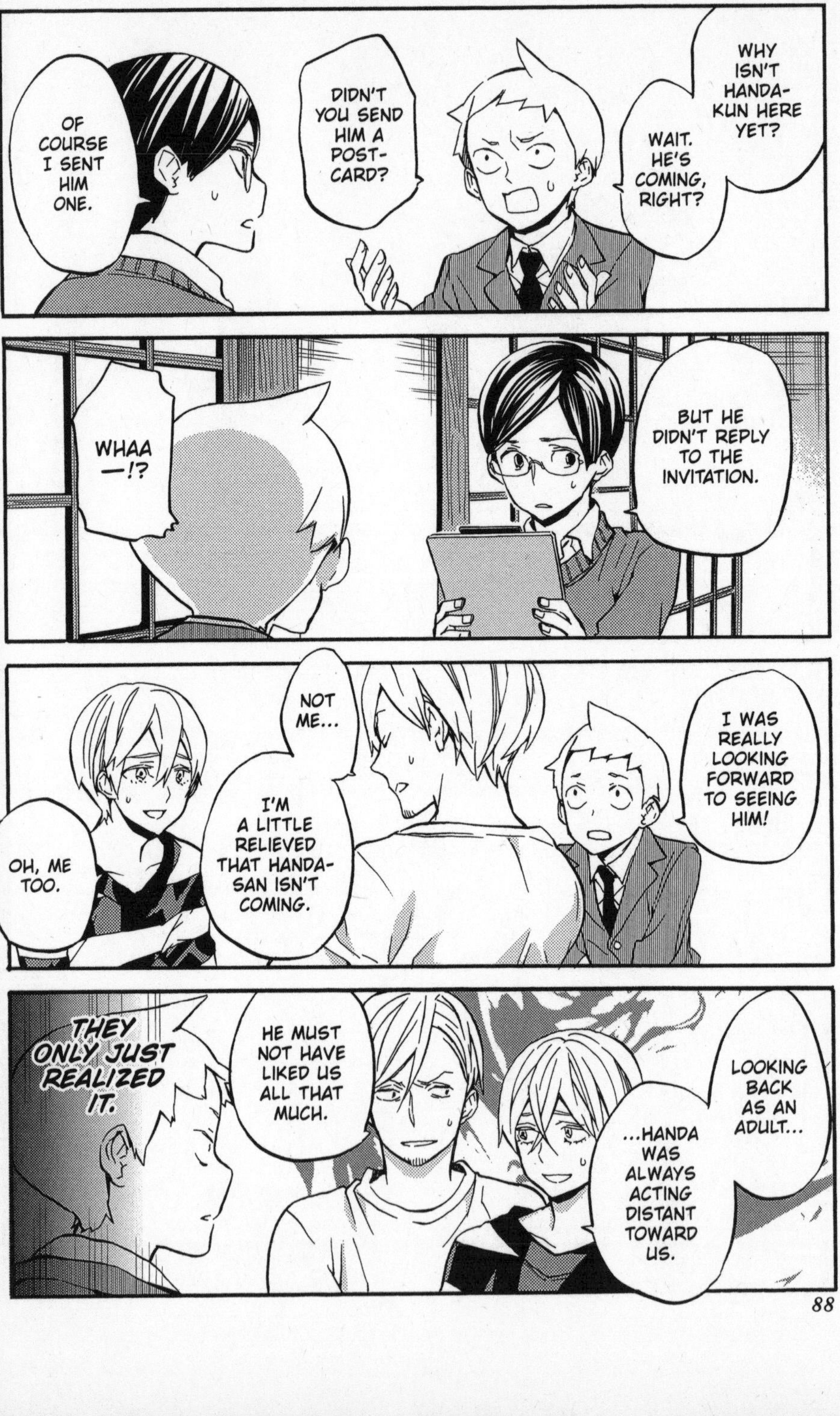
WHY ISN'T HANDA-KUN HERE YET?
WAIT. HE'S COMING, RIGHT?
DIDN'T YOU SEND HIM A POST-CARD?
OF COURSE I SENT HIM ONE.
BUT HE DIDN'T REPLY TO THE INVITATION.
WHAA—!?
I WAS REALLY LOOKING FORWARD TO SEEING HIM!
NOT ME...
I'M A LITTLE RELIEVED THAT HANDA-SAN ISN'T COMING.
OH, ME TOO.
LOOKING BACK AS AN ADULT...
...HANDA WAS ALWAYS ACTING DISTANT TOWARD US.
HE MUST NOT HAVE LIKED US ALL THAT MUCH.
THEY ONLY JUST REALIZED IT.

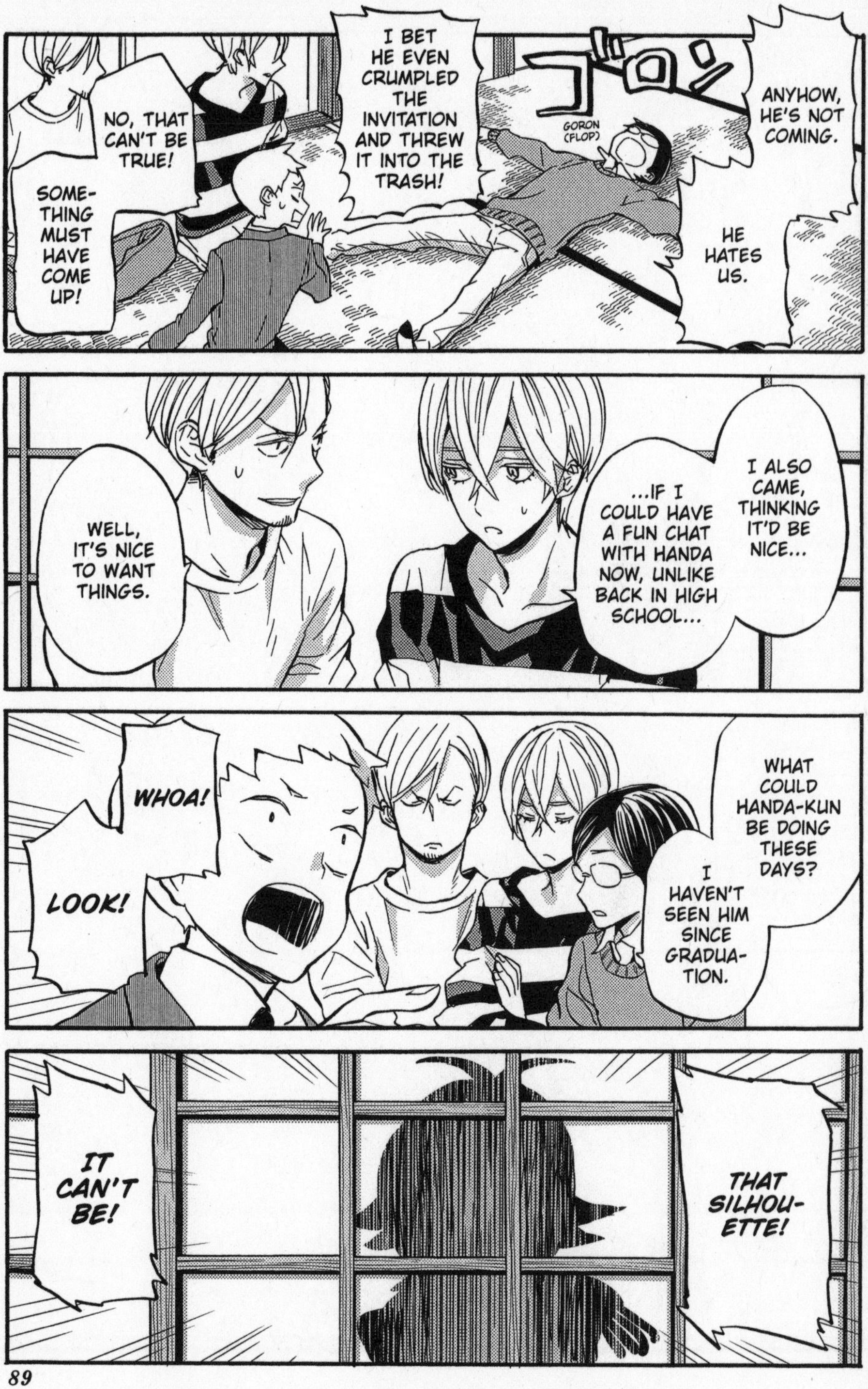

ゴロン
GORON (FLOP)
ANYHOW, HE'S NOT COMING.
HE HATES US.
I BET HE EVEN CRUMPLED THE INVITATION AND THREW IT INTO THE TRASH!
NO, THAT CAN'T BE TRUE!
SOME-THING MUST HAVE COME UP!
I ALSO CAME, THINKING IT'D BE NICE...
...IF I COULD HAVE A FUN CHAT WITH HANDA NOW, UNLIKE BACK IN HIGH SCHOOL...
WELL, IT'S NICE TO WANT THINGS.
WHAT COULD HANDA-KUN BE DOING THESE DAYS?
I HAVEN'T SEEN HIM SINCE GRADUA-TION.
WHOA!
LOOK!
THAT SILHOU-ETTE!
IT CAN'T BE!

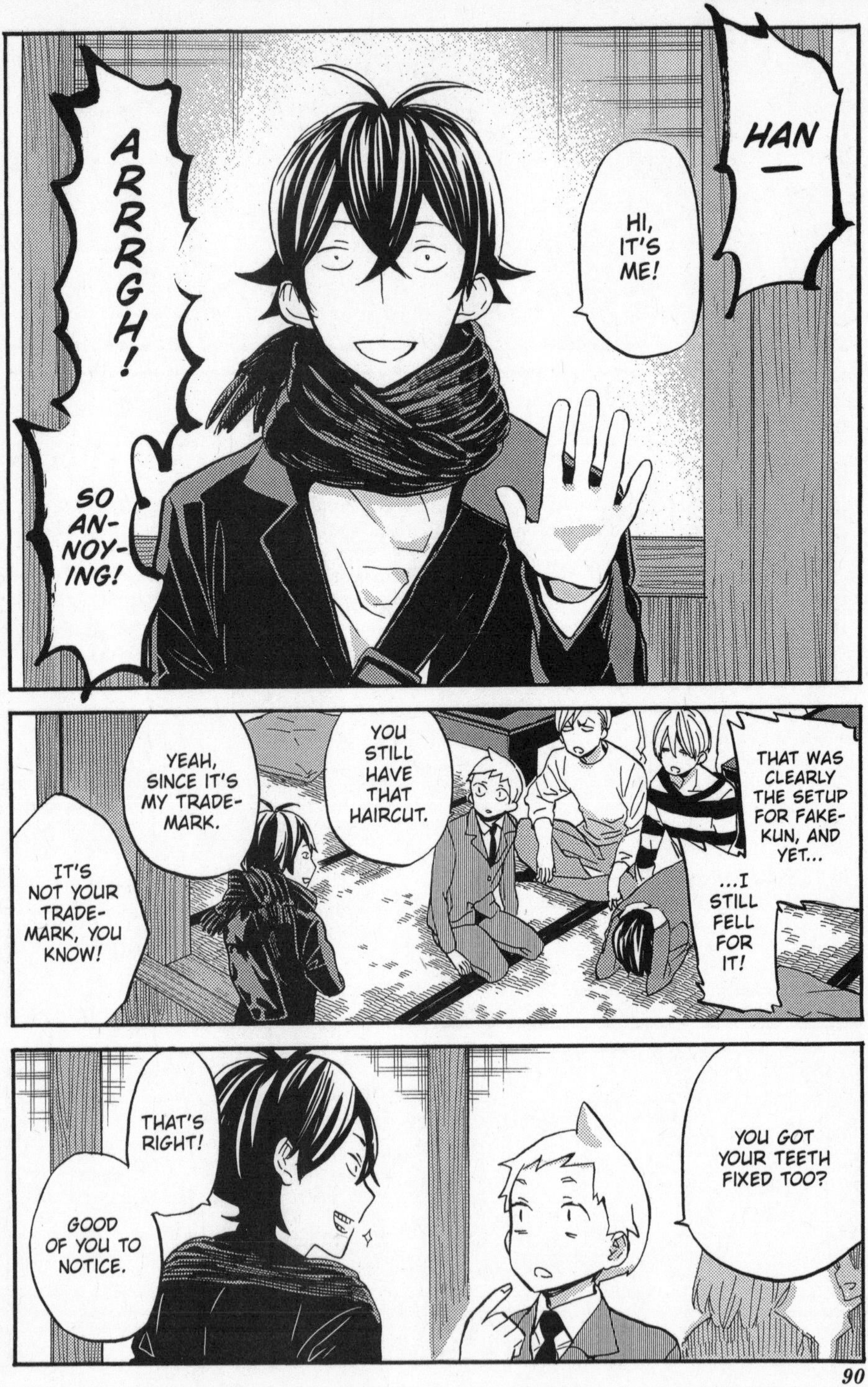
HAN—
HI, IT'S ME!
ARRRGH!
SO AN-NOY-ING!
THAT WAS CLEARLY THE SETUP FOR FAKE-KUN, AND YET...
...I STILL FELL FOR IT!
YOU STILL HAVE THAT HAIRCUT.
YEAH, SINCE IT'S MY TRADE-MARK.
IT'S NOT YOUR TRADE-MARK, YOU KNOW!
YOU GOT YOUR TEETH FIXED TOO?
THAT'S RIGHT!
GOOD OF YOU TO NOTICE.

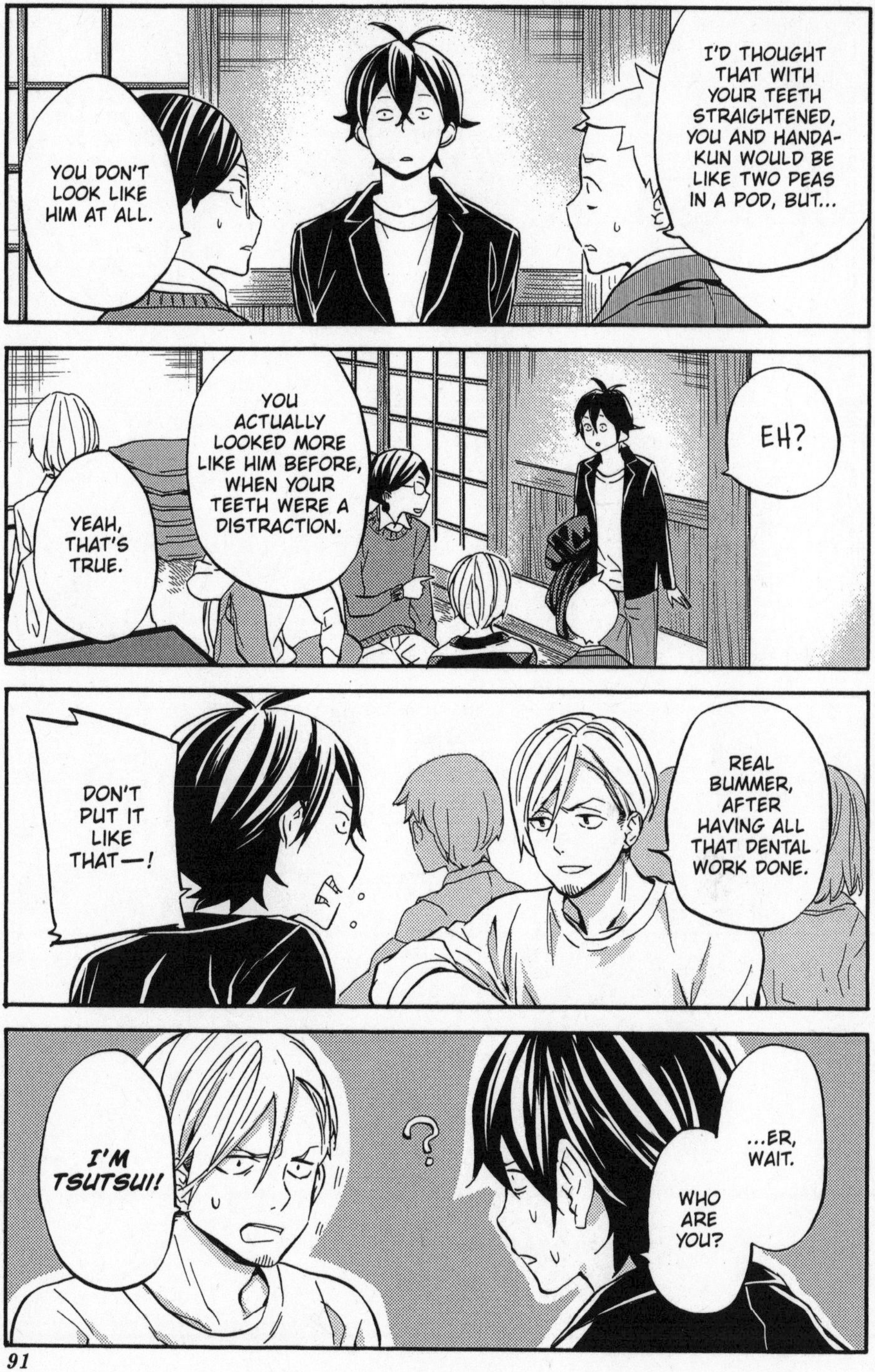
I'D THOUGHT THAT WITH YOUR TEETH STRAIGHTENED, YOU AND HANDA-KUN WOULD BE LIKE TWO PEAS IN A POD, BUT...
YOU DON'T LOOK LIKE HIM AT ALL.
EH?
YOU ACTUALLY LOOKED MORE LIKE HIM BEFORE, WHEN YOUR TEETH WERE A DISTRACTION.
YEAH, THAT'S TRUE.
REAL BUMMER, AFTER HAVING ALL THAT DENTAL WORK DONE.
DON'T PUT IT LIKE THAT—!
...ER, WAIT.
WHO ARE YOU?
?
I'M TSUTSUI!

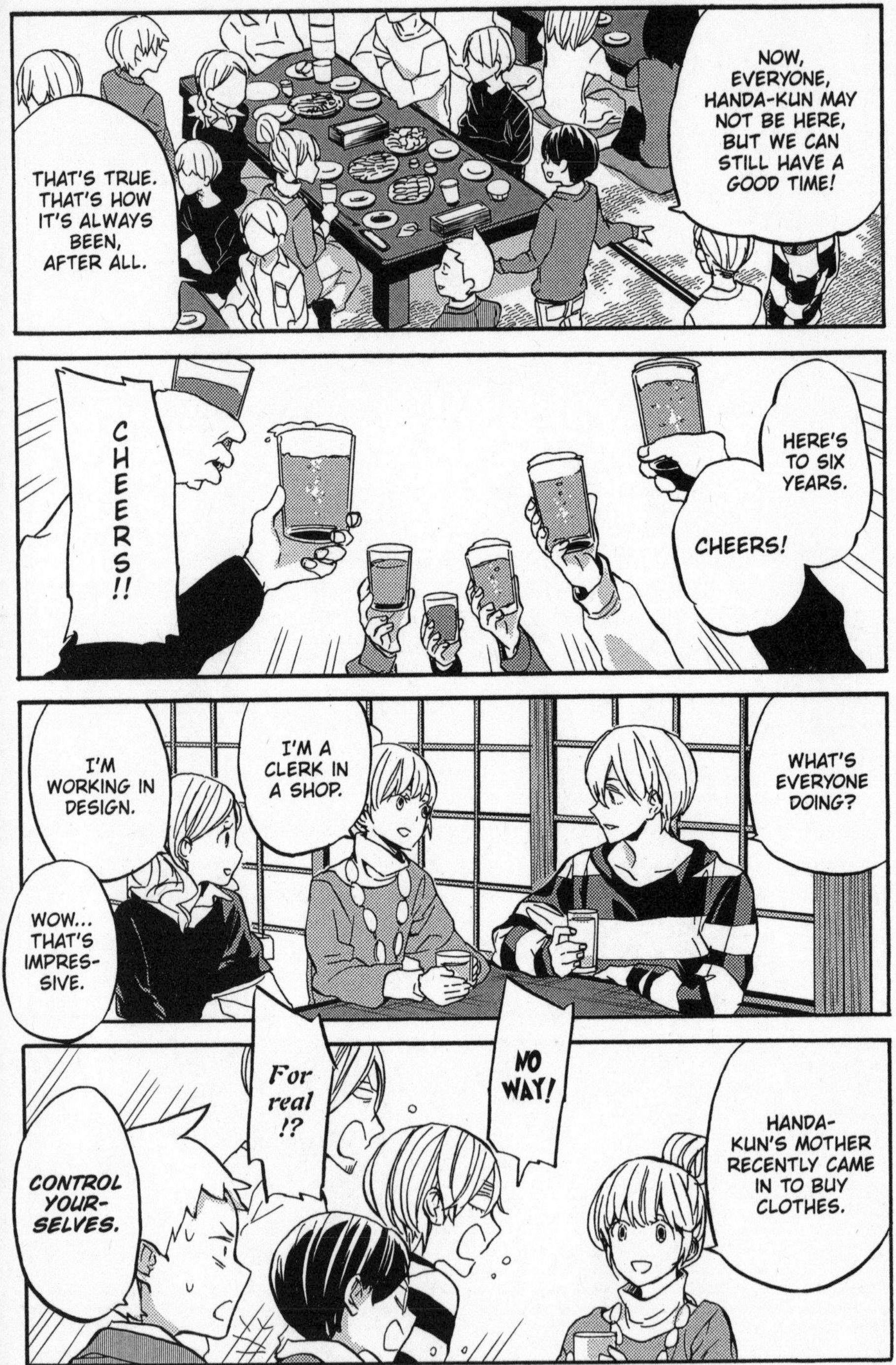
NOW, EVERYONE, HANDA-KUN MAY NOT BE HERE, BUT WE CAN STILL HAVE A GOOD TIME!
THAT'S TRUE. THAT'S HOW IT'S ALWAYS BEEN, AFTER ALL.
HERE'S TO SIX YEARS.
CHEERS!
CHEERS!!
WHAT'S EVERYONE DOING?
I'M A CLERK IN A SHOP.
I'M WORKING IN DESIGN.
WOW... THAT'S IMPRESSIVE.
HANDA-KUN'S MOTHER RECENTLY CAME IN TO BUY CLOTHES.
NO WAY!
For real!?
CONTROL YOURSELVES.

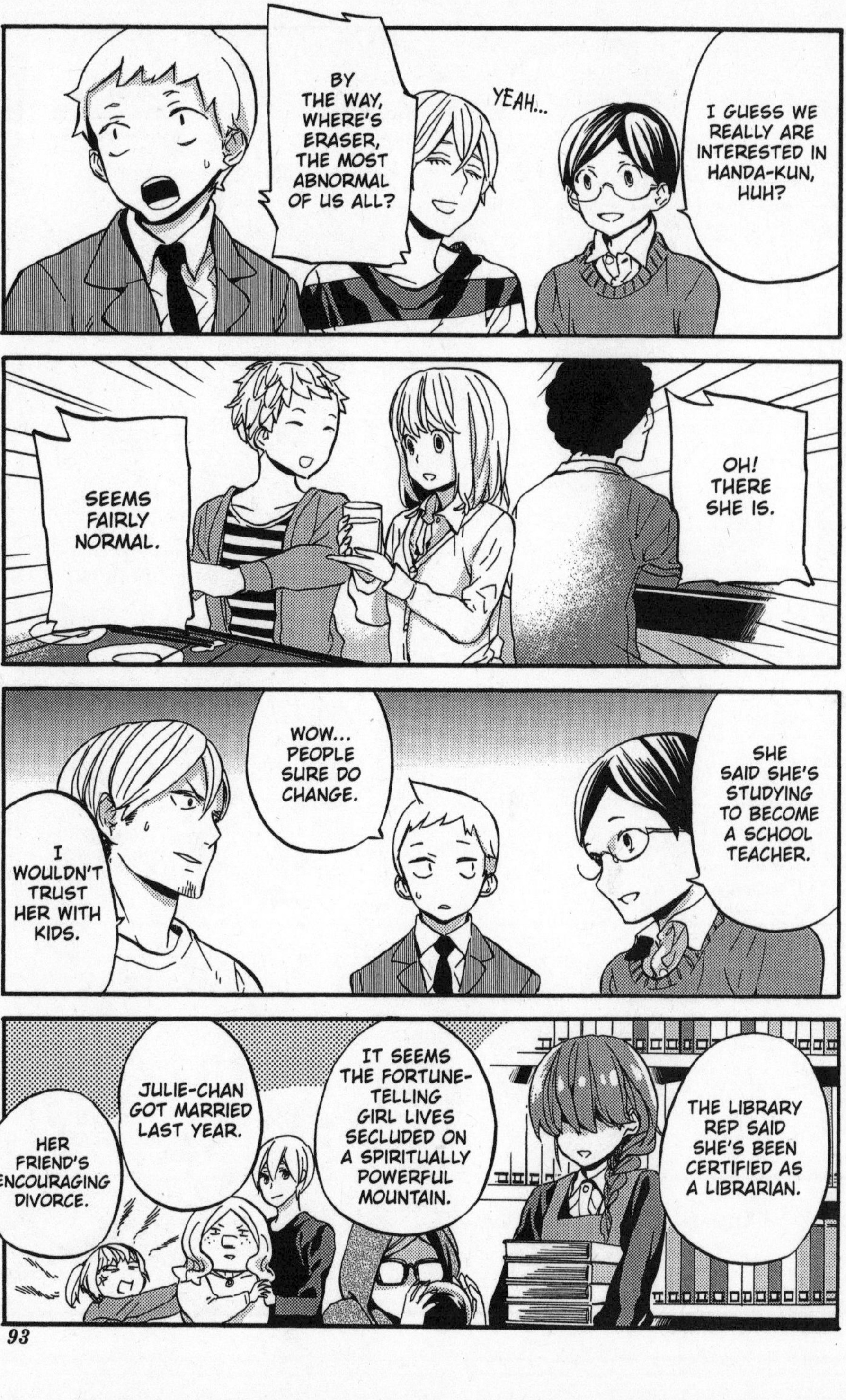
I GUESS WE REALLY ARE INTERESTED IN HANDA-KUN, HUH?
YEAH...
BY THE WAY, WHERE'S ERASER, THE MOST ABNORMAL OF US ALL?
OH! THERE SHE IS.
SEEMS FAIRLY NORMAL.
SHE SAID SHE'S STUDYING TO BECOME A SCHOOL TEACHER.
WOW... PEOPLE SURE DO CHANGE.
I WOULDN'T TRUST HER WITH KIDS.
THE LIBRARY REP SAID SHE'S BEEN CERTIFIED AS A LIBRARIAN.
IT SEEMS THE FORTUNE-TELLING GIRL LIVES SECLUDED ON A SPIRITUALLY POWERFUL MOUNTAIN.
JULIE-CHAN GOT MARRIED LAST YEAR.
HER FRIEND'S ENCOURAGING DIVORCE.

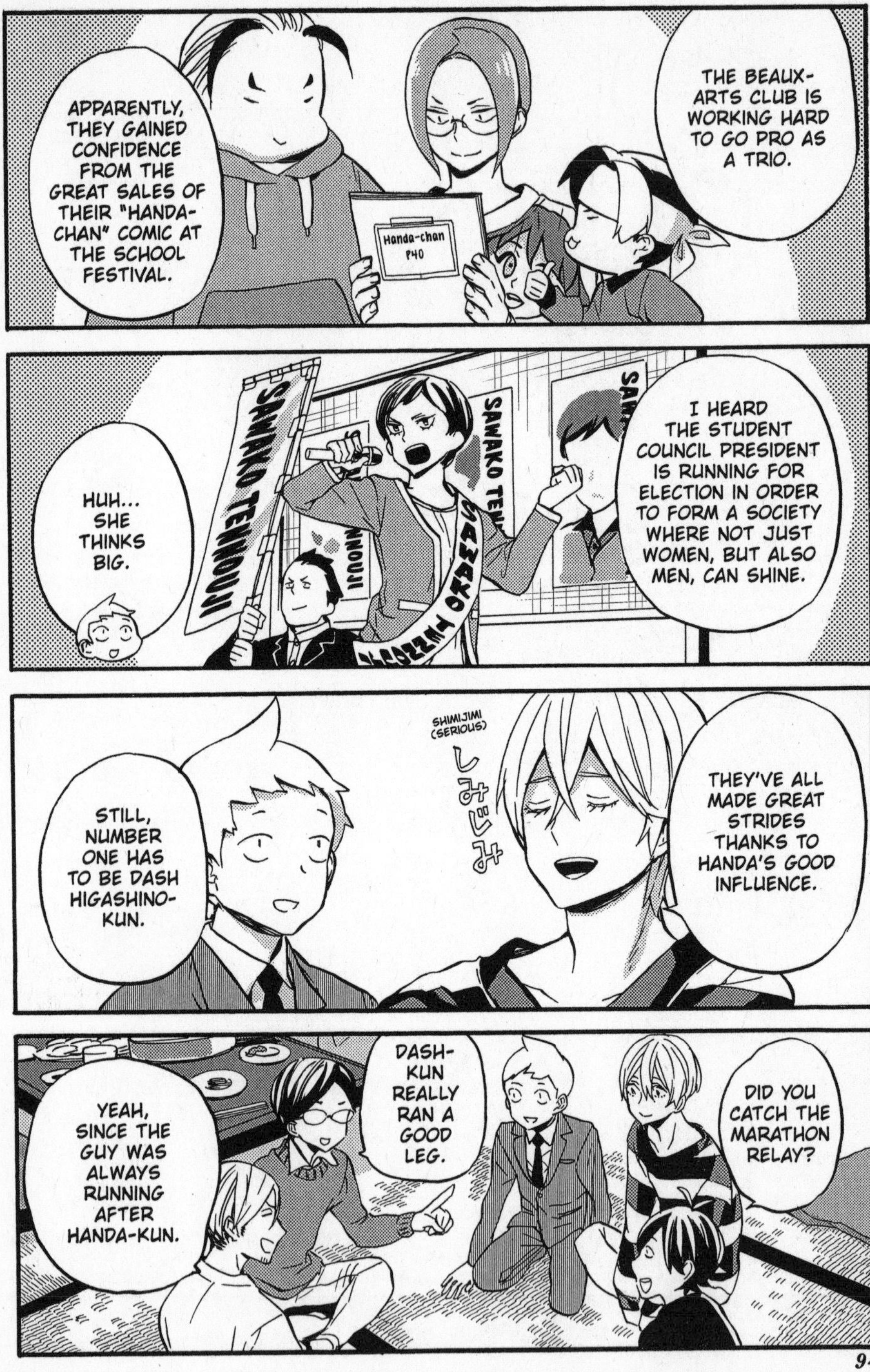
THE BEAUX-ARTS CLUB IS WORKING HARD TO GO PRO AS A TRIO.
Handa-chan P40
APPARENTLY, THEY GAINED CONFIDENCE FROM THE GREAT SALES OF THEIR "HANDA-CHAN" COMIC AT THE SCHOOL FESTIVAL.
I HEARD THE STUDENT COUNCIL PRESIDENT IS RUNNING FOR ELECTION IN ORDER TO FORM A SOCIETY WHERE NOT JUST WOMEN, BUT ALSO MEN, CAN SHINE.
SAWAKO TENNOUJI
HUH... SHE THINKS BIG.
THEY'VE ALL MADE GREAT STRIDES THANKS TO HANDA'S GOOD INFLUENCE.
SHIMIJIMI (SERIOUS)
しみじみ
STILL, NUMBER ONE HAS TO BE DASH HIGASHINO-KUN.
DID YOU CATCH THE MARATHON RELAY?
DASH-KUN REALLY RAN A GOOD LEG.
YEAH, SINCE THE GUY WAS ALWAYS RUNNING AFTER HANDA-KUN.

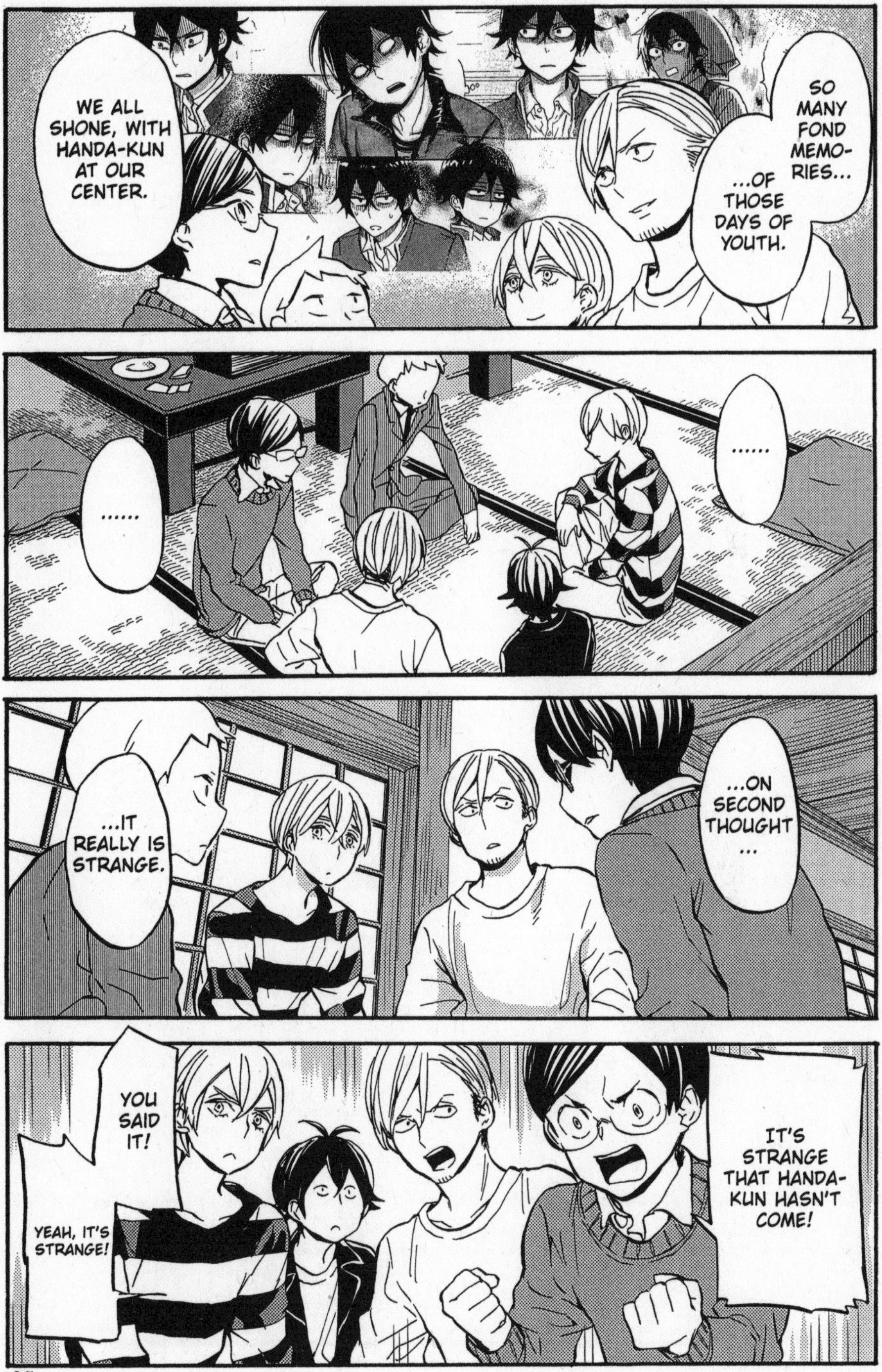
SO MANY FOND MEMORIES...
...OF THOSE DAYS OF YOUTH.
WE ALL SHONE, WITH HANDA-KUN AT OUR CENTER.
......
......
...ON SECOND THOUGHT...
...IT REALLY IS STRANGE.
IT'S STRANGE THAT HANDA-KUN HASN'T COME!
YOU SAID IT!
YEAH, IT'S STRANGE!

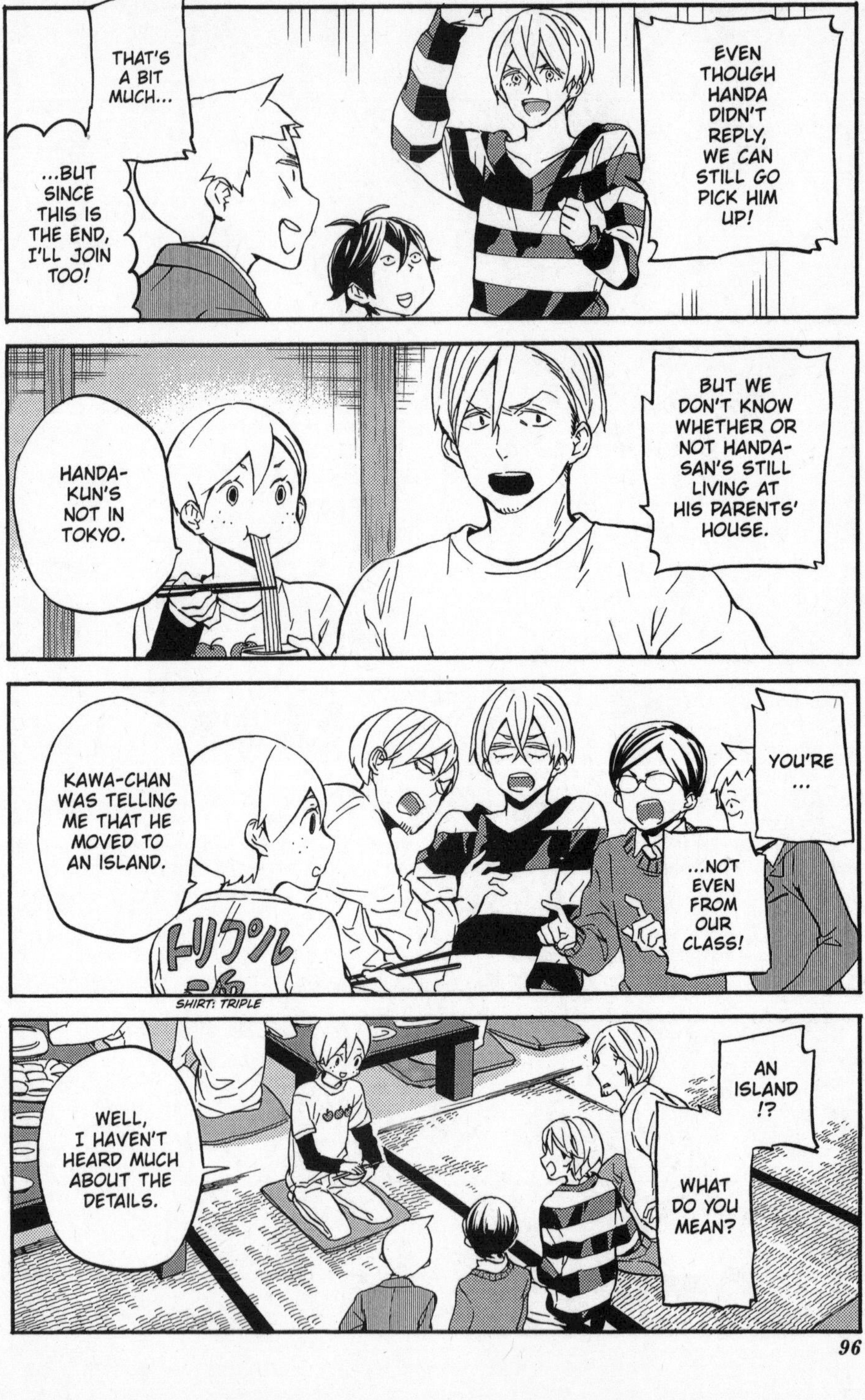
EVEN THOUGH HANDA DIDN'T REPLY, WE CAN STILL GO PICK HIM UP!
THAT'S A BIT MUCH...
...BUT SINCE THIS IS THE END, I'LL JOIN TOO!
BUT WE DON'T KNOW WHETHER OR NOT HANDA-SAN'S STILL LIVING AT HIS PARENTS' HOUSE.
HANDA-KUN'S NOT IN TOKYO.
YOU'RE...
...NOT EVEN FROM OUR CLASS!
KAWA-CHAN WAS TELLING ME THAT HE MOVED TO AN ISLAND.
トリプル
SHIRT: TRIPLE
AN ISLAND!?
WHAT DO YOU MEAN?
WELL, I HAVEN'T HEARD MUCH ABOUT THE DETAILS.

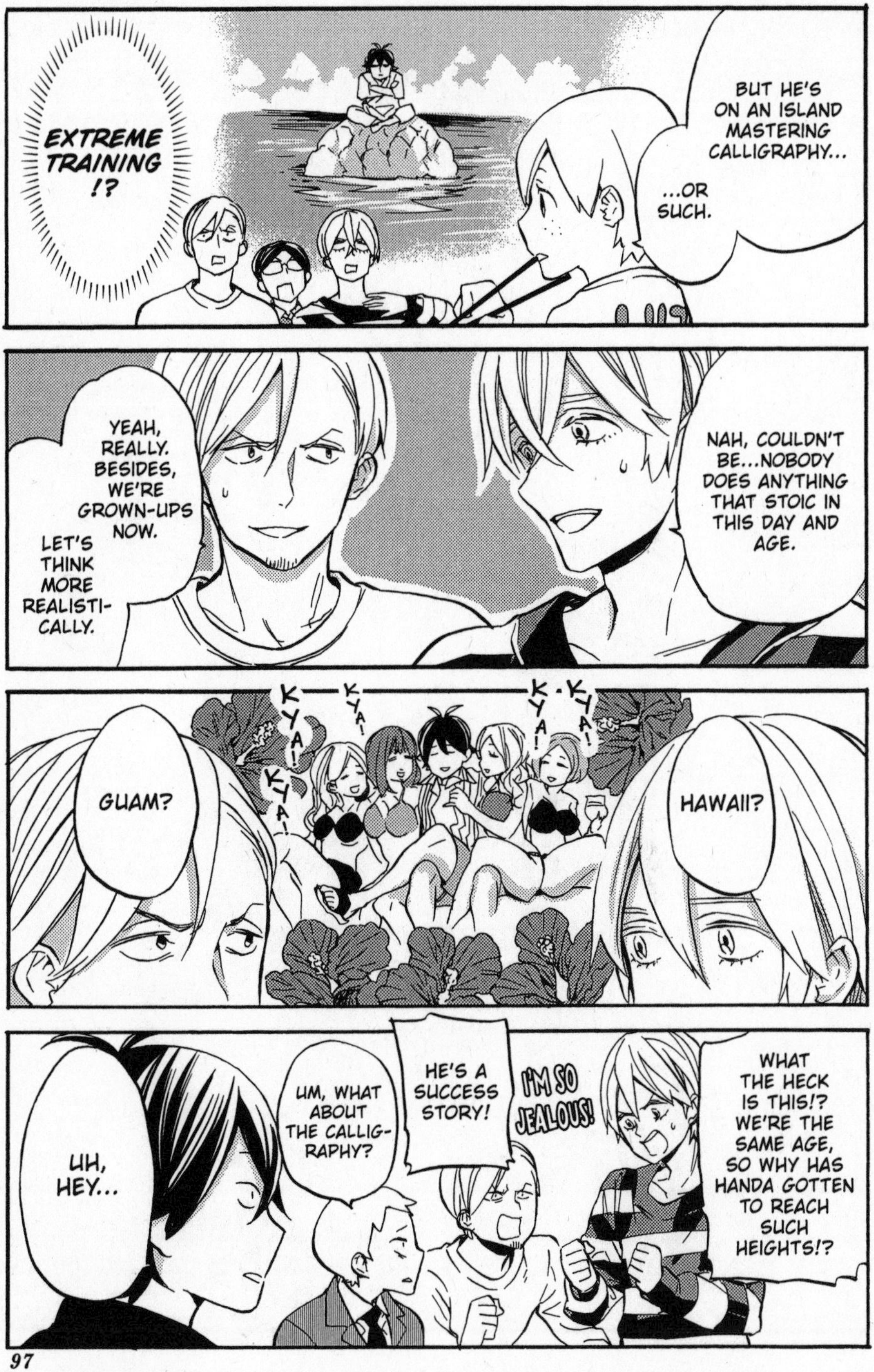
BUT HE'S ON AN ISLAND MASTERING CALLIGRAPHY...
...OR SUCH.
EXTREME TRAINING !?
NAH, COULDN'T BE...NOBODY DOES ANYTHING THAT STOIC IN THIS DAY AND AGE.
YEAH, REALLY. BESIDES, WE'RE GROWN-UPS NOW.
LET'S THINK MORE REALISTI-CALLY.
HAWAII?
KYA!
KYA!
KYA!
KYA!
KYA!
GUAM?
WHAT THE HECK IS THIS!? WE'RE THE SAME AGE, SO WHY HAS HANDA GOTTEN TO REACH SUCH HEIGHTS!?
I'M SO JEALOUS!
HE'S A SUCCESS STORY!
UM, WHAT ABOUT THE CALLIG-RAPHY?
UH, HEY...

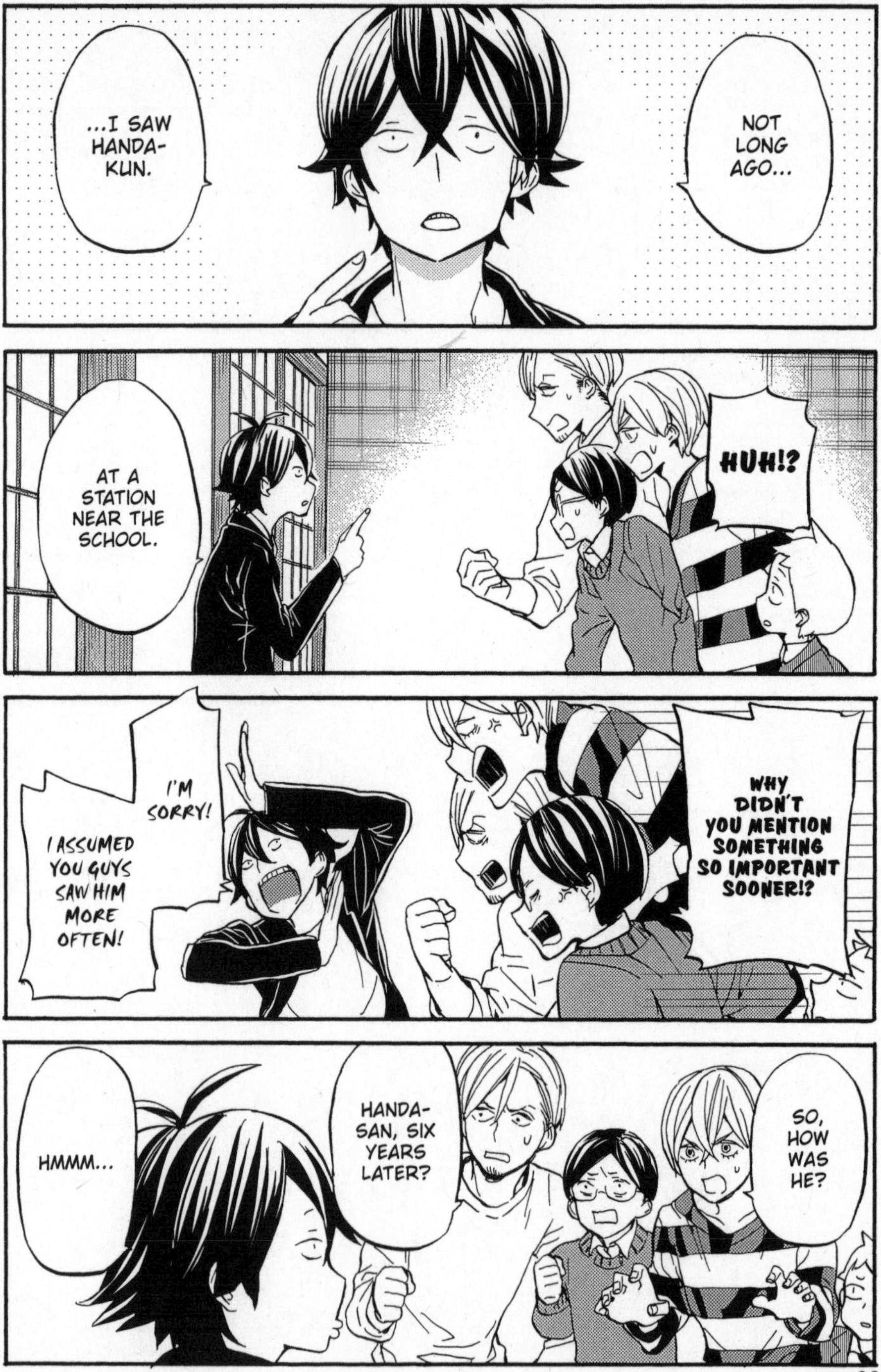
NOT LONG AGO...
...I SAW HANDA-KUN.
AT A STATION NEAR THE SCHOOL.
HUH!?
WHY DIDN'T YOU MENTION SOMETHING SO IMPORTANT SOONER!?
I'M SORRY!
I ASSUMED YOU GUYS SAW HIM MORE OFTEN!
SO, HOW WAS HE?
HANDA-SAN, SIX YEARS LATER?
HMMM...

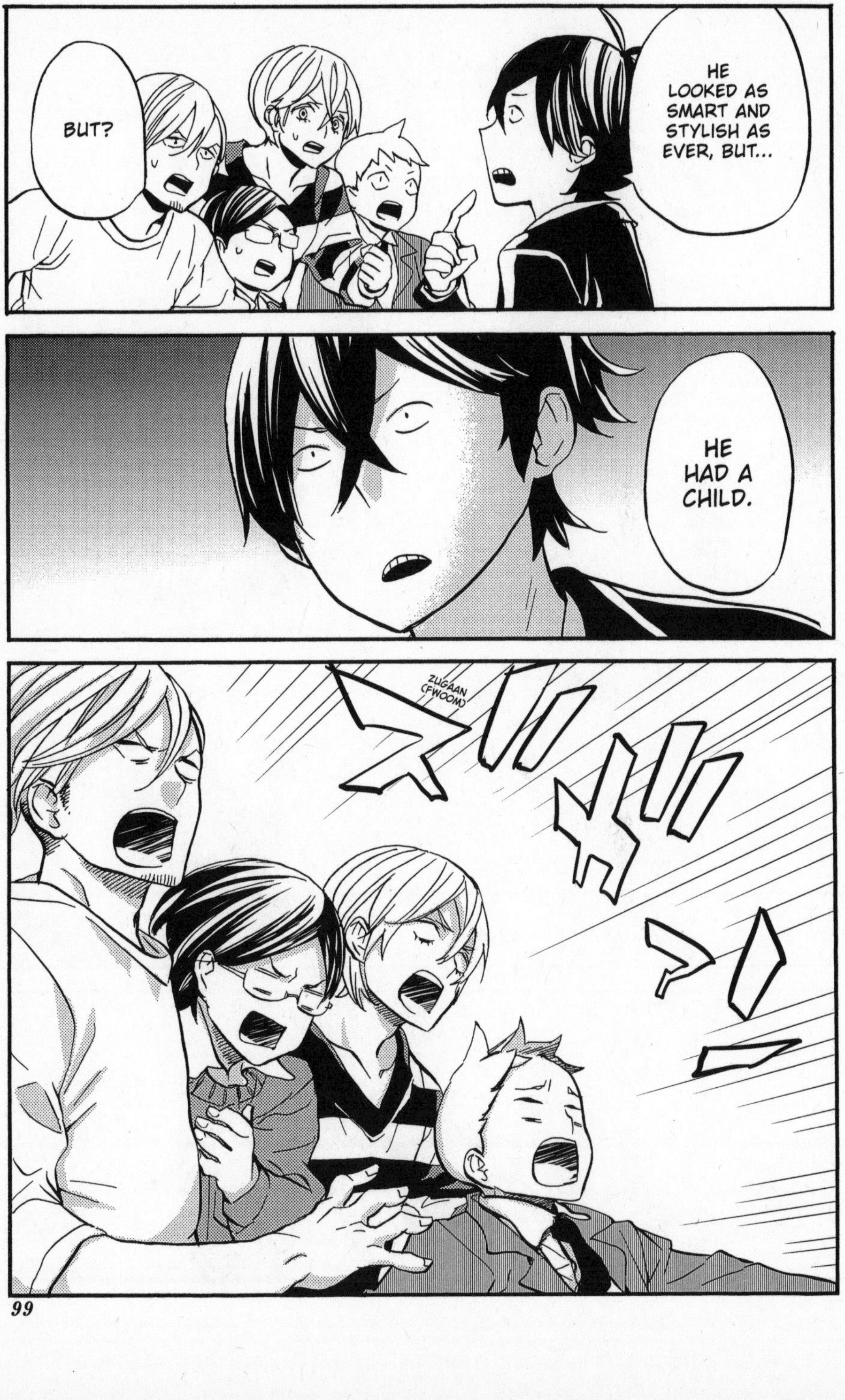
HE LOOKED AS SMART AND STYLISH AS EVER, BUT...
BUT?
HE HAD A CHILD.
ZUGAAN (FWOOM)

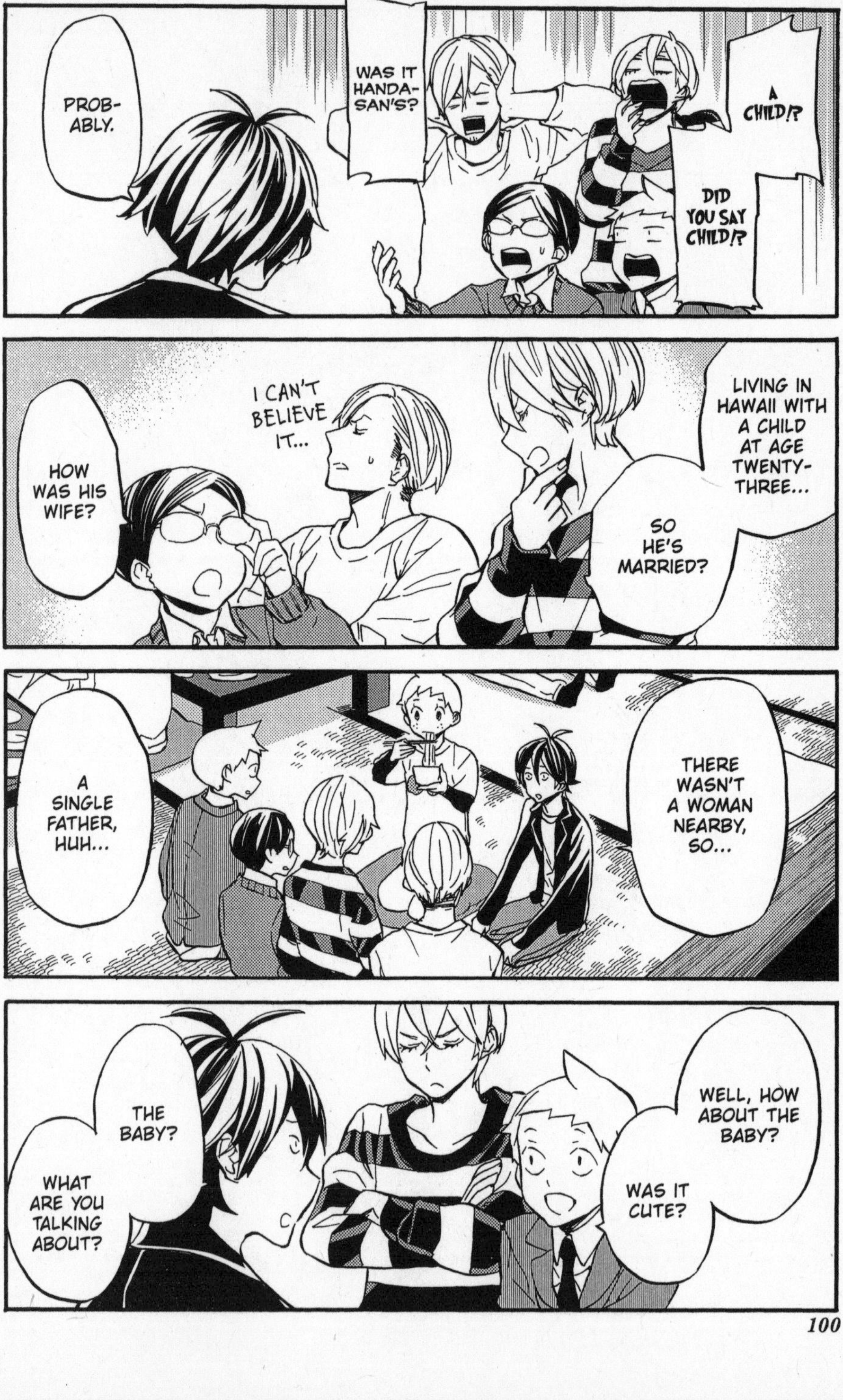
A CHILD!?
DID YOU SAY CHILD!?
WAS IT HANDA-SAN'S?
PROB-ABLY.
LIVING IN HAWAII WITH A CHILD AT AGE TWENTY-THREE...
SO HE'S MARRIED?
I CAN'T BELIEVE IT...
HOW WAS HIS WIFE?
THERE WASN'T A WOMAN NEARBY, SO...
A SINGLE FATHER, HUH...
WELL, HOW ABOUT THE BABY?
WAS IT CUTE?
THE BABY?
WHAT ARE YOU TALKING ABOUT?

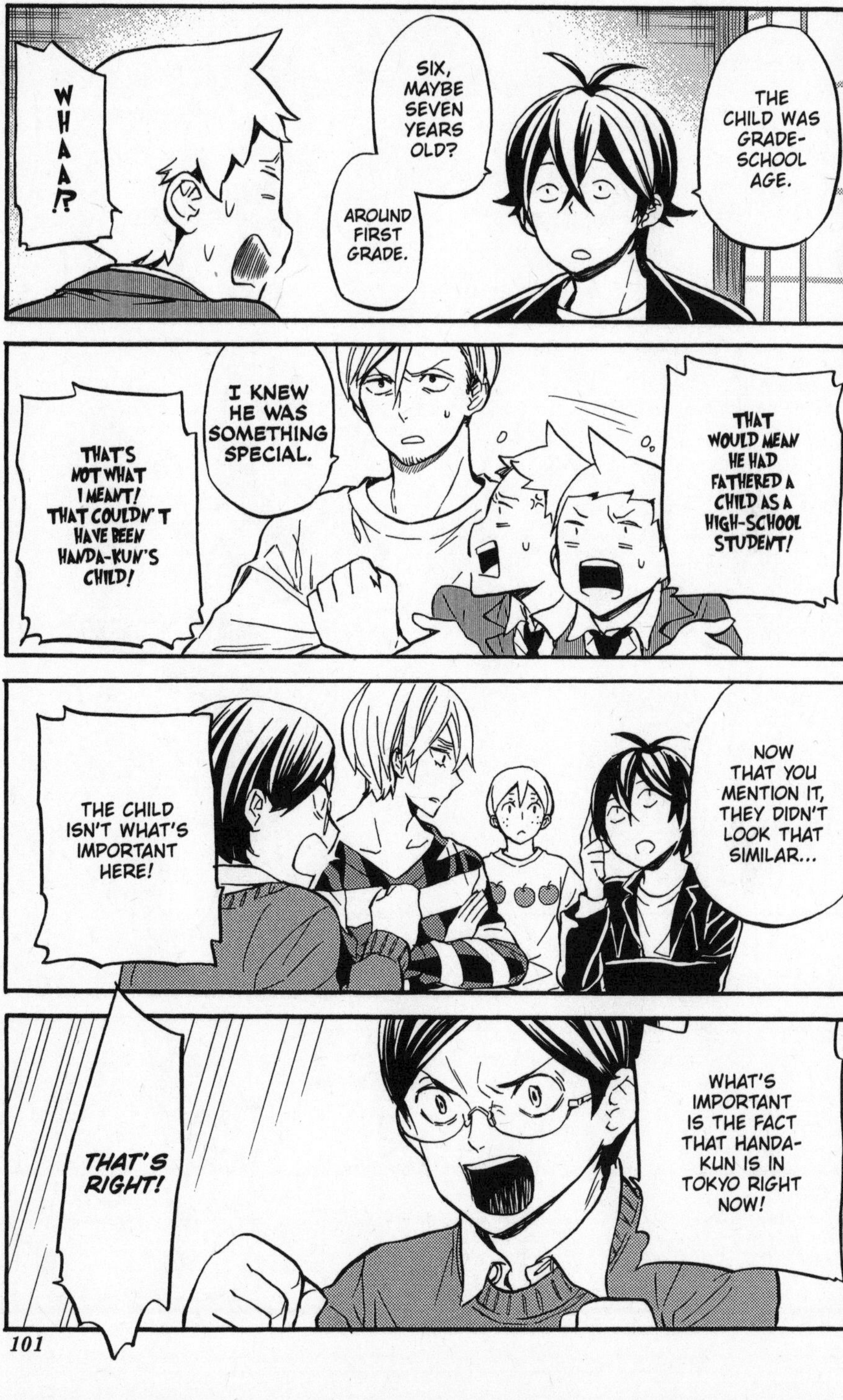
THE CHILD WAS GRADE-SCHOOL AGE.
SIX, MAYBE SEVEN YEARS OLD?
AROUND FIRST GRADE.
WHAAA!?
THAT WOULD MEAN HE HAD FATHERED A CHILD AS A HIGH-SCHOOL STUDENT!
I KNEW HE WAS SOMETHING SPECIAL.
THAT'S NOT WHAT I MEANT! THAT COULDN'T HAVE BEEN HANDA-KUN'S CHILD!
NOW THAT YOU MENTION IT, THEY DIDN'T LOOK THAT SIMILAR...
THE CHILD ISN'T WHAT'S IMPORTANT HERE!
WHAT'S IMPORTANT IS THE FACT THAT HANDA-KUN IS IN TOKYO RIGHT NOW!
THAT'S RIGHT!

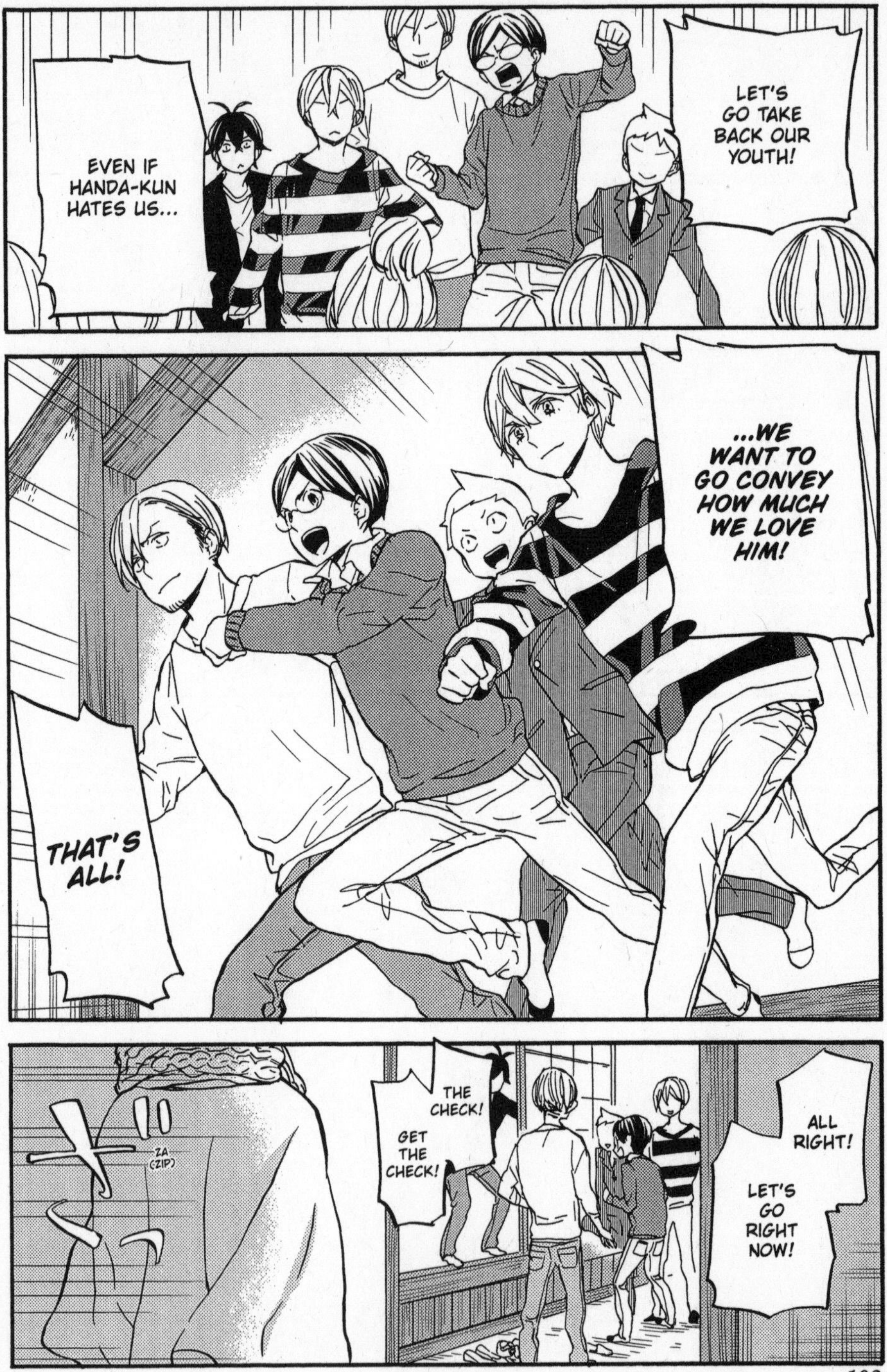
LET'S GO TAKE BACK OUR YOUTH!
EVEN IF HANDA-KUN HATES US...
...WE WANT TO GO CONVEY HOW MUCH WE LOVE HIM!
THAT'S ALL!
ALL RIGHT!
LET'S GO RIGHT NOW!
THE CHECK!
GET THE CHECK!
ZA (ZIP)

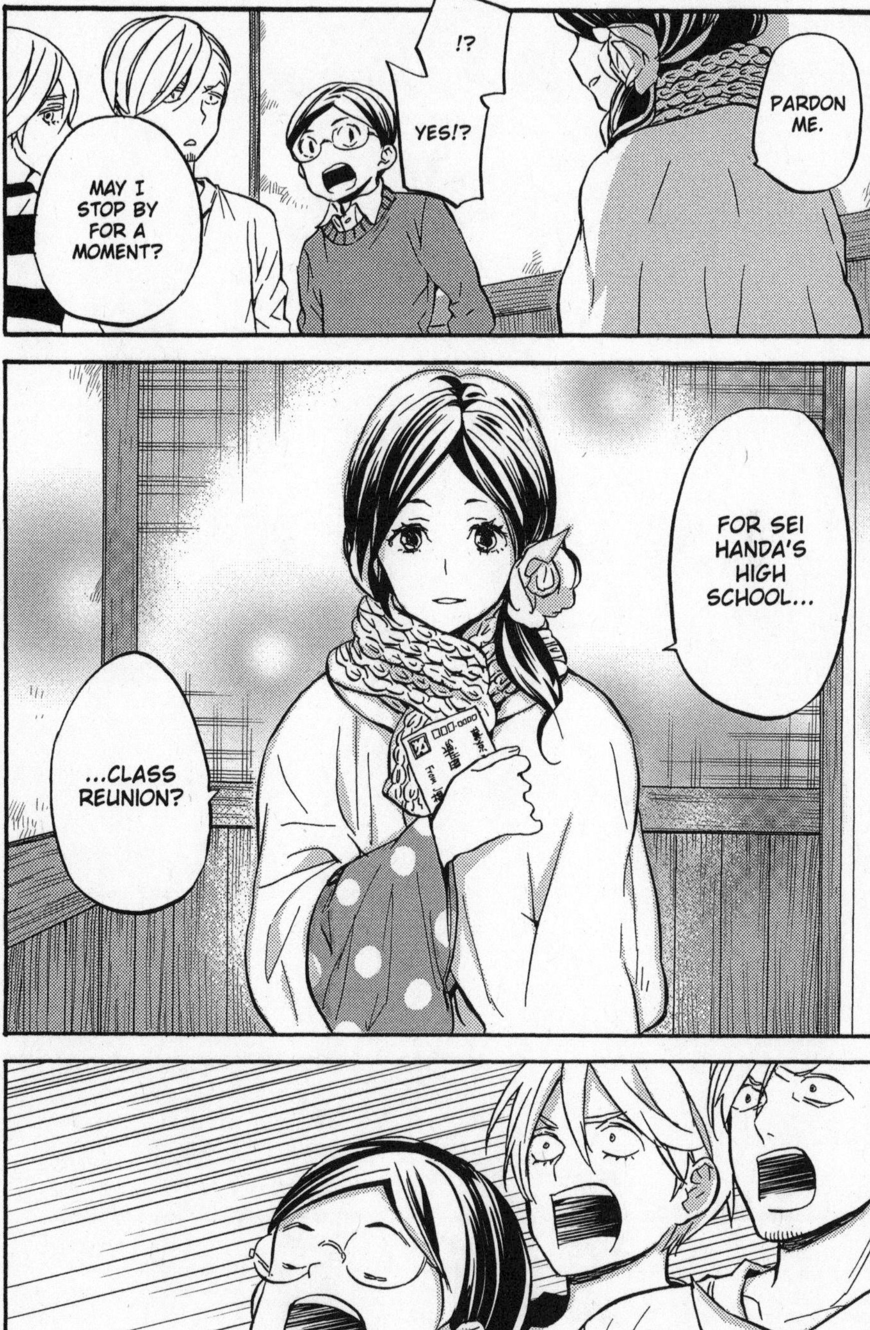
PARDON ME.
!?
YES!?
MAY I STOP BY FOR A MOMENT?
FOR SEI HANDA'S HIGH SCHOOL...
...CLASS REUNION?

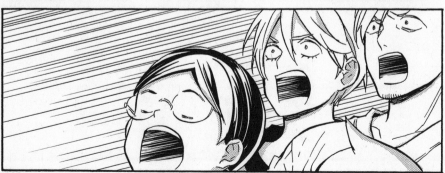

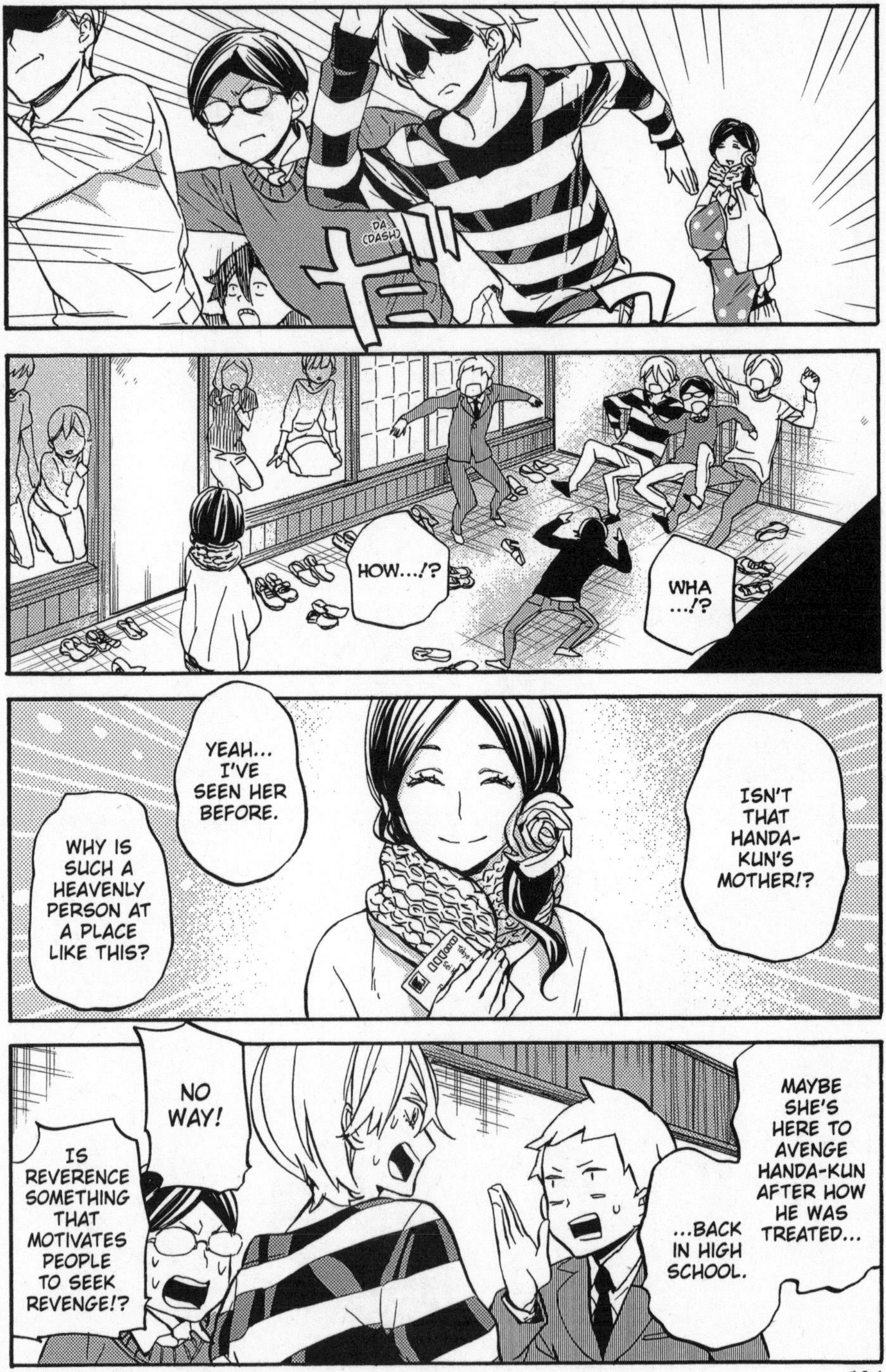
DA (DASH)
WHA...!?
HOW...!?
ISN'T THAT HANDA-KUN'S MOTHER!?
YEAH... I'VE SEEN HER BEFORE.
WHY IS SUCH A HEAVENLY PERSON AT A PLACE LIKE THIS?
MAYBE SHE'S HERE TO AVENGE HANDA-KUN AFTER HOW HE WAS TREATED...
...BACK IN HIGH SCHOOL.
NO WAY!
IS REVERENCE SOMETHING THAT MOTIVATES PEOPLE TO SEEK REVENGE!?

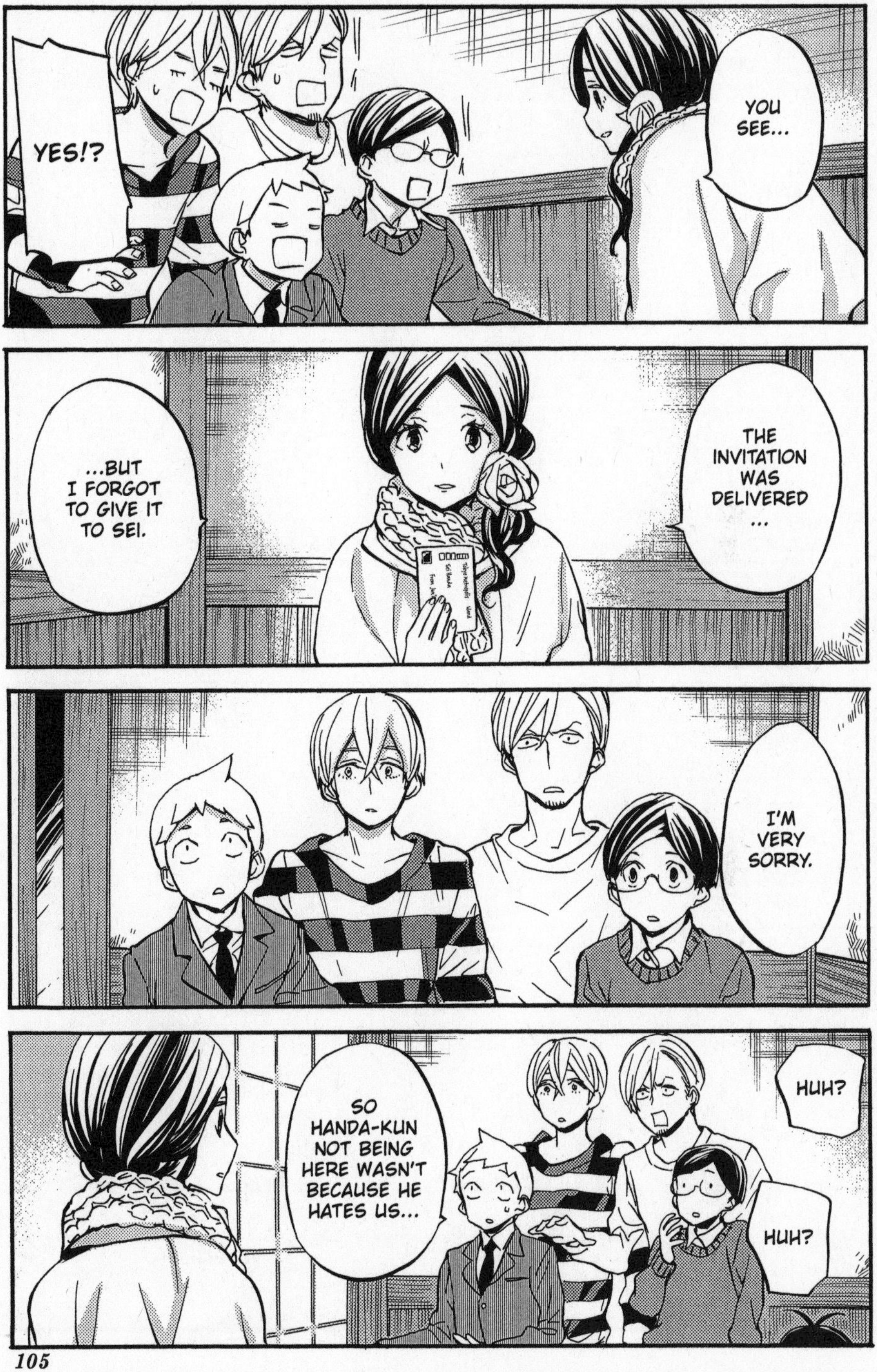
YOU SEE...
YES!?
THE INVITATION WAS DELIVERED...
...BUT I FORGOT TO GIVE IT TO SEI.
I'M VERY SORRY.
SO HANDA-KUN NOT BEING HERE WASN'T BECAUSE HE HATES US...
HUH?
HUH?

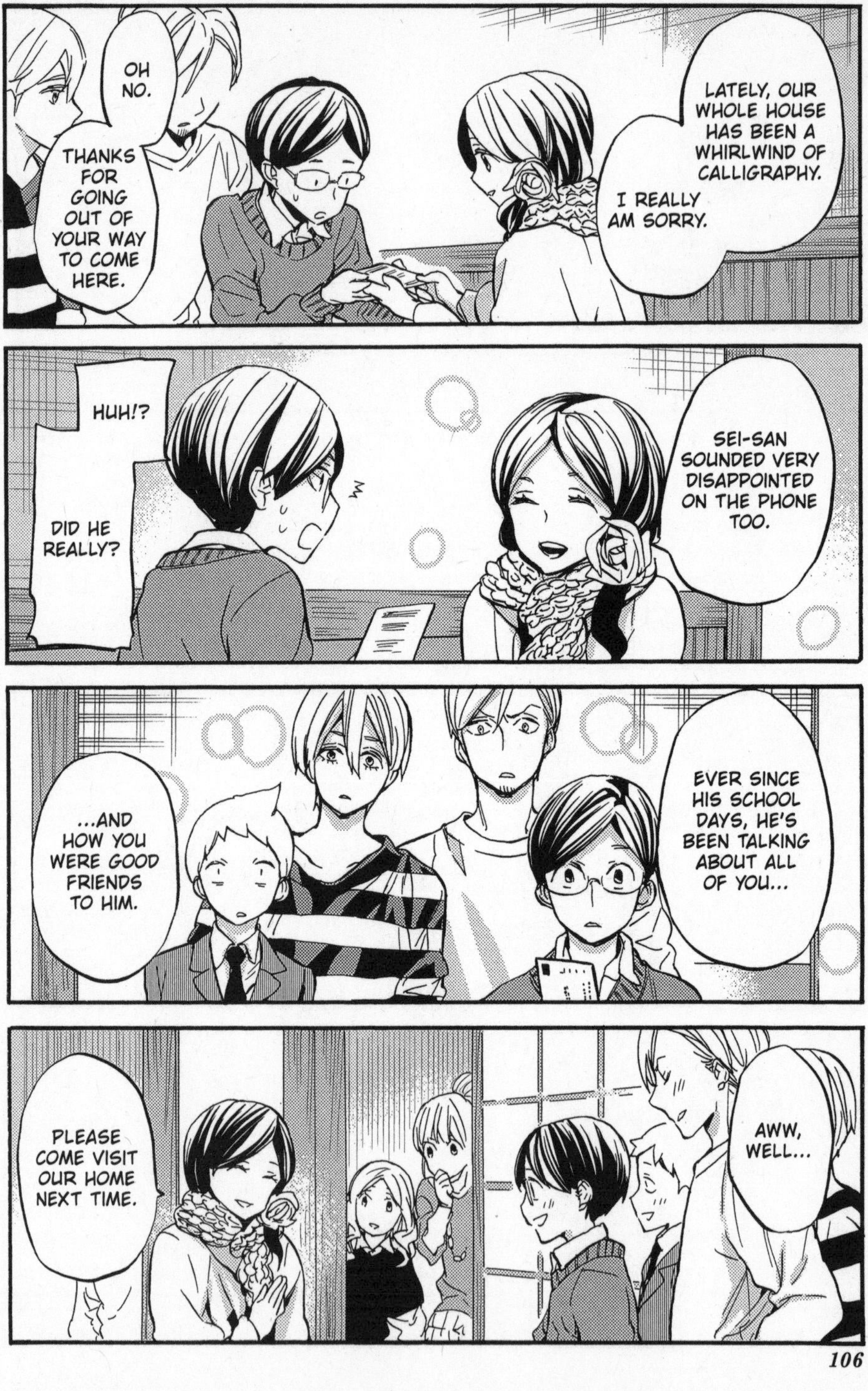
LATELY, OUR WHOLE HOUSE HAS BEEN A WHIRLWIND OF CALLIGRAPHY.
I REALLY AM SORRY.
OH NO.
THANKS FOR GOING OUT OF YOUR WAY TO COME HERE.
SEI-SAN SOUNDED VERY DISAPPOINTED ON THE PHONE TOO.
HUH!?
DID HE REALLY?
EVER SINCE HIS SCHOOL DAYS, HE'S BEEN TALKING ABOUT ALL OF YOU...
...AND HOW YOU WERE GOOD FRIENDS TO HIM.
AWW, WELL...
PLEASE COME VISIT OUR HOME NEXT TIME.

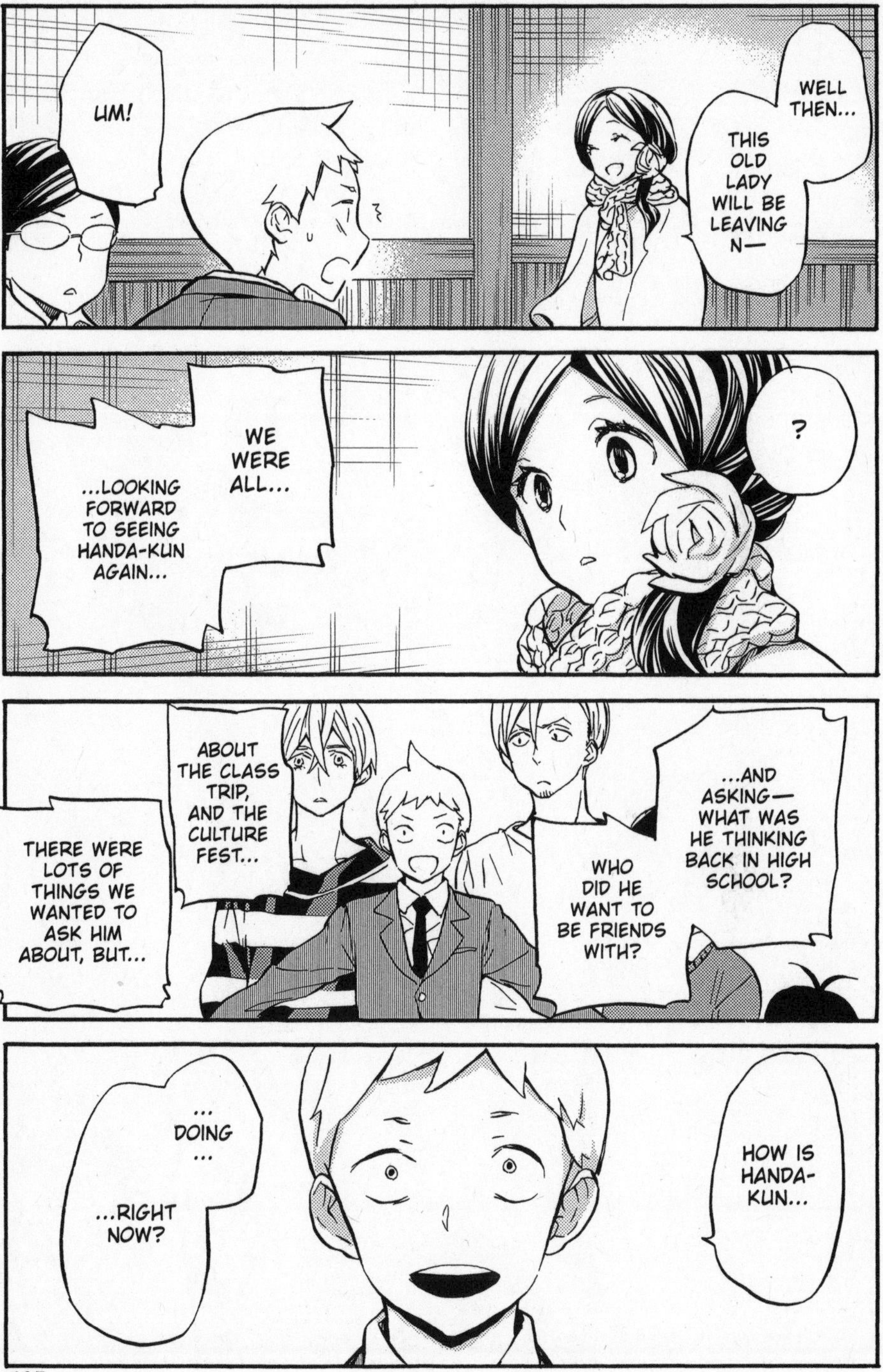
WELL THEN...
THIS OLD LADY WILL BE LEAVING N—
UM!
?
WE WERE ALL...
...LOOKING FORWARD TO SEEING HANDA-KUN AGAIN...
...AND ASKING— WHAT WAS HE THINKING BACK IN HIGH SCHOOL?
WHO DID HE WANT TO BE FRIENDS WITH?
ABOUT THE CLASS TRIP, AND THE CULTURE FEST...
THERE WERE LOTS OF THINGS WE WANTED TO ASK HIM ABOUT, BUT...
HOW IS HANDA-KUN...
...DOING...
...RIGHT NOW?

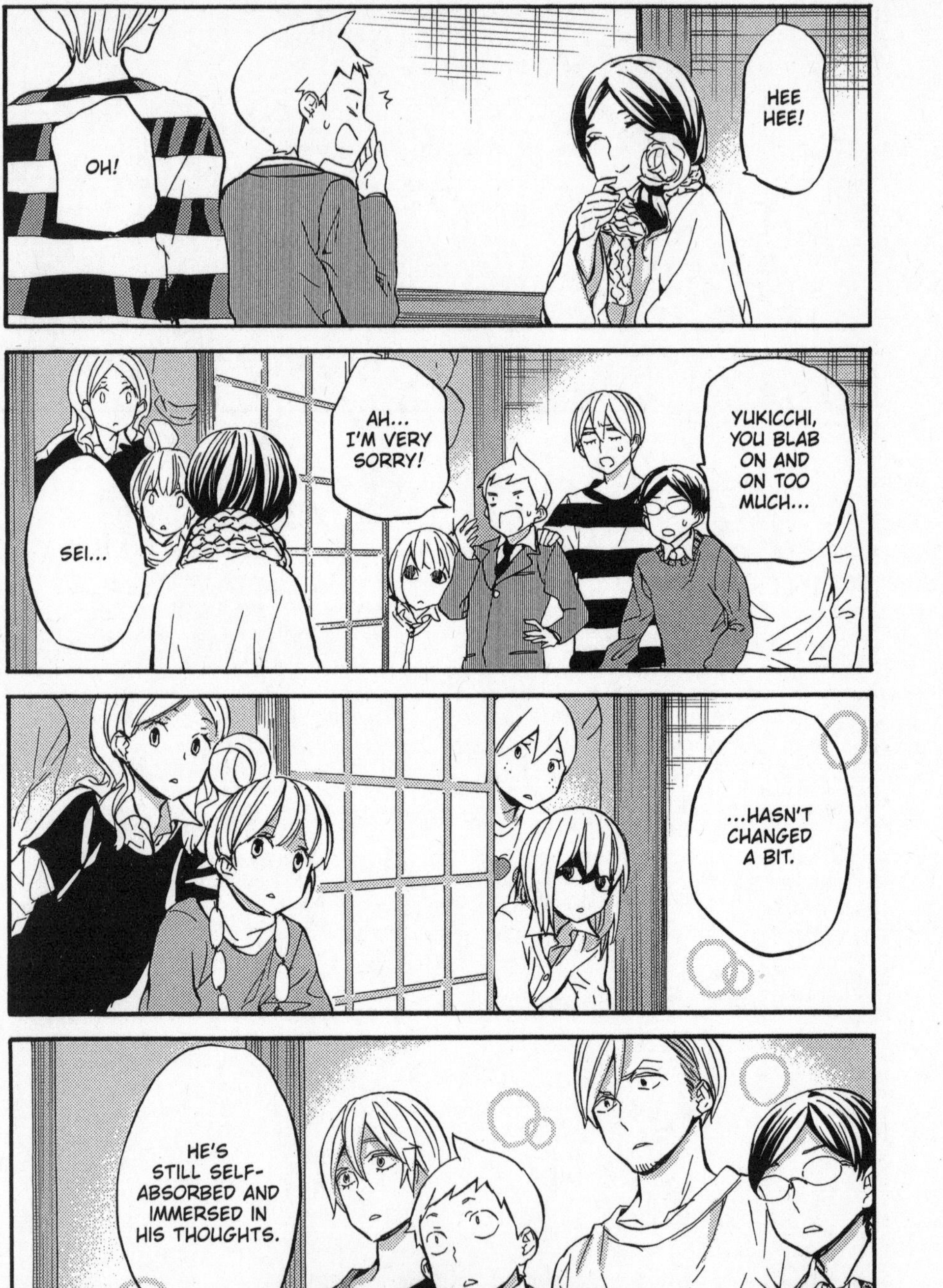
HEE HEE!
OH!
YUKICCHI, YOU BLAB ON AND ON TOO MUCH...
AH... I'M VERY SORRY!
SEI...
...HASN'T CHANGED A BIT.
HE'S STILL SELF-ABSORBED AND IMMERSED IN HIS THOUGHTS.

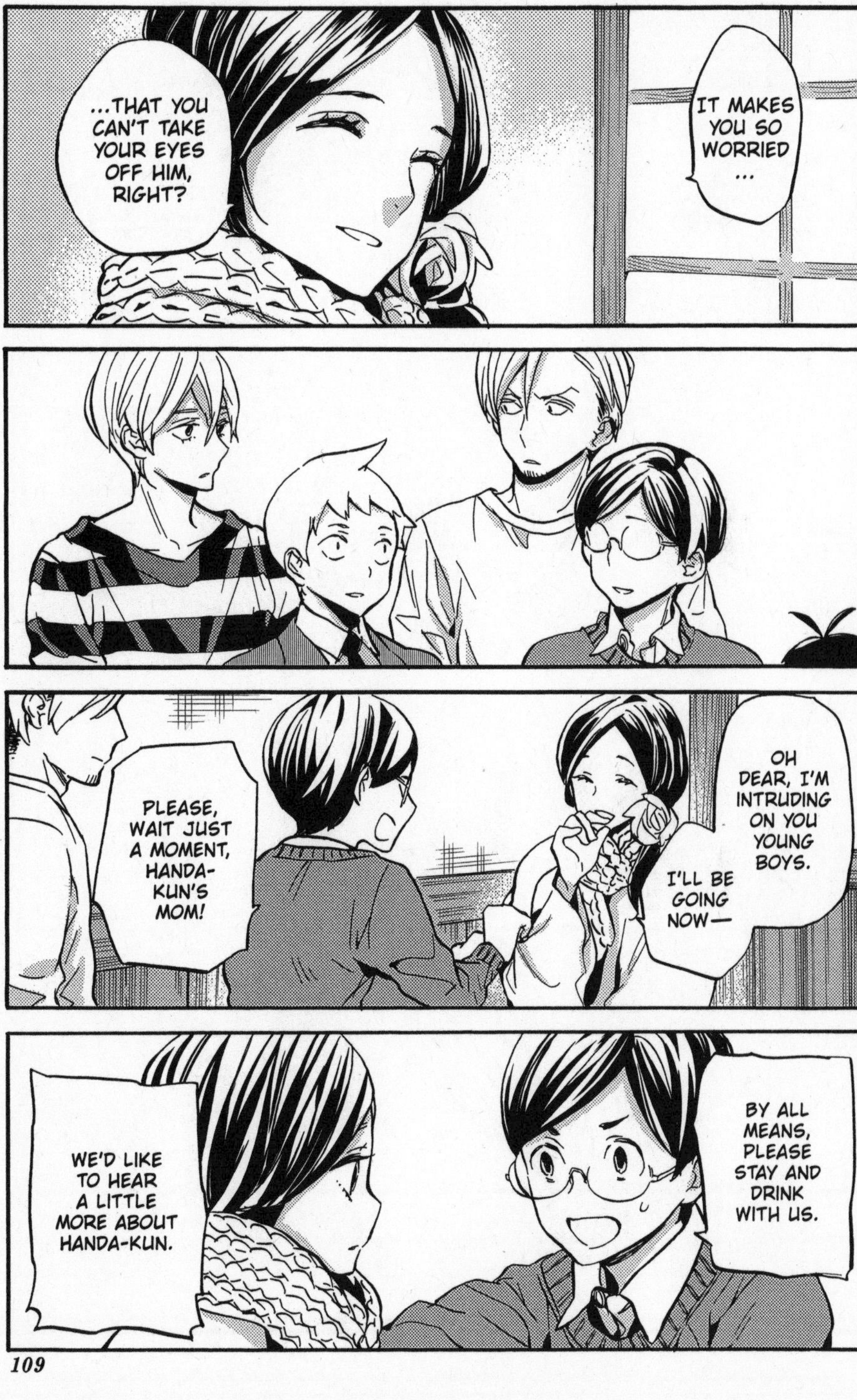
IT MAKES YOU SO WORRIED ...
...THAT YOU CAN'T TAKE YOUR EYES OFF HIM, RIGHT?
OH DEAR, I'M INTRUDING ON YOU YOUNG BOYS.
I'LL BE GOING NOW—
PLEASE, WAIT JUST A MOMENT, HANDA-KUN'S MOM!
BY ALL MEANS, PLEASE STAY AND DRINK WITH US.
WE'D LIKE TO HEAR A LITTLE MORE ABOUT HANDA-KUN.

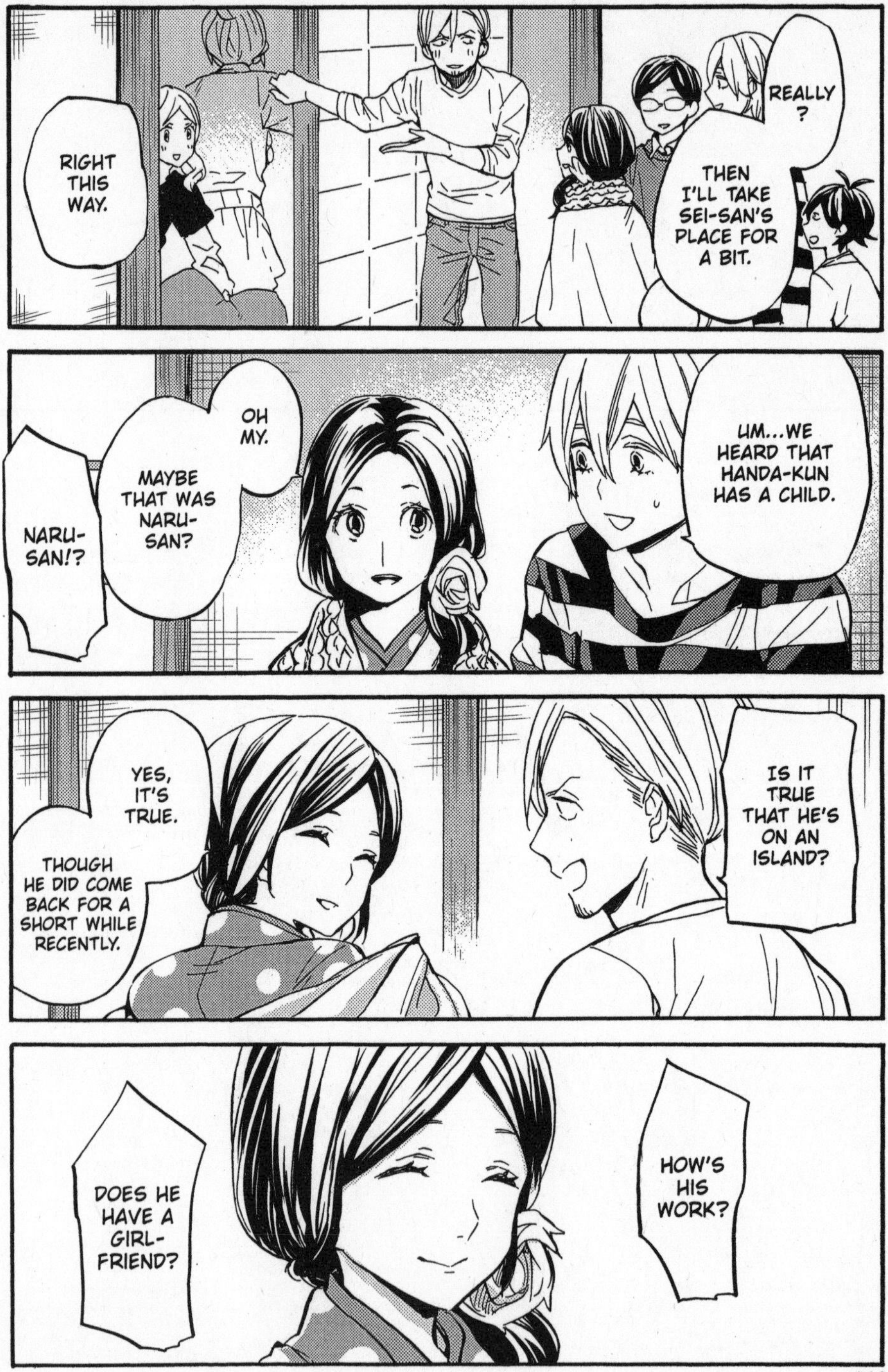
REALLY?
THEN I'LL TAKE SEI-SAN'S PLACE FOR A BIT.
RIGHT THIS WAY.
UM...WE HEARD THAT HANDA-KUN HAS A CHILD.
OH MY.
MAYBE THAT WAS NARU-SAN?
NARU-SAN!?
IS IT TRUE THAT HE'S ON AN ISLAND?
YES, IT'S TRUE.
THOUGH HE DID COME BACK FOR A SHORT WHILE RECENTLY.
HOW'S HIS WORK?
DOES HE HAVE A GIRL-FRIEND?

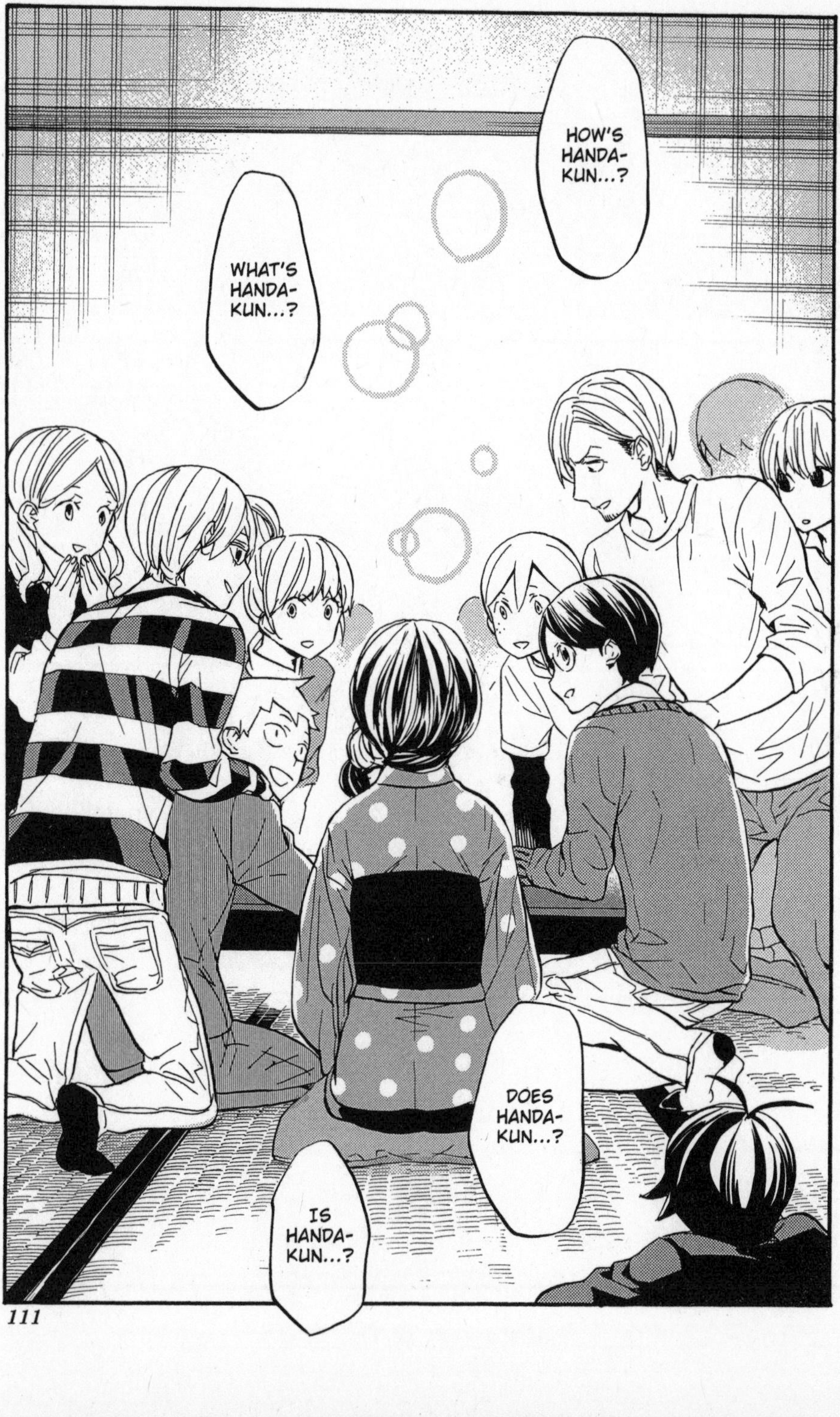
HOW'S HANDA-KUN...?
WHAT'S HANDA-KUN...?
DOES HANDA-KUN...?
IS HANDA-KUN...?

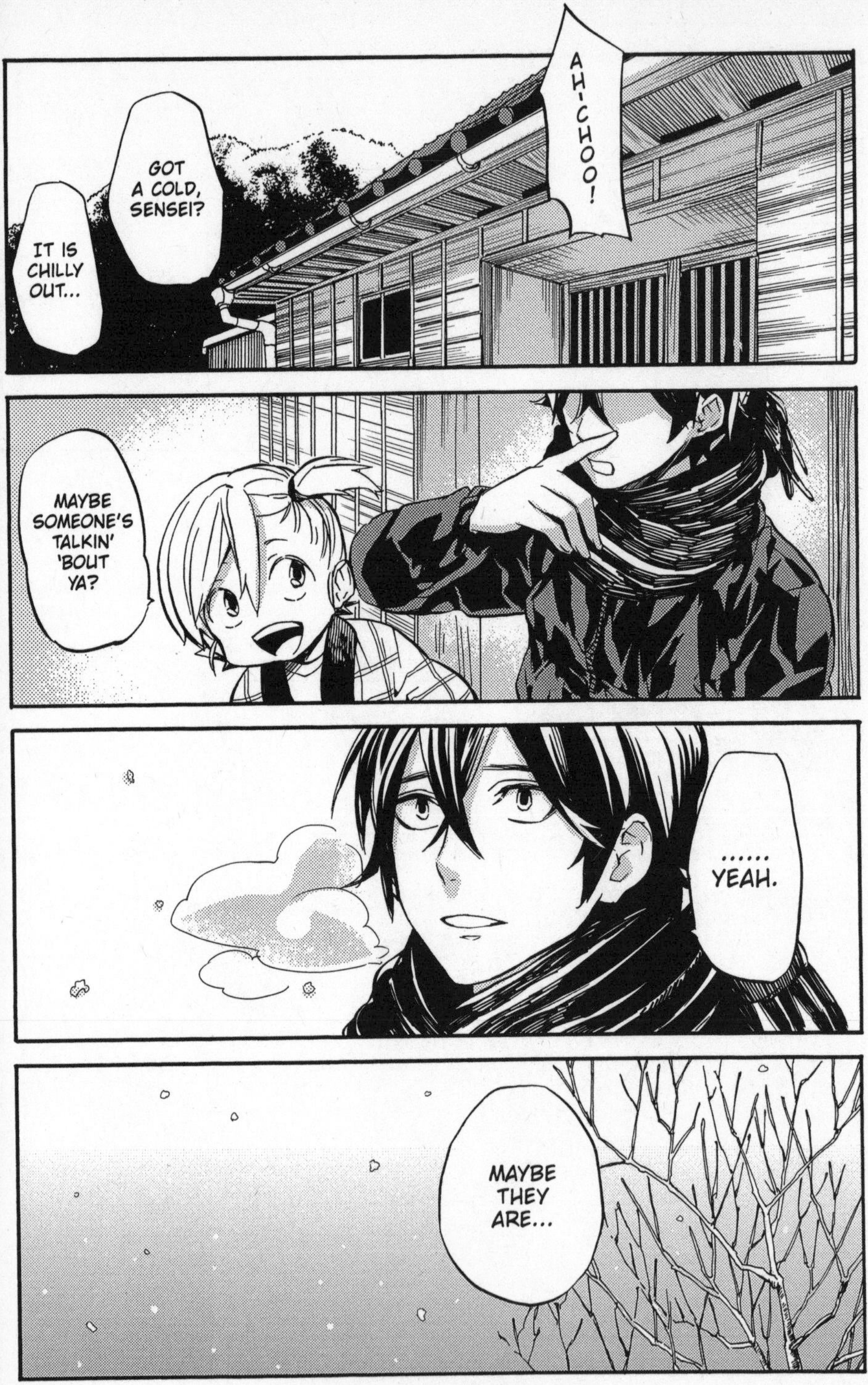
AH-CHOO!
GOT A COLD, SENSEI?
IT IS CHILLY OUT...
MAYBE SOMEONE'S TALKIN' 'BOUT YA?
...... YEAH.
MAYBE THEY ARE...

HANDA-KUN 7 THE END

Since this will really, truly be the very last chapter, I considered ways to surprise the readers without tying everything up cleanly or going deep into the characters, and as a result, decided to draw *Handa-kun* taking place six years later.

While I'd worked hard at the start of the series to make *Handa-kun* consistent with *Barakamon*, it later diverged into a fairly separate thing, so I at least wanted to have the very last of it end in the same place—that's why I drew that final scene.

But if the Handa from *Handa-kun* was to go to the island, doesn't he seem more likely to close off his heart with thoughts like, "There's an ulterior motive behind this kindness...," "The children come by to harass me," or "Rural high schoolers are scary"? Would Handa-kun even be capable of living without locking his door? And then, of course, the Handa Army would invade Gotou, as a purported "trip"...but with no place to spend the night, they'd end up staying at Handa's house!? There'd be a new sect of Handa-ism starting up in the countryside!! ...You know, silly stuff like that. It seems like we could create a new *Barakamon* route, but if I started imagining spin-offs of spin-offs, there'd never be enough Handas to cover all that, so I decided not to think about it much.

Like I wrote in an earlier afterword, when they adapted *Handa-kun* as an anime, I insisted that they avoid making it a second season of *Barakamon*. This was partly because the stories' dynamics were too different, but also because, as a spin-off, that might give the impression that only people who love *Barakamon* are welcome, even though hardly any *Barakamon* characters appear in it. I really didn't want that to happen.

I put the same amount of effort into drawing Handa-kun and the Handa Army because while it may be a spin-off, I still wanted it to be recognized as a manga in its own right—that's why I made that suggestion.

For having listened to my selfish request, I have only words of gratitude for the two separate anime staffs and casts of *Barakamon* and *Handa-kun*. It was a truly valuable experience to get the chance to see how tough it is to make an anime and how amazing of a job the pros do. I would like to take this opportunity to thank all of you very much for what you've done for me.

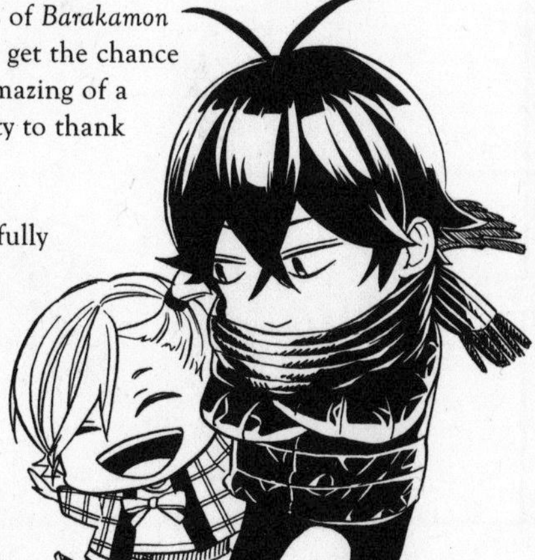

As I drew the spin-off *Handa-kun*, I feel as though I fully grasped the fact that a manga is not something completed by one lone artist. I received lots of feedback from all of you readers. I'm glad that it made you laugh, and even if it didn't...
I am sincerely grateful that you shared even a moment of your time with me.

If the time comes when I draw another spin-off or a completely different manga, I hope to go in swinging the bat at full strength once more! Thank you so much for coming along for the ride!!!

SATSUKI YOSHINO

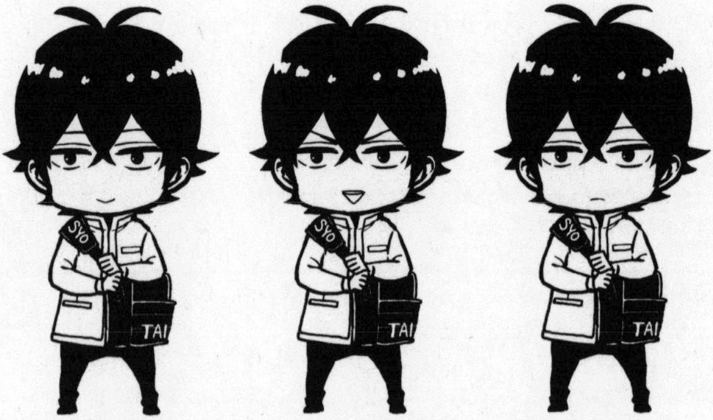
SYO
TAI
SYO
TAI
SYO
TAI

HANDA-KUN SPECIAL

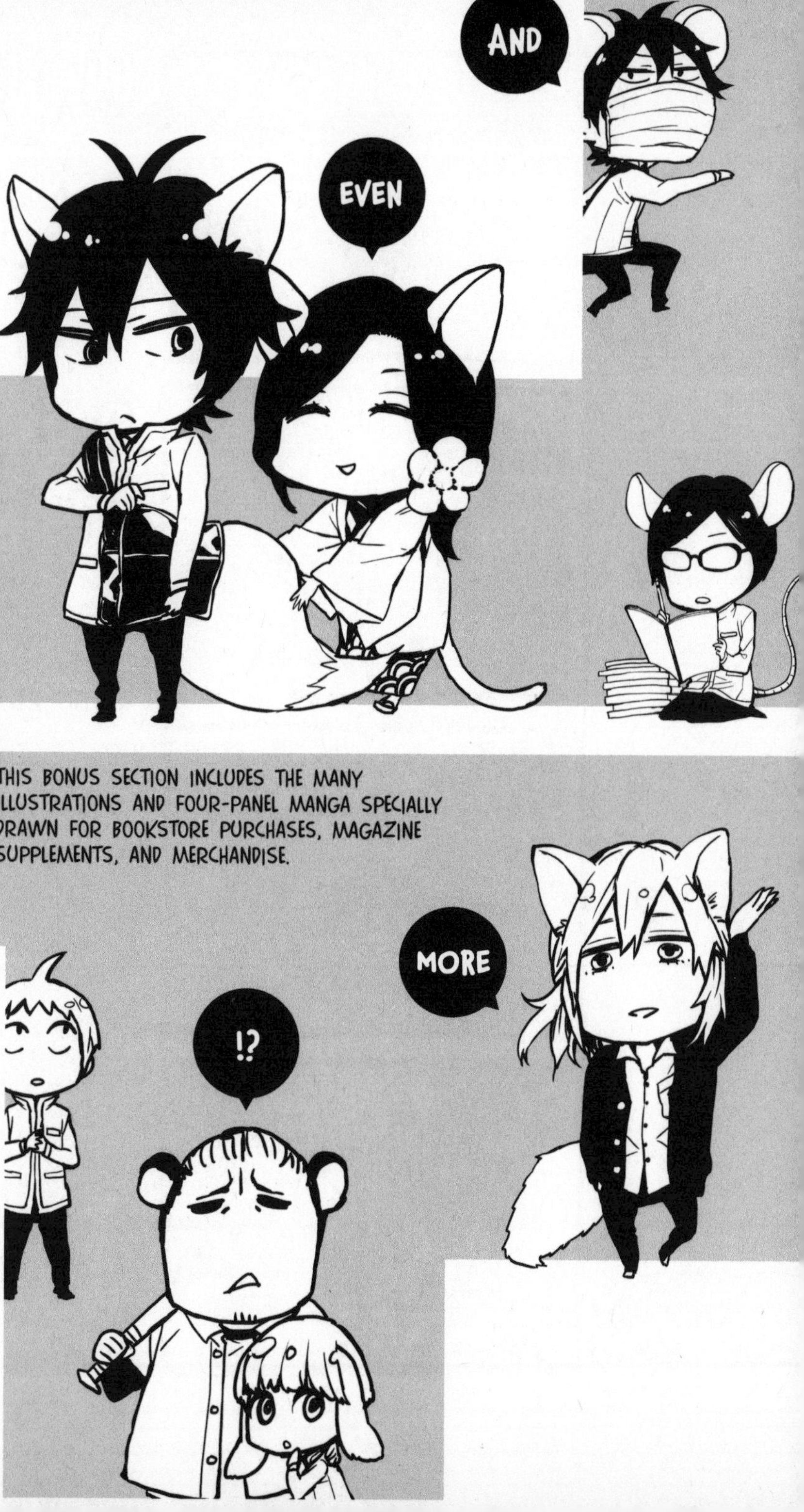
AND
EVEN
MORE
!?

THIS BONUS SECTION INCLUDES THE MANY ILLUSTRATIONS AND FOUR-PANEL MANGA SPECIALLY DRAWN FOR BOOKSTORE PURCHASES, MAGAZINE SUPPLEMENTS, AND MERCHANDISE.

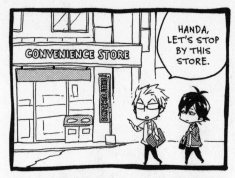

HANDA-KUN VOLUME 1 BONUS COMIC

※ PLEASE ENJOY AFTER READING VOLUME 1

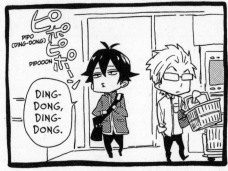

CONVENIENCE STORE
SWEET DUMPLINGS
HANDA, LET'S STOP BY THIS STORE.
ピポピポーン
PIPO (DING-DONG)
PIPOOON
DING-DONG, DING-DONG.
ピポピポーン
PIPO
PIPOOON
DING-DONG, DING-DONG.
ピポピポーン
PIPO
PIPOOON
DING-DONG, DING-DONG.
HE KEEPS UNCONSCIOUSLY MIMICKING THAT SOUND. SHOULD I SAY SOMETHING...?

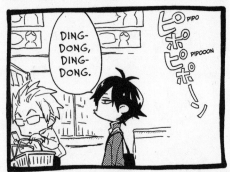

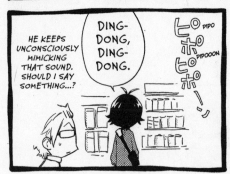

HANDA-KUN VOLUME 1 BONUS COMIC

※ PLEASE ENJOY AFTER READING VOLUME 1

OUR SCHOOL'S BOYS' UNIFORM IS JUST SO PLAIN.
TRIED IT ON.
I MEAN, A GRAY GAKURAN JACKET...
YEAH, REALLY!
YOU HAVE NO IDEA, DO YOU?
(VICE) CLASS REP!
A FAMOUS FASHION DESIGNER CREATED THIS UNIFORM ESPECIALLY FOR HANDA-KUN!
OH, I SEE!
I BELIEVE IT'S BASED ON THE IMPRESSION OF INK.
SO THEY'RE BLAMING ME FOR OUR LAME UNIFORMS...

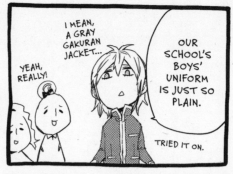

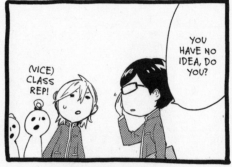

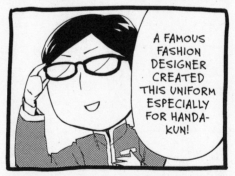

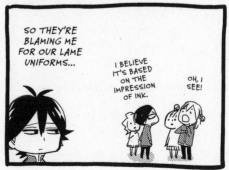

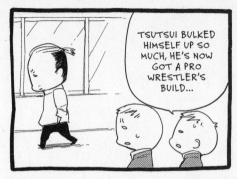

HANDA-KUN VOLUME 2 BONUS COMIC

※ PLEASE ENJOY AFTER READING VOLUME 2

TSUTSUI BULKED HIMSELF UP SO MUCH, HE'S NOW GOT A PRO WRESTLER'S BUILD...
I WANT HIM TO BE MOUSY LIKE HE USED TO BE!
WAAAAAHH!
NO CRYING!! IT'S OUR OWN FAULT FOR TEASING HIM SO MUCH HE GOT DRIVEN TO THIS.
TAKE A LOOK! HE'S STILL MOUSY, EVEN NOW!
GUH ...!
RATTAIL
WHUT?

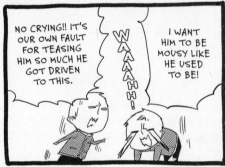

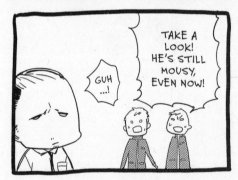

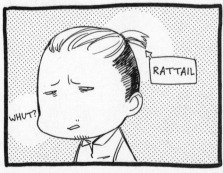

HANDA-KUN VOLUME 2 BONUS COMIC

※ PLEASE ENJOY AFTER READING VOLUME 2

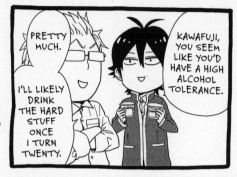

KAWAFUJI, YOU SEEM LIKE YOU'D HAVE A HIGH ALCOHOL TOLERANCE.
PRETTY MUCH.
I'LL LIKELY DRINK THE HARD STUFF ONCE I TURN TWENTY.
LIKE TEQUILA, AND DOM PERIGNON...
I'LL BE QUAFFING THEM ALL DOWN.
KUI (TIP)
KAWAFUJI REALLY IS AN AMAZING GUY!
THREE YEARS LATER
CONGRATS ON TURNING TWENTY, KAWAFUJI!
CHEERS!
TO MY LEGAL BOOZE!
HERE WE GO!
GUBI (GULP)
BATAN (WHACK)
ZZZ...
KAWA-FUJI!?
EH!? KAWA-FUJI!?

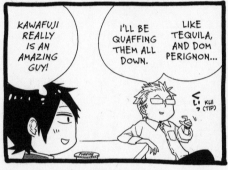

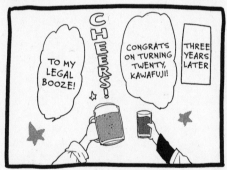

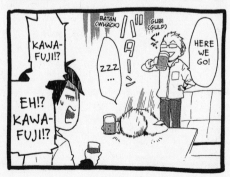

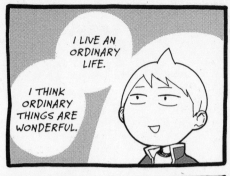

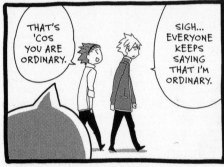

HANDA-KUN VOLUME 2 BONUS COMIC

※ PLEASE ENJOY AFTER READING VOLUME 2

I LIVE AN ORDINARY LIFE.
I THINK ORDINARY THINGS ARE WONDERFUL.
SIGH... EVERYONE KEEPS SAYING THAT I'M ORDINARY.
THAT'S 'COS YOU ARE ORDINARY.
MAN, AND I EVEN DYED MY HAIR BLOND AND ALL!
TRY ALL YOU LIKE, PIROSHI, YOU'LL STILL BE ORDINARY.
OKAY, MAYBE NOT ALL ORDINARY THINGS.

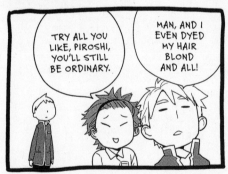

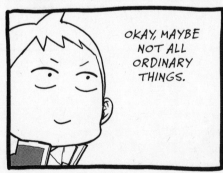

HANDA-KUN VOLUME 2 BONUS COMIC

※ PLEASE ENJOY AFTER READING VOLUME 2

YUKICCHI, I THINK YOU'D BE MORE ATTRACTIVE IF YOU DRESSED STYLISHLY.
I DUNNO ...
"YUKI-CCHI"?
LEAVE IT TO ME, THE FORMER MODEL!
I'LL GIVE YOU A TOTAL WARDROBE MAKEOVER!
SHOPPE
WAIT, WHAAA!?
THIS IS EMBARRASSING!
THERE WE ARE!
REO-STYLE: YUKI-YUKI SPRING FASHION!
HUH? THIS GUY LOOKS LAME AS HELL.
LOOKING GOOD, YUKICCHI!

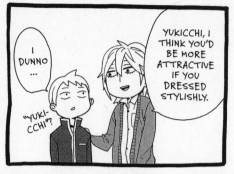

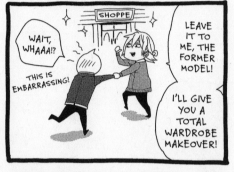

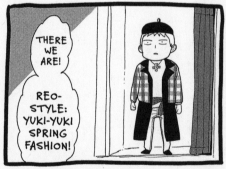

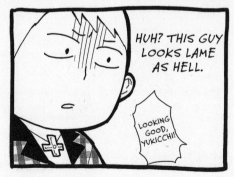

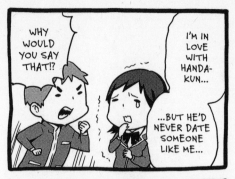

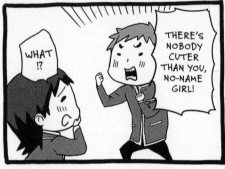

HANDA-KUN VOLUME 3 BONUS COMIC

※ PLEASE ENJOY AFTER READING VOLUME 3

I'M IN LOVE WITH HANDA-KUN...
...BUT HE'D NEVER DATE SOMEONE LIKE ME...
WHY WOULD YOU SAY THAT!?
THERE'S NOBODY CUTER THAN YOU, NO-NAME GIRL!
WHAT !?
BUT I JUST KNOW THAT HE'LL REJECT ME, AND CRUELLY TOO!
THEN DARE TO GET REJECTED!!
I'LL BE THERE TO CATCH YOU, NO-NAME GIRL...
OH, NO-NAME BOY...
イラ
IRA (IRK)
イラ
IRA
NOTHING IS MORE ANNOYING THAN COUPLES BLOCKING THE HALLWAY.

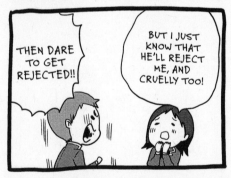

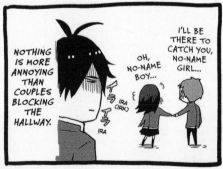

HANDA-KUN VOLUME 3 BONUS COMIC

※ PLEASE ENJOY AFTER READING VOLUME 3

HOW COME HANDA-KUN DOESN'T NOTICE HIS FEMALE FANS' ADVANCES?
SA (ZIP)
TRASH

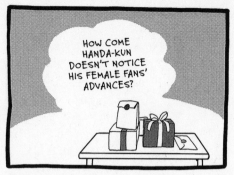

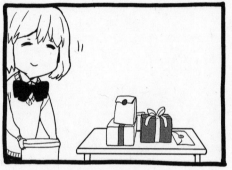

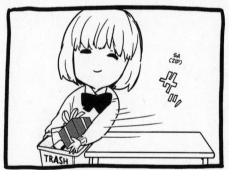

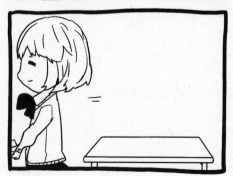

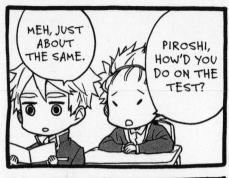

HANDA-KUN VOLUME 3 BONUS COMIC

※ PLEASE ENJOY AFTER READING VOLUME 3

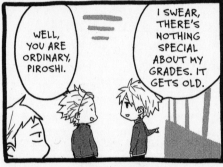

PIROSHI, HOW'D YOU DO ON THE TEST?
MEH, JUST ABOUT THE SAME.
I SWEAR, THERE'S NOTHING SPECIAL ABOUT MY GRADES. IT GETS OLD.
WELL, YOU ARE ORDINARY, PIROSHI.
BUT AREN'T YOU IN THE TOP OF OUR GRADE?
BUT NOT THE VERY BEST. BEING THE LOWEST WOULD MAKE ME MORE SPECIAL.
WHAT EVEN IS "ORDINARY"?

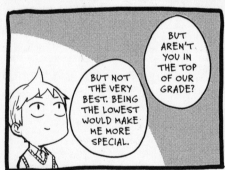

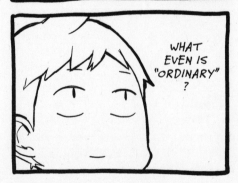

HANDA-KUN VOLUME 4 BONUS COMIC

※ PLEASE ENJOY AFTER READING VOLUME 4

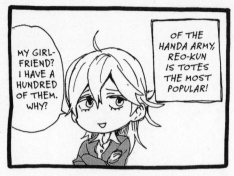

OF THE HANDA ARMY, REO-KUN IS TOTES THE MOST POPULAR!
MY GIRL-FRIEND? I HAVE A HUNDRED OF THEM. WHY?
THESE TWO ARE MY GIRLFRIENDS AS WELL.
SAY WHAT? WE'RE NOT YOUR GIRL-FRIENDS!
WE'RE NOT EVEN SURE WE'RE YOUR FRIENDS.
ER...
REALLY?

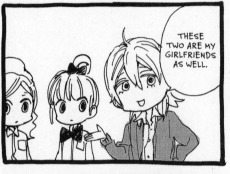

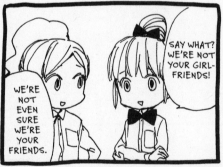

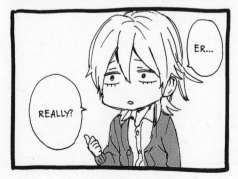

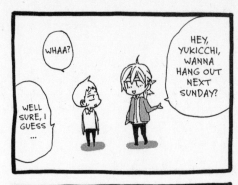

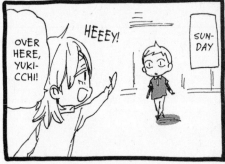

HANDA-KUN VOLUME 4 BONUS COMIC

※ PLEASE ENJOY AFTER READING VOLUME 4

HEY, YUKICCHI, WANNA HANG OUT NEXT SUNDAY?
WHAA?
WELL SURE, I GUESS...
SUN-DAY
HEEEY!
OVER HERE, YUKI-CCHI!
SO I BROUGHT ALONG MY MODEL FRIENDS TOO.
SURAAARI (SLIM)
スラーーリ
WOW, HE REALLY DOES HAVE THAT ORDINARY LOOK.
IMAGE DISPARITY
YOU SEE? NOW THAT'S WHAT I CALL ORDINARY!
REO GETS THE DEATH PENALTY.
YEAH, HE'S ORDINARY AS HELL.

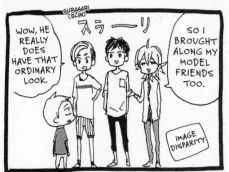

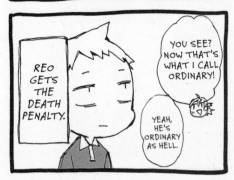

HANDA-KUN VOLUME 4 BONUS COMIC

※ PLEASE ENJOY AFTER READING VOLUME 4

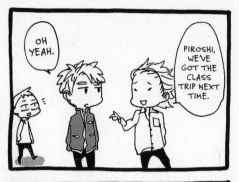

PIROSHI, WE'VE GOT THE CLASS TRIP NEXT TIME.
OH YEAH.
I'LL GO HANG OUT IN THE GIRLS' ROOMS...
...AND TRY PEEPING ON THE GIRLS' BATH.
JUST LIKE WE DID BACK IN MIDDLE SCHOOL, HUH?
I SWEAR ...
...ALL THAT HAPPENS TO ME IS ORDINARY STUFF LIKE YOU SEE IN MANGA.
CAN MY LIFE EVEN GET MORE ORDINARY THAN THIS?
WELL HEY, YOU'RE ORDINARY.
HIS STANDARDS FOR "ORDINARY" AREN'T ORDINARY AT ALL...

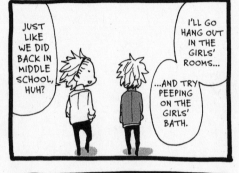

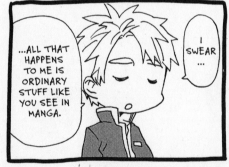

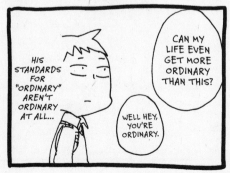

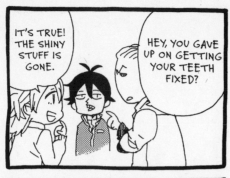

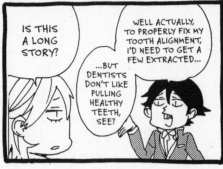

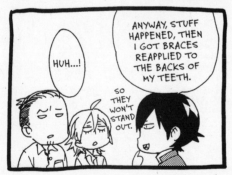

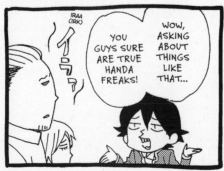

HANDA-KUN VOLUME 5 BONUS COMIC

※ PLEASE ENJOY AFTER READING VOLUME 5

HEY, YOU GAVE UP ON GETTING YOUR TEETH FIXED?
IT'S TRUE! THE SHINY STUFF IS GONE.
WELL ACTUALLY, TO PROPERLY FIX MY TOOTH ALIGNMENT, I'D NEED TO GET A FEW EXTRACTED...
...BUT DENTISTS DON'T LIKE PULLING HEALTHY TEETH, SEE?
IS THIS A LONG STORY?
ANYWAY, STUFF HAPPENED, THEN I GOT BRACES REAPPLIED TO THE BACKS OF MY TEETH.
SO THEY WON'T STAND OUT.
HUH...!
WOW, ASKING ABOUT THINGS LIKE THAT...
YOU GUYS SURE ARE TRUE HANDA FREAKS!
イラァ
IRAA (IRK)

HANDA-KUN VOLUME 5 BONUS COMIC

※ PLEASE ENJOY AFTER READING VOLUME 5

THIS CLASS TRIP'S PRETTY FUN, PIROSHI.
YEAH. NICE, ORDINARY FUN.
I TOOK AN ORDINARY WALK...
...AND GOT AN ORDINARY LOVE LETTER FROM YET ANOTHER GIRL.
SURE, SHE WAS AN ORDINARY BEAUTY...
...BUT THEN, I'M AN ORDINARY GUY.
AGAIN, IN WHAT WORLD IS THAT "ORDINARY"!?
WE'LL START DATING LIKE AN ORDINARY COUPLE.
WHA!?
WOW, YOU'RE SO ORDI-NARY!

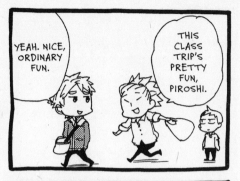

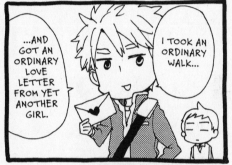

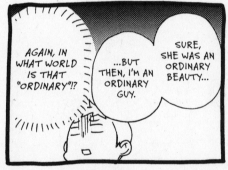

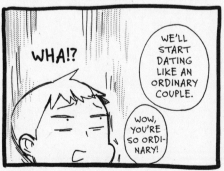

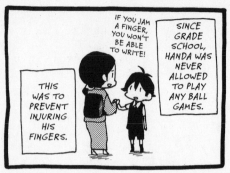

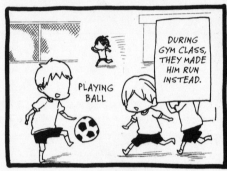

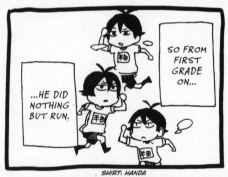

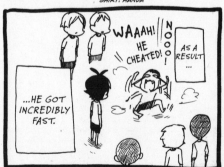

HANDA-KUN VOLUME 5 BONUS COMIC

※ PLEASE ENJOY AFTER READING VOLUME 5

SINCE GRADE SCHOOL, HANDA WAS NEVER ALLOWED TO PLAY ANY BALL GAMES.
IF YOU JAM A FINGER, YOU WON'T BE ABLE TO WRITE!
THIS WAS TO PREVENT INJURING HIS FINGERS.
DURING GYM CLASS, THEY MADE HIM RUN INSTEAD.
PLAYING BALL
SO FROM FIRST GRADE ON...
...HE DID NOTHING BUT RUN.
SHIRT: HANDA
AS A RESULT...
NOOOO!
WAAAH! HE CHEATED!
...HE GOT INCREDIBLY FAST.

HANDA-KUN VOLUME 6 BONUS COMIC

※ PLEASE ENJOY AFTER READING VOLUME 6

WHAT DOES HANDA-KUN MEAN TO YOU?
SOMETHING MORE IMPORTANT THAN STUDYING, PERHAPS.
THERE ARE THINGS YOU CAN'T LEARN FROM JUST SITTING AT A DESK.
WHAT DOES HANDA-KUN MEAN TO YOU?
THE JOY OF CAMARADERIE.
WHAT DOES HANDA-KUN MEAN TO YOU?
A WAY TO KILL TIME AFTER SCHOOL, I GUESS?
THOUGH IT'S GOTTEN TO BE MY MAIN DEAL.
HANDA'S A PART OF OUR YOUTH, ISN'T HE?
LIKE WE'RE IN HIS PARTY.

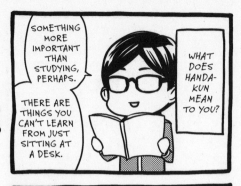

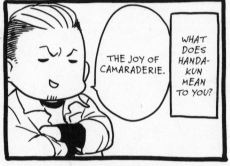

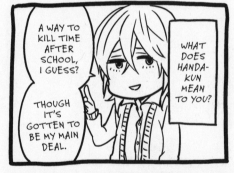

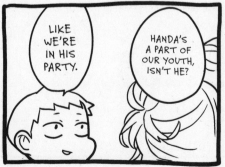

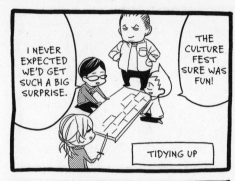

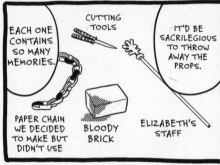

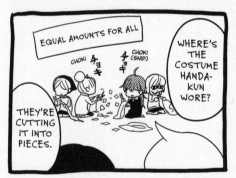

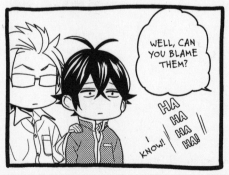

HANDA-KUN VOLUME 6 BONUS COMIC

※ PLEASE ENJOY AFTER READING VOLUME 6

THE CULTURE FEST SURE WAS FUN!
I NEVER EXPECTED WE'D GET SUCH A BIG SURPRISE.
TIDYING UP
IT'D BE SACRILEGIOUS TO THROW AWAY THE PROPS.
CUTTING TOOLS
EACH ONE CONTAINS SO MANY MEMORIES.
ELIZABETH'S STAFF
BLOODY BRICK
PAPER CHAIN WE DECIDED TO MAKE BUT DIDN'T USE
WHERE'S THE COSTUME HANDA-KUN WORE?
EQUAL AMOUNTS FOR ALL
チョキ CHOKI (SNIP)
チョキ CHOKI
THEY'RE CUTTING IT INTO PIECES.
WELL, CAN YOU BLAME THEM?
HA HA HA HA!
I KNOW!

HANDA-KUN VOLUME 6 BONUS COMIC

※ PLEASE ENJOY AFTER READING VOLUME 6

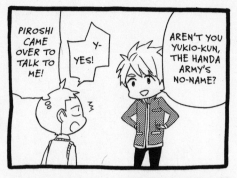

AREN'T YOU YUKIO-KUN, THE HANDA ARMY'S NO-NAME?
Y- YES!
PIROSHI CAME OVER TO TALK TO ME!
I BET YOU ANGUISH OVER HOW YOU'RE TOO ORDINARY JUST LIKE I DO, HUH?
UH...
I DON'T REALLY...
BUT, YOU'VE GOT MORE INDIVIDU-ALITY THAN ME!
THIS HORN THING'S EXTREMELY UNIQUE!
IT'S AMAZ-ING!
AN AMAZING-LY UNIQUE ...
I ENVY YOU!
... HORN?
A UNIQUE HORN!
THIS GUY HAS LET BEING ORDINARY DEVOLVE INTO LOSING SIGHT OF HIMSELF.

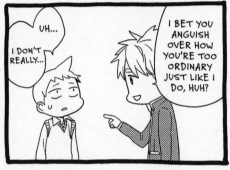

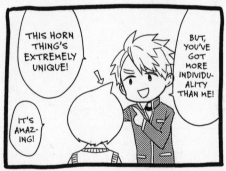

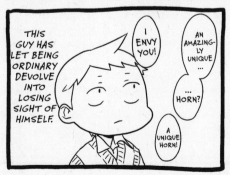

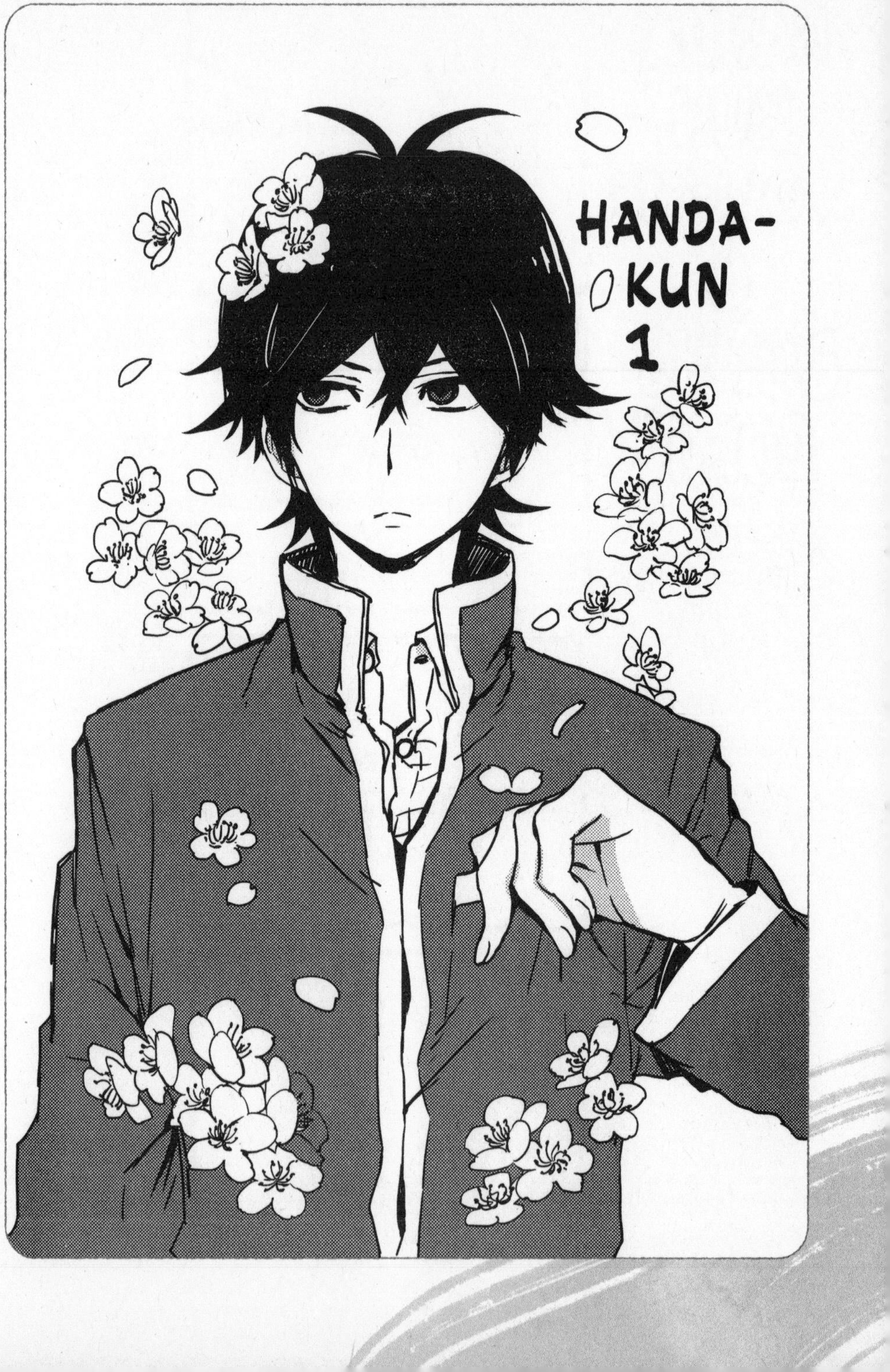
HANDA-
KUN
1

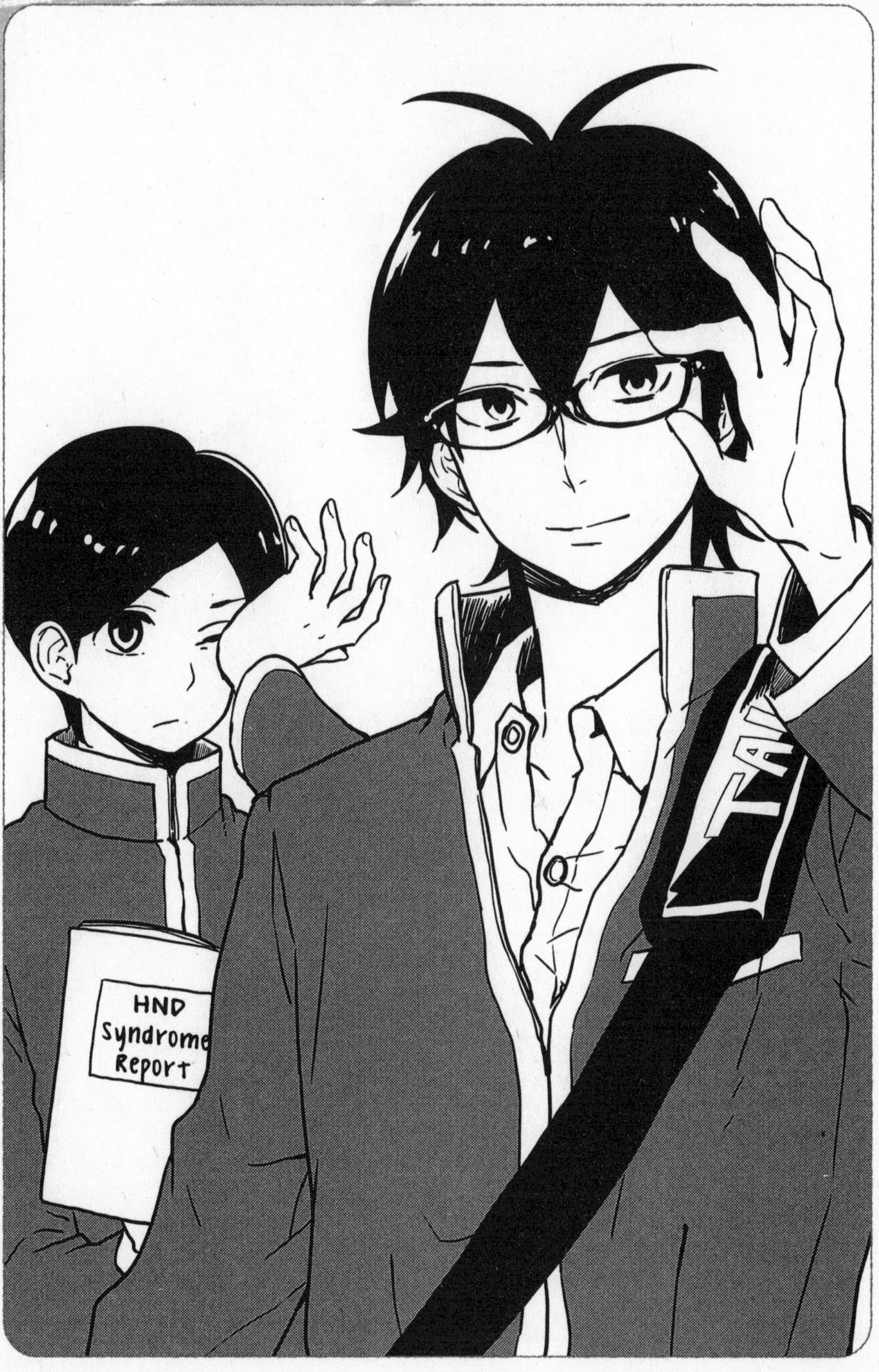
HND
Syndrome
Report

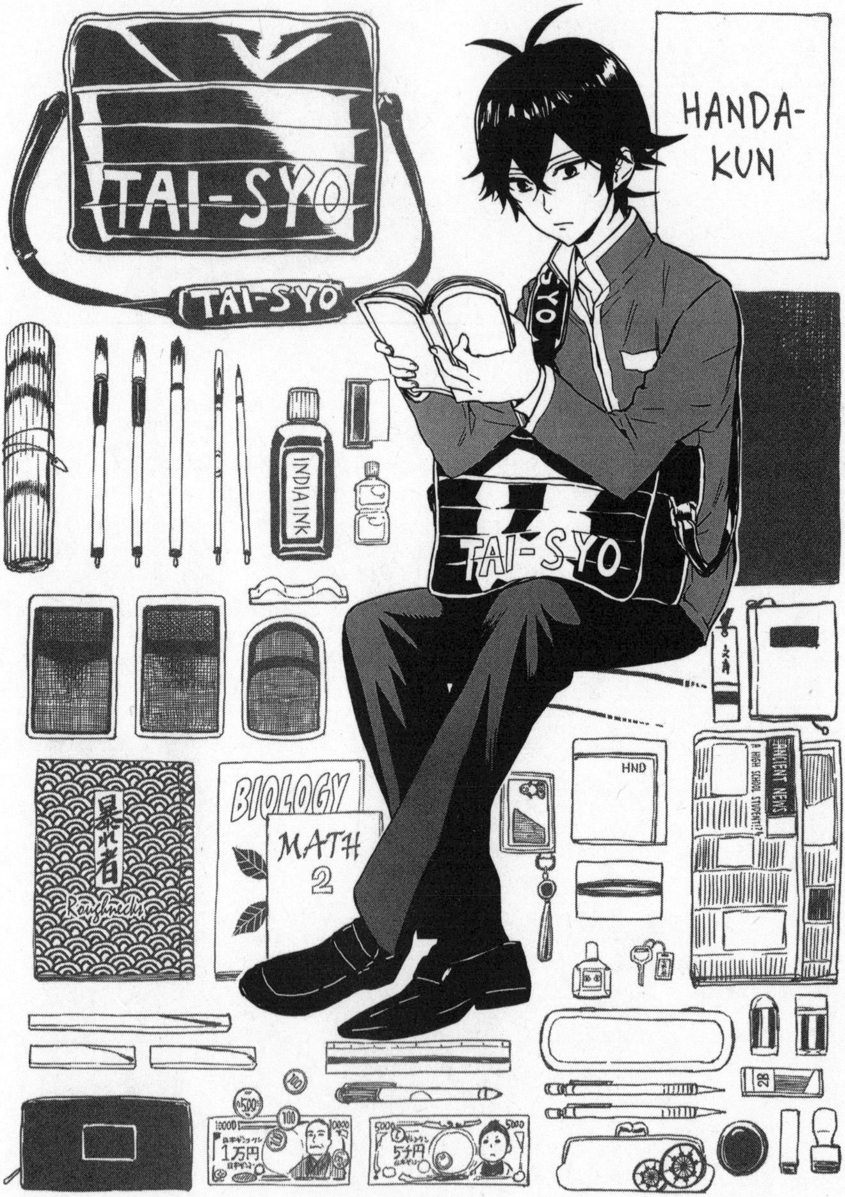
HANDA-
KUN
TAI-SYO
TAI-SYO
INDIA INK
TAI-SYO
BIOLOGY
MATH
2
Roughnecks
HND
A HIGH SCHOOL STUDENT!?

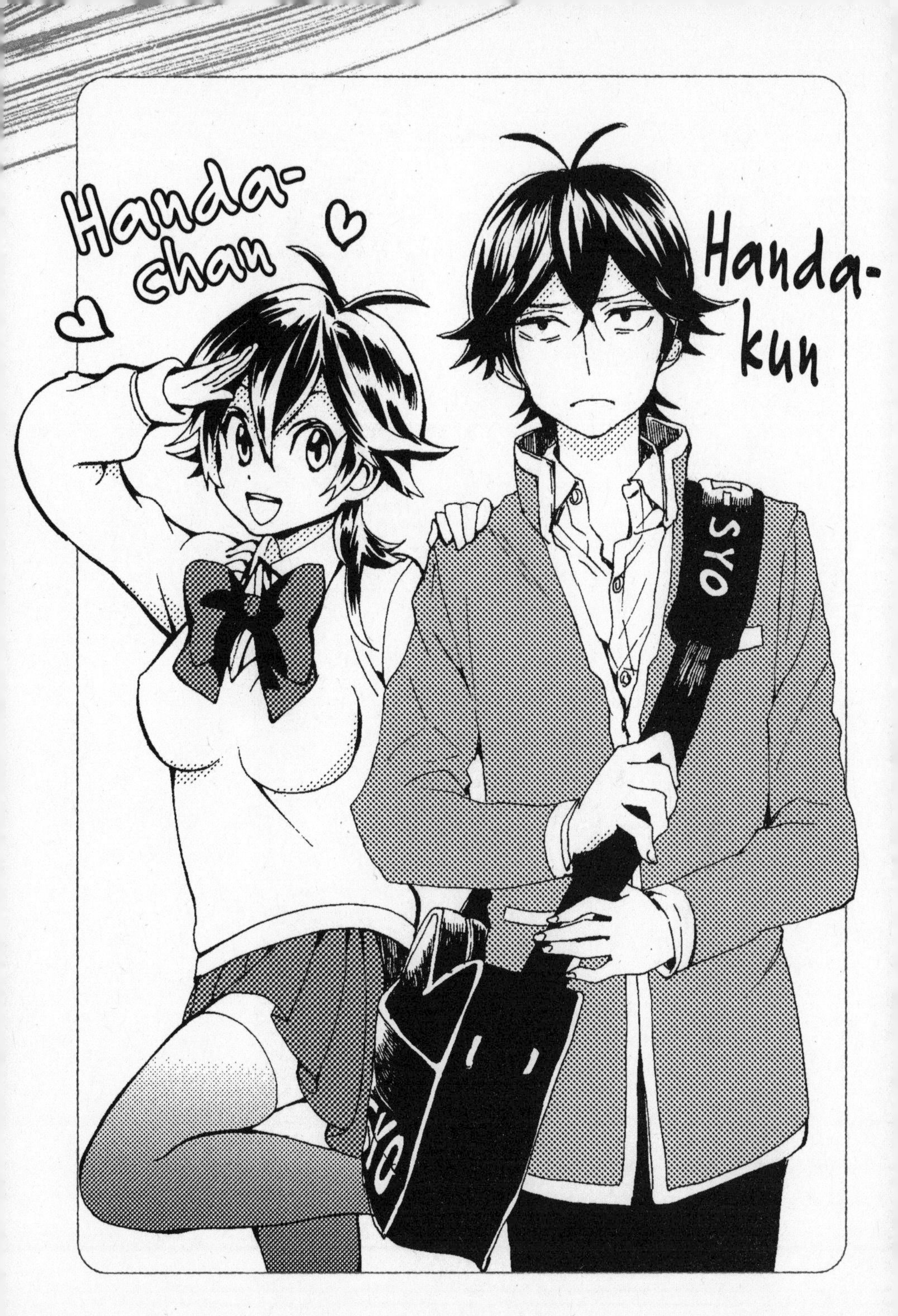
Handa-chan
Handa-kun
SYO
SYO
SYO

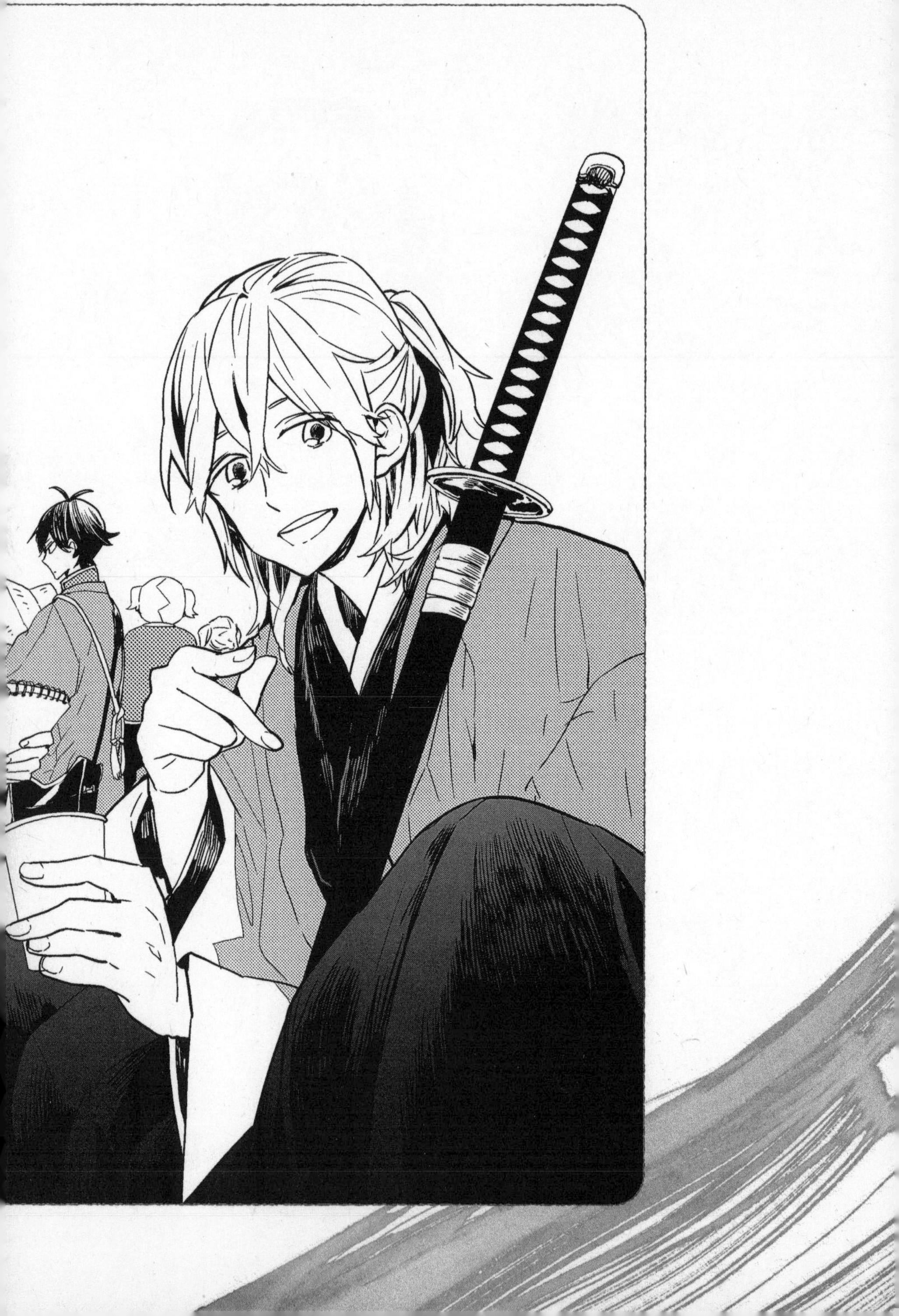

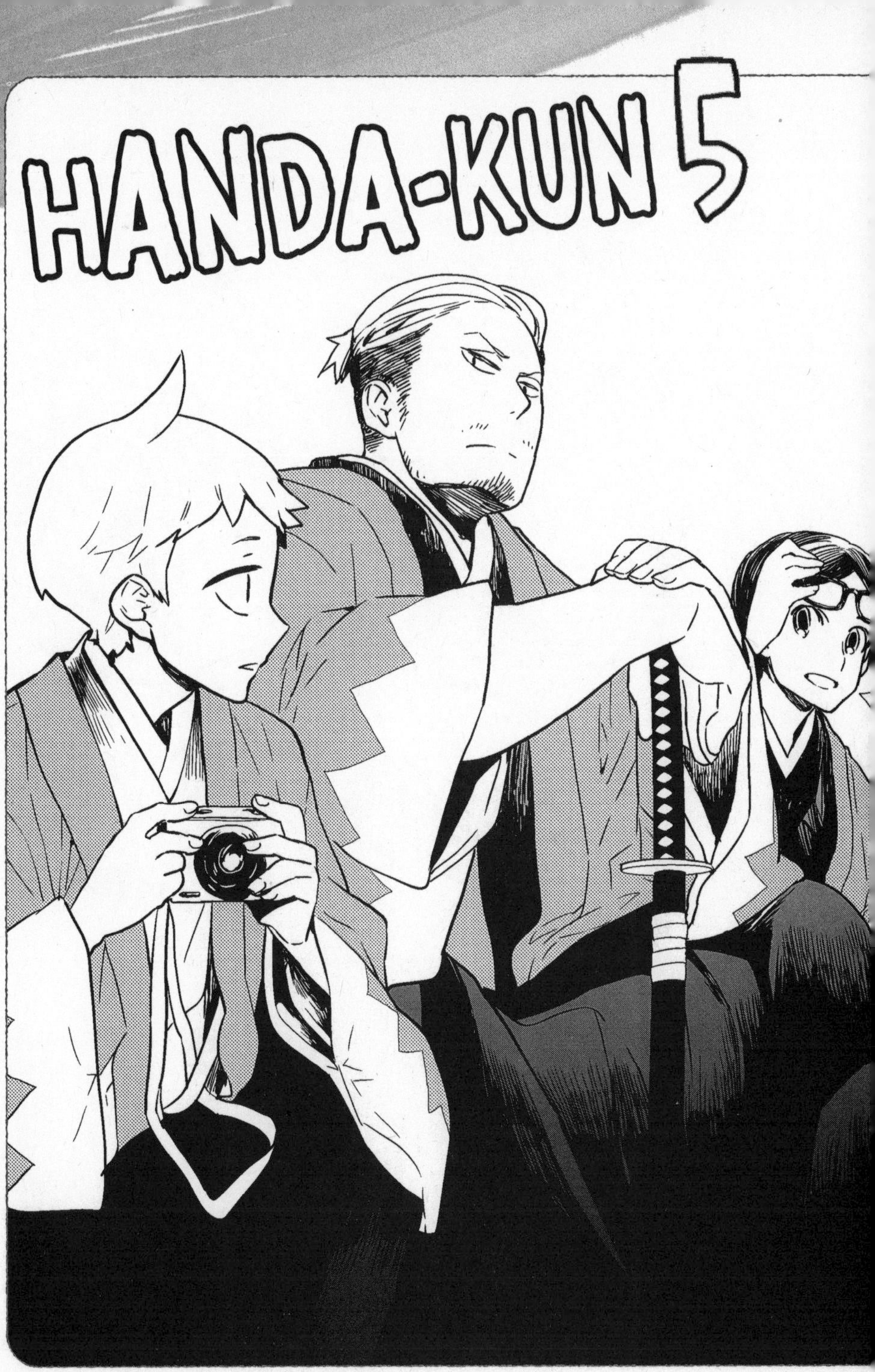
HANDA-KUN 5

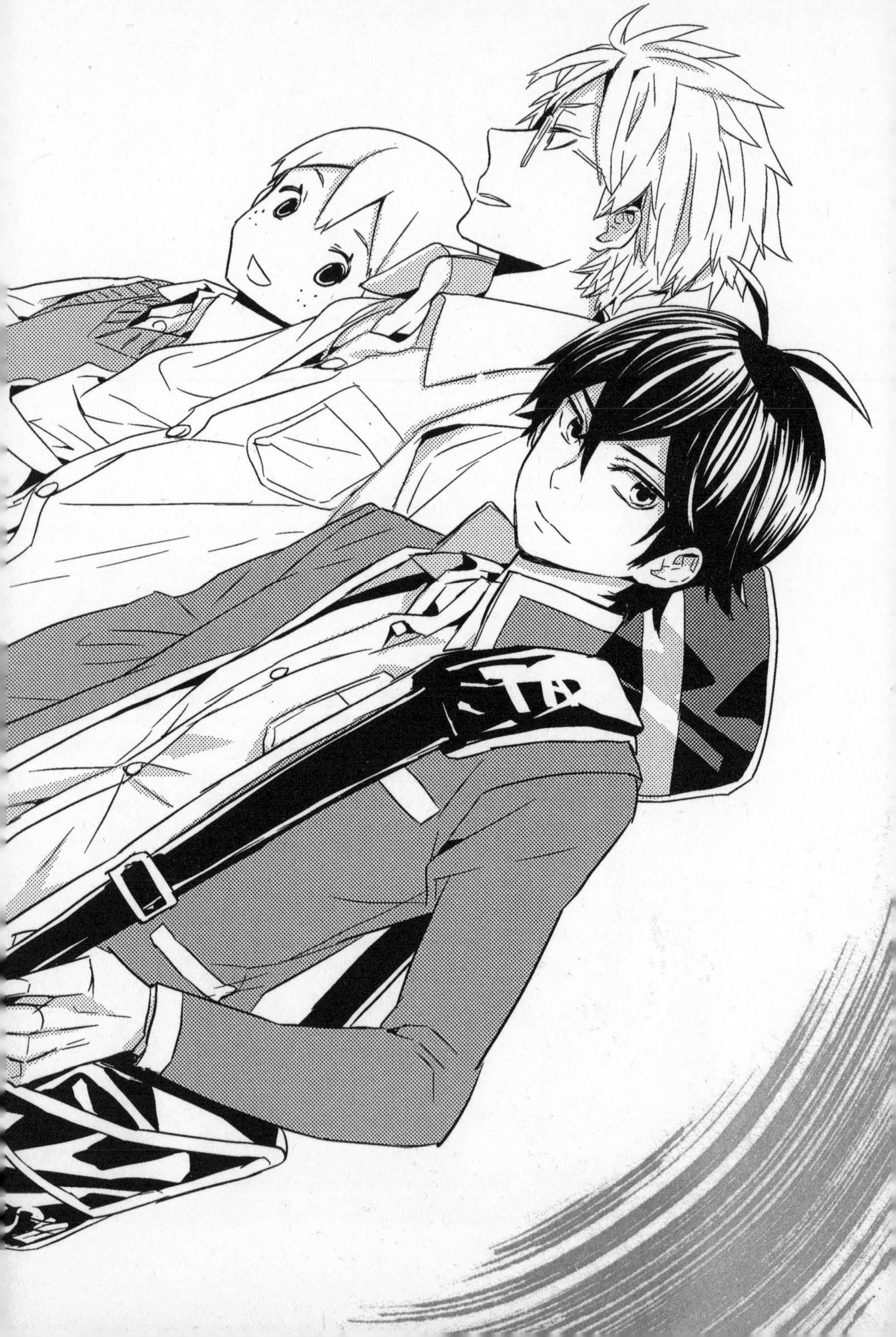

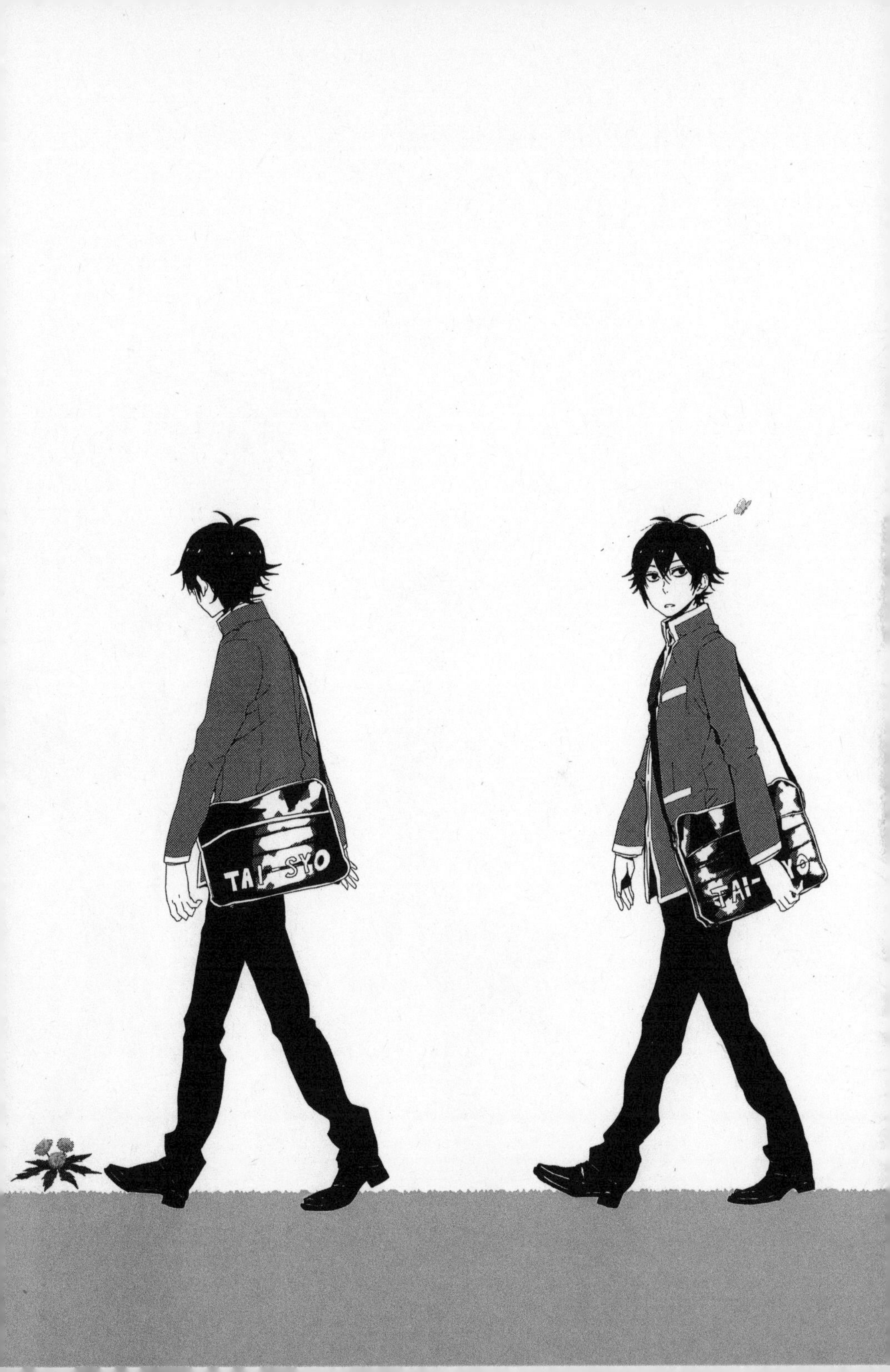
TAI-SYO
TAI-SYO

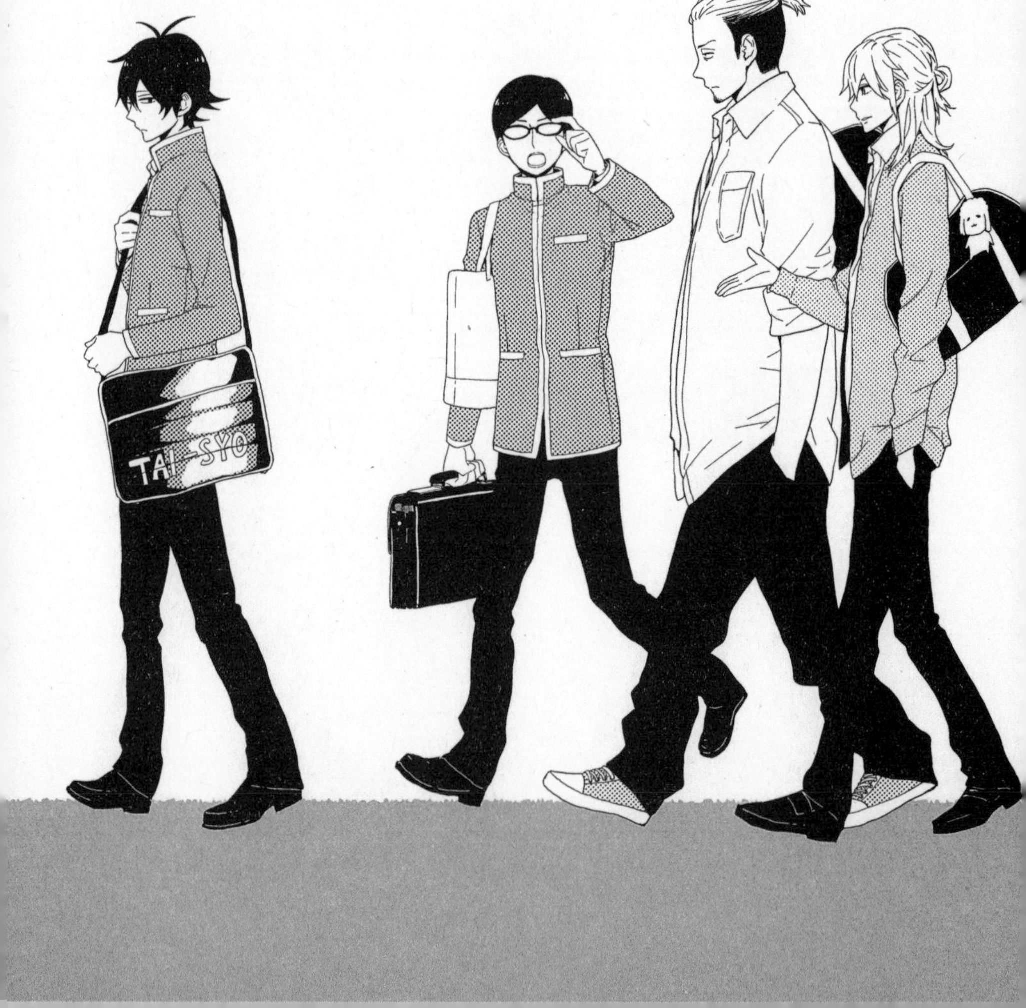
TAI-SYO

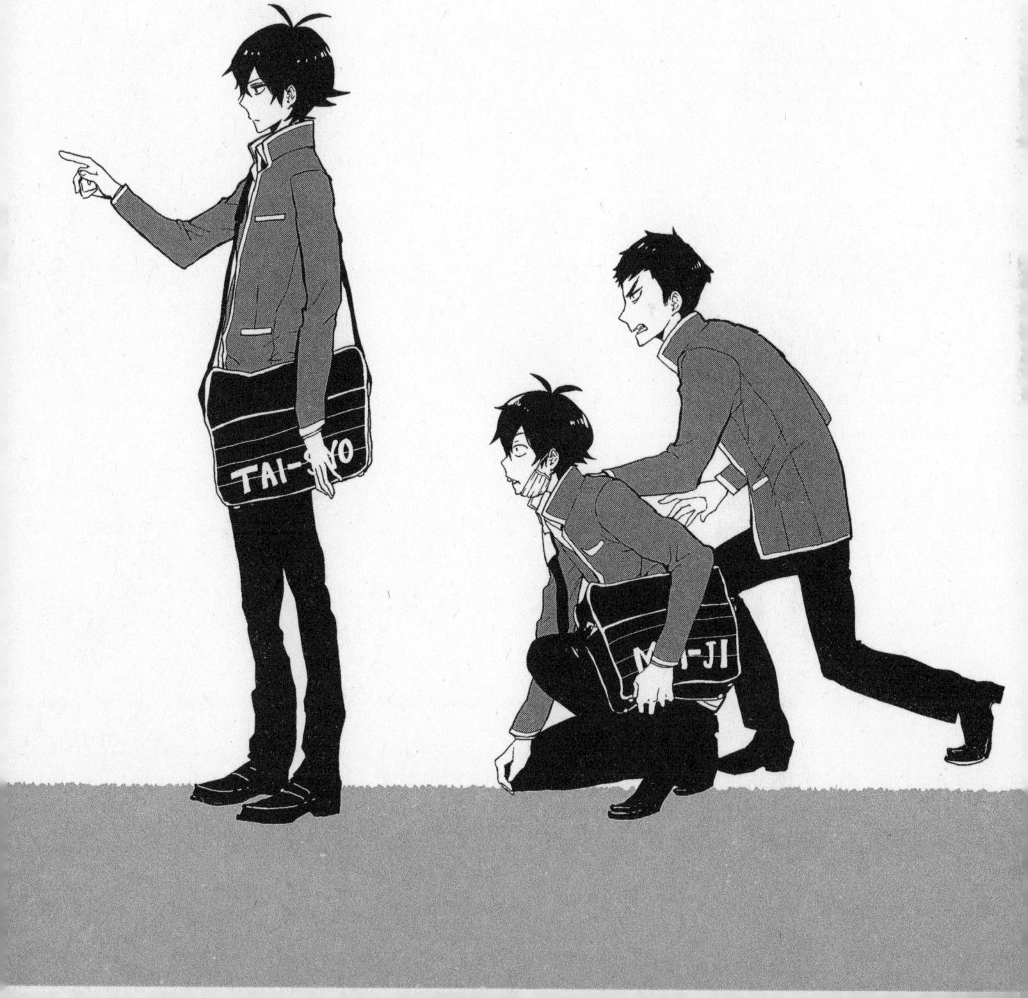

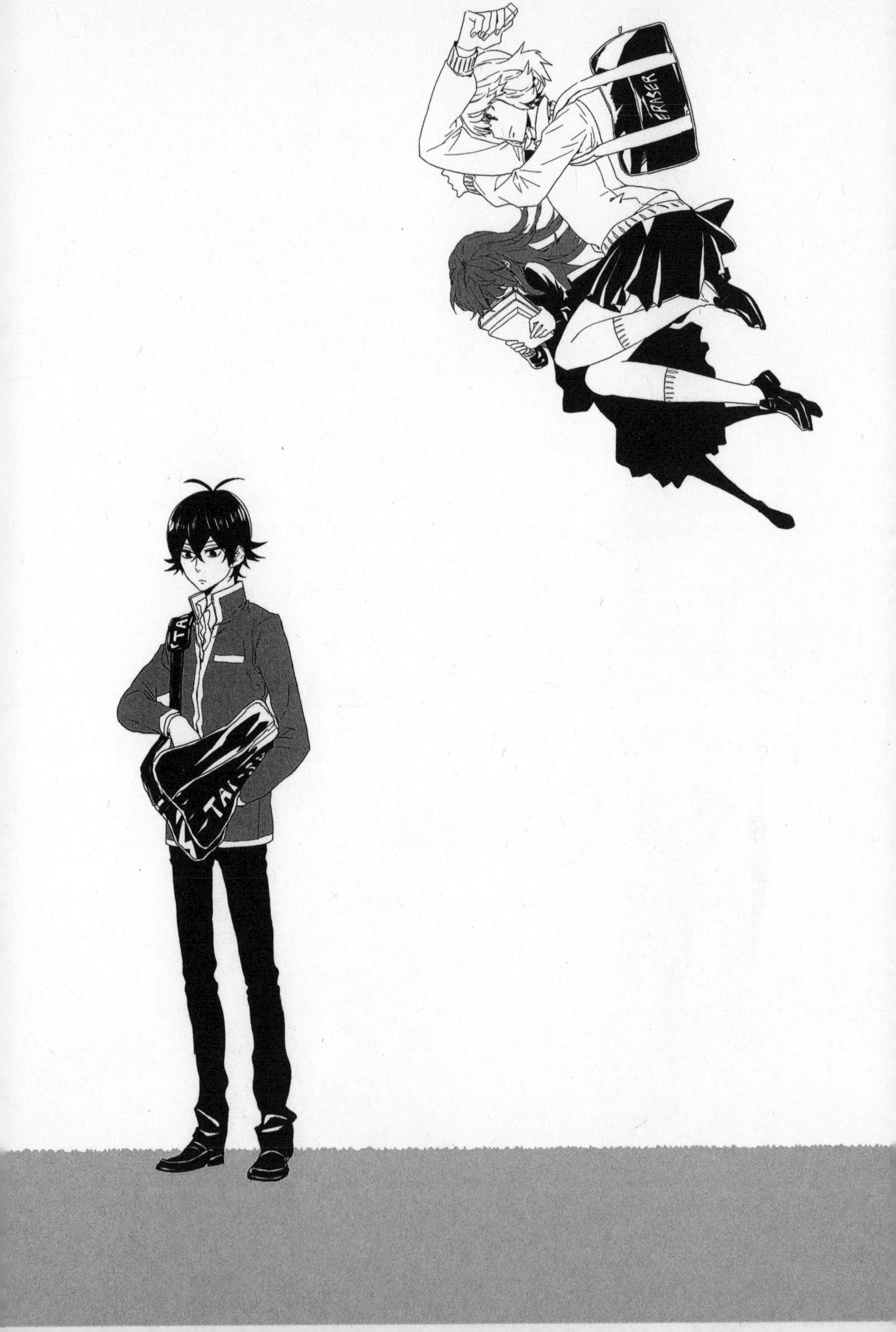
ERASER

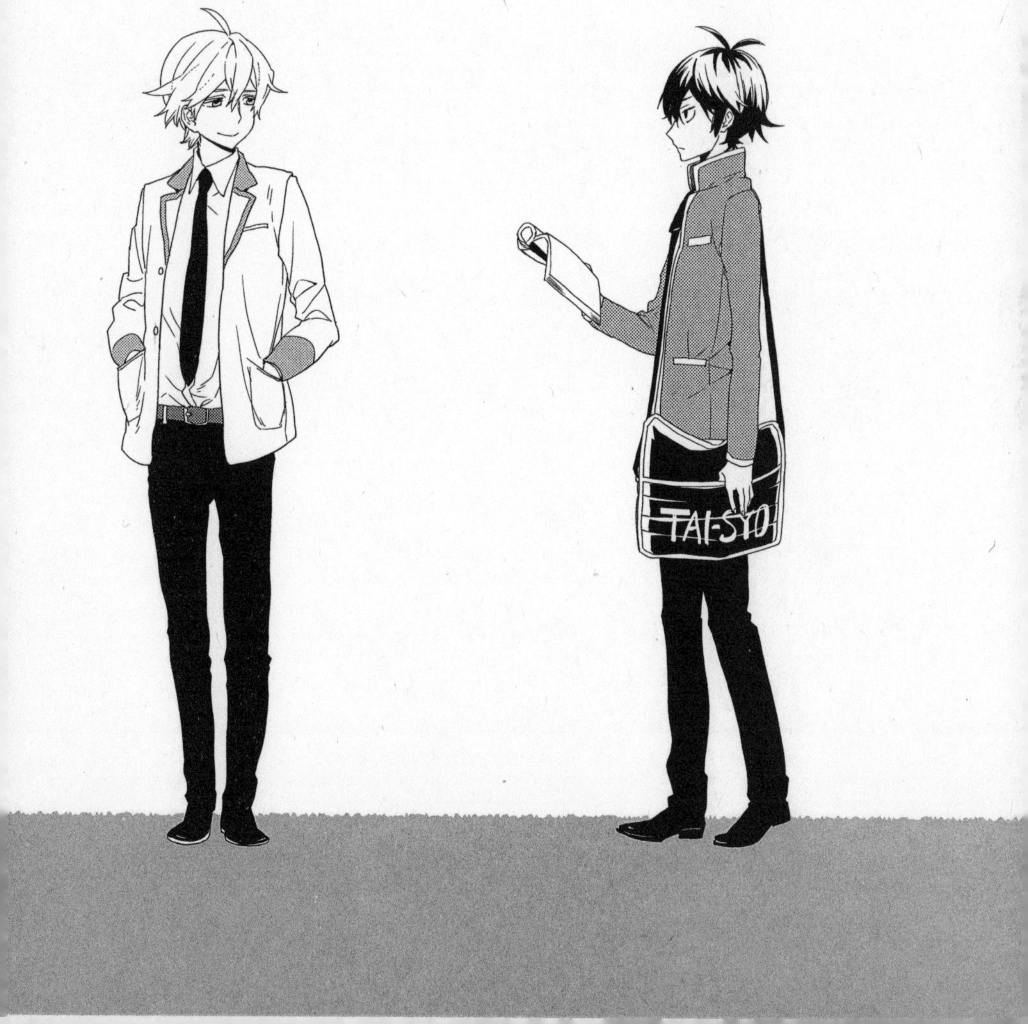
TAI-SYO

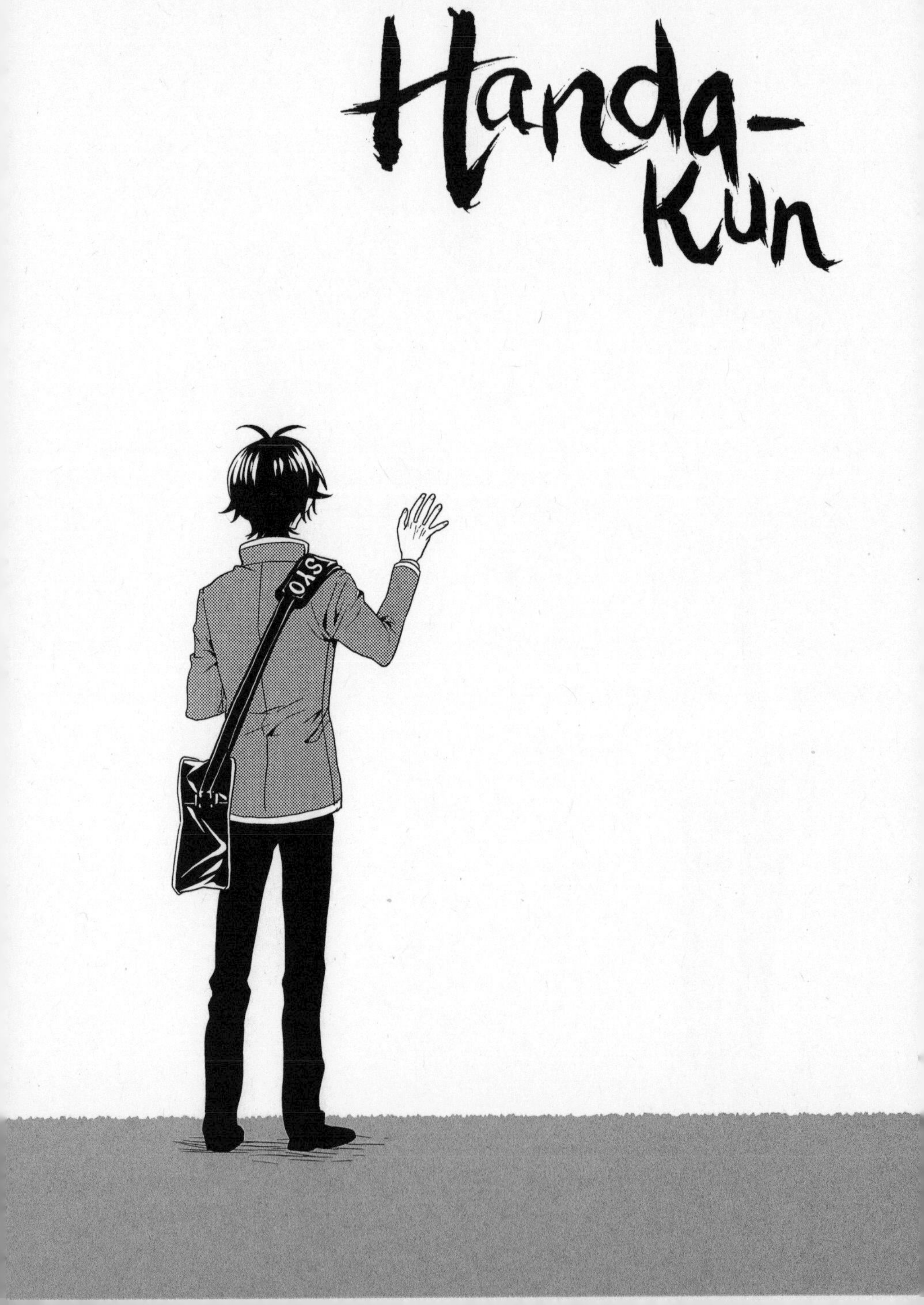
Handa-Kun
SYO

Handa-
Kun

Thank You, Handa Army!!

HANDA-KUN NEWS

Of the Handa Army, by the Handa Army & for the Handa Army (which includes all you readers):

HANDA-BOOK!!

Vol.HND

Everyone, thank you very much for buying *HANDA-KUN* Volume 7! I truly have only words of gratitude. For all you ultimate Handa Army members who've seen us through to the final volume, as a final mop-up, we've made the ultimate volume, crammed full of all things Handa!! The *HANDA-BOOK* was made with our love for Handa and our gratitude to all of you, and we would be very grateful if you kept a copy by your side as a timeless collector's edition in addition to this final volume.

With Volume 7, *HANDA-KUN* has really and truly reached its final ending. Thank you very much for staying with us until now. We bid you adieu until the day we can meet again sometime, somewhere...!!

Monthly Shounen Gangan Oct. issue, now on sale to popular acclaim!!

Series' Final	Cover & Opening Color Pages!!
Special Double Pack-in	*HANDA-KUN* Deluxe Publicity Photo Set
	HANDA-KUN Deluxe Overlapping Book Cover
Send-Away Item	*HANDA-KUN* Deluxe Pin-Button Set

All Specially Drawn!!

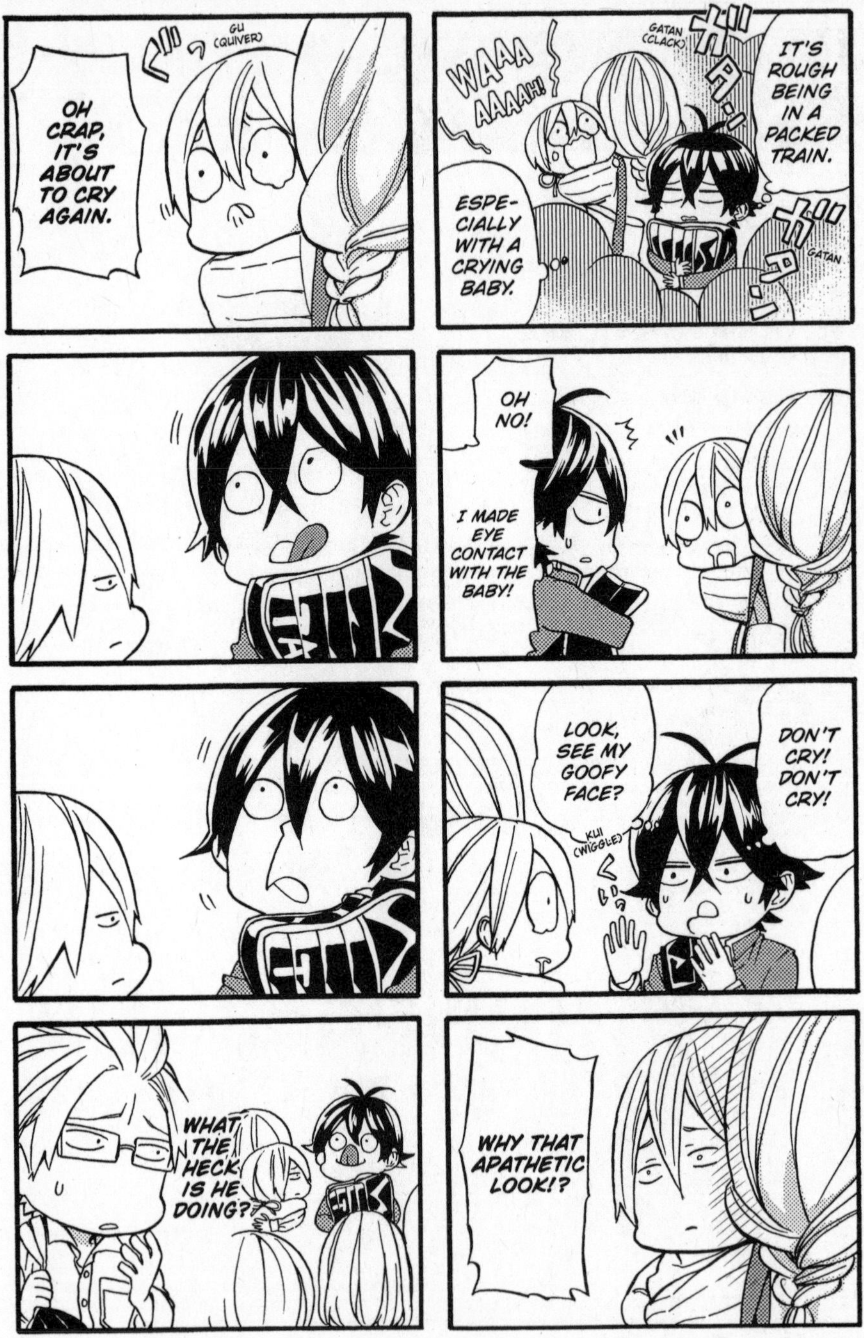
GATAN (CLACK)
IT'S ROUGH BEING IN A PACKED TRAIN.
WAAAAAAAH!
ESPE-CIALLY WITH A CRYING BABY.
GATAN
GU (QUIVER)
OH CRAP, IT'S ABOUT TO CRY AGAIN.
OH NO!
I MADE EYE CONTACT WITH THE BABY!
DON'T CRY! DON'T CRY!
LOOK, SEE MY GOOFY FACE?
KUI (WIGGLE)
WHY THAT APATHETIC LOOK!?
WHAT THE HECK IS HE DOING?

Handa-Kun

7

FINAL

SATSUKI YOSHINO

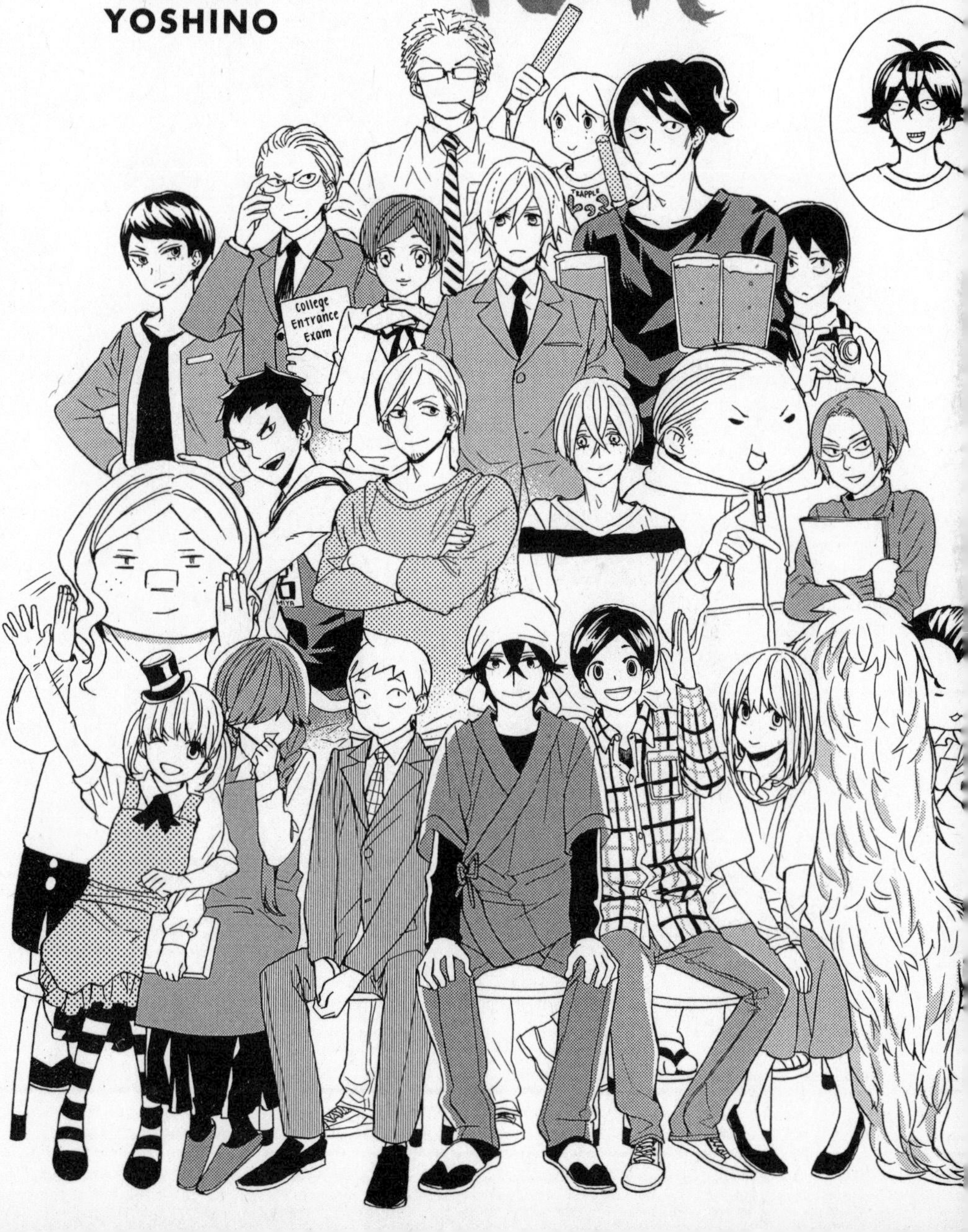
College Entrance Exam

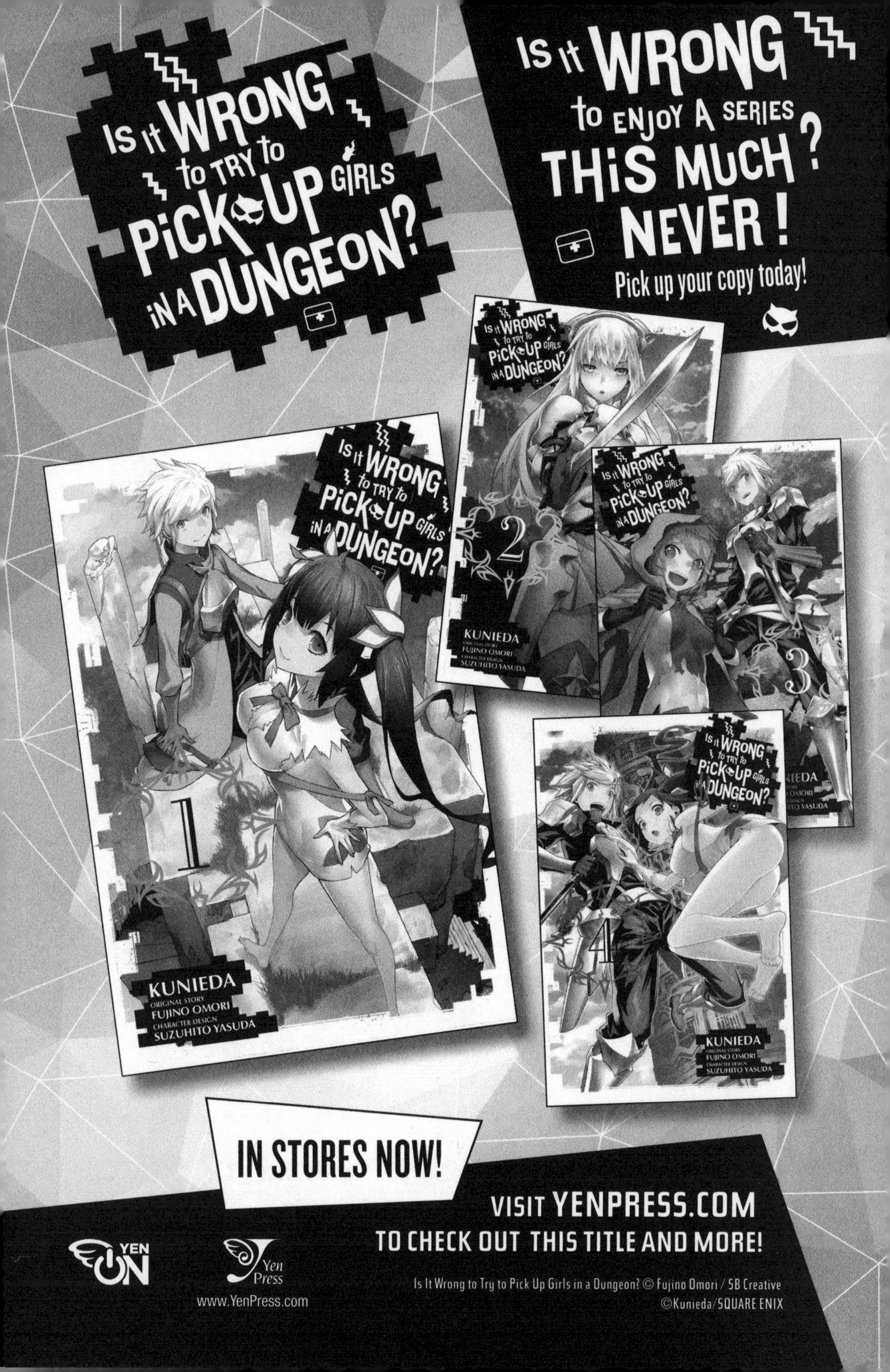
Is it WRONG to Try to PiCK UP GIRLS iN A DUNGEON?
Is it WRONG to ENJOY A SERIES THIS MUCH?
NEVER!
Pick up your copy today!
Is it WRONG to Try to PiCK UP GIRLS iN A DUNGEON?
1
KUNIEDA
ORIGINAL STORY FUJINO OMORI
CHARACTER DESIGN SUZUHITO YASUDA
Is it WRONG to Try to PiCK UP GIRLS iN A DUNGEON?
2
KUNIEDA
ORIGINAL STORY FUJINO OMORI
CHARACTER DESIGN SUZUHITO YASUDA
Is it WRONG to Try to PiCK UP GIRLS iN A DUNGEON?
3
Is it WRONG to Try to PiCK UP GIRLS iN A DUNGEON?
4
KUNIEDA
ORIGINAL STORY FUJINO OMORI
CHARACTER DESIGN SUZUHITO YASUDA
IN STORES NOW!
VISIT YENPRESS.COM
TO CHECK OUT THIS TITLE AND MORE!
YEN ON
Yen Press
www.YenPress.com
Is It Wrong to Try to Pick Up Girls in a Dungeon? © Fujino Omori / SB Creative
©Kunieda/SQUARE ENIX

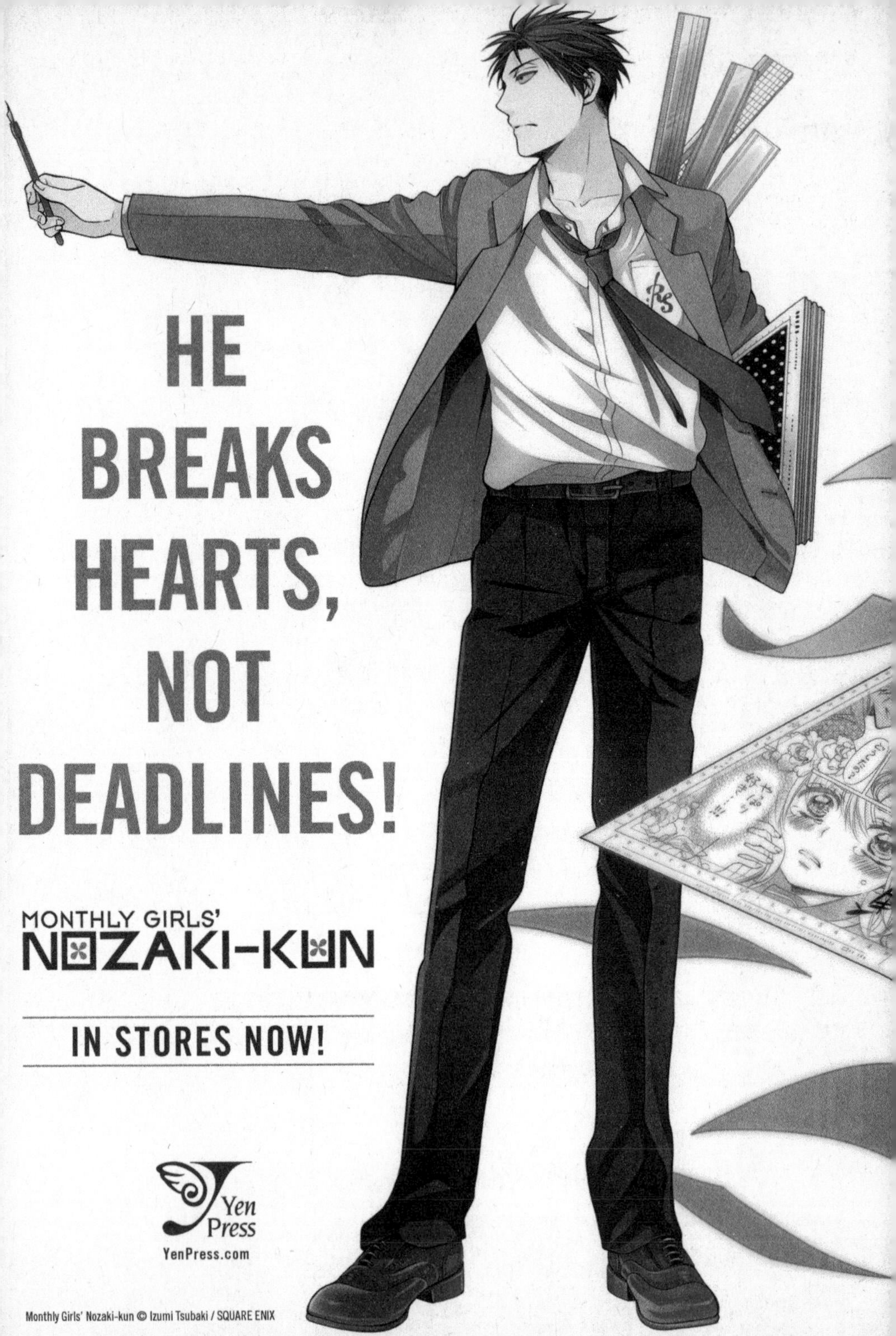
HE BREAKS HEARTS, NOT DEADLINES!
MONTHLY GIRLS' NOZAKI-KUN
IN STORES NOW!
Yen Press
YenPress.com

Satsuki Yoshino

Translation/Adaptation: Krista Shipley, Karie Shipley
Lettering: Lys Blakeslee

Handa-kun Vol.7 ©2016 Satsuki Yoshino/SQUARE ENIX CO., LTD. First published in Japan in 2016 by SQUARE ENIX CO., LTD. English translation rights arranged with SQUARE ENIX CO., LTD. and Yen Press, LLC through Tuttle-Mori Agency, Inc.

English translation ©2017 by SQUARE ENIX CO., LTD.

Yen Press
1290 Avenue of the Americas
New York, NY 10104

Visit us at yenpress.com
facebook.com/yenpress
twitter.com/yenpress
yenpress.tumblr.com
instagram.com/yenpress

First Yen Press Print Edition: September 2017
The chapters in this volume were originally published as ebooks by Yen Press.

Yen Press is an imprint of Yen Press, LLC.
The Yen Press name and logo are trademarks of Yen Press, LLC.

The publisher is not responsible for websites (or their content) that are not owned by the publisher.

Library of Congress Control Number: 2015952606

ISBNs: 978-0-316-47340-8 (paperback)
        978-0-316-47341-5 (ebook)

10 9 8 7 6 5 4 3 2

BVG

Printed in the United States of America